THE MERCHANT OF VENICE

THE MERCHANT OF VENICE

William Shakespeare

a *Broadview Anthology of British Literature* edition

Contributing Editor, *The Merchant of Venice*:
Julie Sutherland, Cape Breton University

General Editors,
Broadview Anthology of British Literature:
Joseph Black, University of Massachusetts, Amherst
Leonard Conolly, Trent University
Kate Flint, University of Southern California
Isobel Grundy, University of Alberta
Don LePan, Broadview Press
Roy Liuzza, University of Toronto
Jerome J. McGann, University of Virginia
Anne Lake Prescott, Barnard College
Barry V. Qualls, Rutgers University
Claire Waters, University of California, Davis

broadview press

Library and Archives Canada Cataloguing in Publication

Shakespeare, William, 1564-1616, author
The merchant of Venice / William Shakespeare ; contributing editor,
The Merchant of Venice: Julie Sutherland (Cape Breton University) ; general
editors, Broadview Anthology of British Literature: Joseph Black (University
of Massachusetts, Amherst), Leonard Conolly (Trent University), Kate Flint
(University of Southern California), Isobel Grundy (University of Alberta),
Don LePan (Broadview Press), Roy Liuzza (University of Toronto),
Jerome J. McGann (University of Virginia), Anne Lake Prescott (Barnard
College), Barry V. Qualls (Rutgers University), Claire Waters (University of
California, Davis).

(Broadview anthology of British literature edition)
Includes bibliographical references.
ISBN 978-1-55481-212-7 (pbk.)

1. Shylock (Fictitious character)—Drama. 2. Jews—Italy—Drama.
3. Moneylenders—Drama. 4. Venice (Italy)—Drama. 5. Comedies—
I. Sutherland, Julie, 1976-, editor II. Title. III. Series: Broadview
anthology of British literature (Series)

PR2825.A1 2015   822.3'3   C2014-907408-5

Broadview Press is an independent, international publishing house, incorporated in 1985.

We welcome comments and suggestions regarding any aspect of our publications—please feel free to contact us at the addresses below or at broadview@broadviewpress.com.

North America	PO Box 1243, Peterborough, Ontario K9J 7H5, Canada
	555 Riverwalk Parkway, Tonawanda, NY 14150, USA
	Tel: (705) 743-8990; Fax: (705) 743-8353
	email: customerservice@broadviewpress.com
UK, Europe, Central Asia,	Eurospan Group, 3 Henrietta St., London WC2E 8LU, UK
Middle East, Africa, India,	Tel: 44 (0) 1767 604972; Fax: 44 (0) 1767 601640
and Southeast Asia	email: eurospan@turpin-distribution.com
Australia and New Zealand	Footprint Books
	1/6a Prosperity Parade, Warriewood, NSW 2102, Australia
	Tel: 1300 260 090; Fax: 02 9997 3185
	email: info@footprint.com.au

www.broadviewpress.com

Broadview Press acknowledges the financial support of the Government of Canada through the Canada Book Fund for our publishing activities.

Developmental Editors: Laura Buzzard and Don LePan

PRINTED IN CANADA

Contents

Introduction

William Shakespeare
1564–1616

The plays of William Shakespeare are foundational works of Western culture; in the English-speaking world they have influenced subsequent literary culture more broadly and more deeply than any other group of texts except the books of the Bible. The language and imagery of the plays; their ways of telling stories; their innovative dramatic qualities; the characters that populate them (and the ways in which these characters are created); the issues and ideas the plays explore (and the ways in which they explore them)—all these have powerfully shaped English literature and culture over the past four centuries. This shaping influence has continually touched popular culture as well as more "elevated" literary and academic worlds. From the eighteenth century on Shakespeare's plays have held the stage with far greater frequency than those of any other playwright, and in the twentieth century many have been made into popular films (some of the best of which are films in Japanese and in Russian). Even outside the English-speaking world the plays of Shakespeare receive unparalleled exposure; in the Netherlands, for example, his plays have been performed in the late twentieth and early twenty-first centuries more than twice as often as those of any other playwright. In 2000 he headed the list both on the BBC "person of the millennium" poll and on the *World Almanac*'s poll listing the 10 "most influential people of the second millennium." The fact that a playwright, a member of the popular entertainment industry, has continued to enjoy this kind of cultural status—ranked above the likes of Isaac Newton, Winston Churchill, Galileo Galilei, and Albert Einstein—is worth pausing over. Why are these plays still performed, read, watched, filmed, studied, and appropriated four centuries after they were written? What is the source of his ongoing cultural currency?

There are many ways to answer these questions. One is surely that the plays tell great stories: fundamental, psychologically sophisticated stories about love, death, growing up, families, communities, guilt, revenge, jealousy, order and disorder, self-knowledge, and identity. Another, just as surely, is that they tell them with extraordinary verbal facility in almost all respects: Shakespeare is generally regarded as unsurpassed in his choice of individual words and his inventiveness in conjuring up striking images; in his structuring of the rhythm of poetic lines; in balancing sentences rhetorically; in shaping long speeches; and in crafting sparkling dialogue. A third is that the characters within the stories are uniquely engaging and memorable. In large part this can be attributed to Shakespeare's ingenuity: within the English literary tradition he more or less invented the psychologically realistic literary character; within the European literary tradition he more or less also invented the strong, independent female character. The bare bones of his characters are typically provided by other sources, but the flesh and blood is of Shakespeare's making. Fourth, and perhaps most important of all, Shakespeare's plays tell their stories in ways that are open-ended emotionally and intellectually: no matter how neatly the threads of story may be knitted together at the end, the threads of idea and of emotion in Shakespeare's plays are never tied off. It is this openness of the plays, their availability for reinterpretation, that enables them to be endlessly restaged, rewritten, reinterpreted—and to yield fresh ideas and fresh feelings time and time again.

Given the centrality of Shakespeare to Western culture, the wish of many readers to know far more than we do about his life is understandable. In fact we do know a fair amount about the facts of his life—given late sixteenth- and early seventeenth-century norms, perhaps more than we might expect to know of someone of his class and background. But we know a good deal less of Shakespeare than we do of some other leading writers of his era—Ben Jonson, for example, or John Donne. And, perhaps most frustrating of all, we know almost nothing of an intimate or personal nature about Shakespeare.

Shakespeare (whose surname also appears on various documents as Shakespear, Shakspere, Shaxpere, and Shagspere) was baptized in Stratford-upon-Avon on 26 April 1564. Reasonable conjecture, given the customs of the time, suggests that he was born two-to-four days earlier; the date that has been most frequently advanced is 23

April (the same day of the year on which he died in 1616, and also the day on which St. George, England's patron saint, is traditionally honored). His father, John, was a glove-maker and also a local politician: first an alderman and then bailiff, a position equivalent to mayor. Some scholars have argued that he had remained a Catholic in newly Protestant England, and that Shakespeare thus grew up in a clandestinely Catholic home; though the evidence for this is suggestive, it is not conclusive. (If Shakespeare had grown up Catholic, that background might lead readers to see some of his history plays in a different perspective, and might lend even greater poignancy to images such as that of the "bare ruined choirs" of Sonnet 73, with its suggestion of the destruction of the monasteries dissolved by Henry VIII following the break with Rome.)

Stratford-upon-Avon had a good grammar school, which is generally presumed to have provided Shakespeare's early education, though no records exist to confirm this. Not surprisingly, he did not go on to university, which at the time it would have been unusual for a person from the middle class to attend. (Even Ben Jonson, one of the finest classicists of the period, did not attend university.) Shakespeare's first exposure to theater was probably through the troupes of traveling players that regularly toured the country at that time.

On 28 November 1582, when Shakespeare was eighteen, he was married to Anne Hathaway, who was eight years his senior. Six months later, in May of 1583, Anne gave birth to their first daughter, Susanna; given the timing, it seems reasonable to speculate that an unexpected pregnancy may have prompted a sudden marriage. In February 1585, twins, named Hamnet (Shakespeare's only son, who was to die at the age of eleven) and Judith, were born. Some time later, probably within the next three years, Shakespeare moved to London, leaving his young family behind. There has been considerable speculation as to his reasons for leaving Stratford-upon Avon, but no solid evidence has been found to support any of the numerous theories. Certainly London was then (as now) a magnet for ambitious young men, and in the late 1580s it was effectively the only English city conducive to the pursuit of a career as a writer or in the theater.

It is not known exactly when Shakespeare joined the professional theater in London, but by 1592 several of his plays had reached the stage—the three parts of *Henry VI*, probably *The Comedy of Errors* and

Titus Andronicus, possibly others. The earliest extant mention of him in print occurs in 1592: a sarcastic jibe by an embittered older playwright, Robert Greene. Greene calls Shakespeare "an upstart crow beautified with our feathers," probably referring to Shakespeare's work on the series of *Henry VI* plays, which may well have involved the revision of material by other writers who had originally worked on the play. In any case, from 1594 on, Will Shakespeare is listed as a member of the company called The Lord Chamberlain's Men (later called The King's Men, when James I became its patron).

Professional theater in London did not become firmly established until 1576, when the first permanent playhouses opened. By the late 1580s four theaters were in operation—an unprecedented level of activity, and one that in all probability helped to nurture greater sophistication on the part of audiences. Certainly it was a hothouse that nurtured an extraordinary growth of theatrical agility on the part of Elizabethan playwrights. Shakespeare, as both playwright and actor in The Lord Chamberlain's Men, was afforded opportunities of forging, testing, and revising his written work in the heat of rehearsals and performances—opportunities that were not open to other playwrights.[1] And in Christopher Marlowe he had a rival playwright of a most extraordinary sort. It seems safe to conjecture that the two learned a good deal about play construction from each other. In the late 1580s and early 1590s they both adopt virtually simultaneously the practice of having their characters express their intentions in advance of the unfolding action, thereby encouraging the formation of audience expectations; they also begin to make it a practice to interpose some other action between the exit and the re-entry of any character, thereby further fostering the creation of a sense of temporal and spatial illusion of a sort quite new to the English stage.

---

1   From the nineteenth century onwards (though, perhaps tellingly, never before that), the suggestion has occasionally been put forward that Shakespeare never wrote the plays attributed to him, and that someone else—perhaps Francis Bacon, perhaps Edward de Vere, 17th Earl of Oxford—was actually the author. These conspiracy theories have sometimes gained popular currency, but the vast majority of scholars have never found any reason whatsoever to credit any of them. One of the many reasons such theories lack credibility follows from our sure knowledge that Shakespeare was an actor in many of the plays that bear his name as author. If Shakespeare had not written the plays himself it would surely have been impossibly difficult to conceal that fact from all the members of the rest of the company, in rehearsal as well as in performance, over the course of many, many years.

In his early years in London Shakespeare also established himself as a non-dramatic poet—and sought aristocratic patronage in doing so. In the late sixteenth century the writing of poetry was accorded considerable respect, the writing of plays a good deal less. It was conventional for those not of aristocratic birth themselves to seek a patron for their writing—as Shakespeare evidently did with the Earl of Southampton, a young noble to whom he dedicated two substantial poems of mythological narrative, *Venus and Adonis* (1593) and *The Rape of Lucrece* (1594). (It is a measure of the magnitude of Shakespeare's achievement that these poems, which would be regarded as major works of almost any other writer of the period, are an afterthought in most considerations of Shakespeare's work.) Before the end of the century Shakespeare was also circulating his sonnets, as we know from the praise of Francis Meres, who wrote in 1598 that the "sweet, witty soul" of the classical poet of love, Ovid, "lives in mellifluous and honey-tongued Shakespeare, witness his Venus and Adonis, his Lucrece, his sugared sonnets among his private friends, etc." Such circulation among "private friends" was common practice at the time, and was not necessarily followed by publication. When Shakespeare's sonnets were finally published, in 1609, the dedication was from the printer rather than the author, suggesting that Shakespeare may not have authorized their publication.

There are thirty-eight extant plays by Shakespeare (if *Two Noble Kinsmen* is included in the total). Unlike most other playwrights of the age, he wrote in every major dramatic genre. His history plays (most of them written in the 1590s) include *Richard III, Henry IV, Part 1 and Part 2,* and *Henry V.* He wrote comedies throughout his playwriting years; the succession of comedies that date from the years 1595 to 1601, including *Much Ado about Nothing, As You Like It,* and *Twelfth Night,* may represent his most successful work in this genre, though some have argued that *The Merchant of Venice* (c. 1596) and the "dark comedies" which date from between 1601 and 1604 (including *All's Well That Ends Well* and *Measure for Measure*) resonate even more deeply. The period of the "dark comedies" substantially overlaps with the period in which Shakespeare wrote a succession of great tragedies. *Hamlet* may have been written as early as 1598–99, but *Othello, King Lear,* and *Macbeth* were written in succession between 1601 and 1606. Several of his last plays are romance-comedies—notably *Cymbeline,*

The Winter's Tale, and *The Tempest* (all of which date from the period 1608–11).

Shakespeare was a shareholder in The Lord Chamberlain's Men, and it was in that capacity rather than as a playwright or actor that he made a good deal of money. There was at the time no equivalent to modern laws of copyright, or to modern conventions of payment to the authors of published works. Nineteen of Shakespeare's plays were printed individually during Shakespeare's lifetime, but it is clear that many of these publications did not secure his cooperation. It has often been hypothesized that some of the most obviously defective texts (referred to by scholars as "bad quartos") are pirated editions dictated from memory to publishers by actors; there is some evidence to support this theory, though even if correct it leaves many textual issues unresolved.

The first publication of Shakespeare's collected works did not occur until 1623, several years after his death, when two of his fellow actors, John Heminges and Henry Condell, arranged to have printed the First Folio, a carefully prepared volume (by the standards of the time) that included thirty-six of Shakespeare's plays. Eighteen of these were appearing for the first time, and four others for the first time in a reliable edition. (*Two Noble Kinsmen*, which was written in collaboration with a younger playwright, John Fletcher, and *Pericles*, of which it appears Shakespeare was not the sole author, were both excluded, although the editors did include *Henry VIII*, which is now generally believed to have been another work in which Fletcher had a hand.)

A vital characteristic of Shakespeare's plays is their extraordinary richness of language. After several centuries of forging a new tongue out of its polyglot sources, the English language in the sixteenth century had entered a period of steady growth in its range, as vocabulary expanded to meet the needs of an increasingly complex society. Yet its structure over this same time (no doubt in connection with the spread of print culture) was becoming increasingly stable. When we compare the enormous difference between the language of Chaucer, who was writing in the late fourteenth century, and that of Shakespeare, writing in the late sixteenth century, it is remarkable to see how greatly the language changed over those two centuries—considerably more than it has changed in the four centuries from Shakespeare's time to our own. English was still effectively a new language in his time, with immense and largely unexplored possibilities for conveying subtleties of meaning. More than any other, Shakespeare embarked on that exploration; his reading was clearly very wide,[1] as was his working vocabulary. But he expanded the language as well as absorbing it; a surprising number of the words Shakespeare used are first recorded as having been used in his work.

The popular image of Shakespeare's last few years is that first expressed by Nicholas Rowe in 1709:

> The latter part of his life was spent, as all men of good sense wish theirs may be, in ease, retirement, and the conversation of his friends. He had the good fortune to gather together an estate equal to his occasion, and, in that, to his wish; and is said to have spent some years before his death at his native Stratford.

We know for a fact that around 1610 Shakespeare moved from London to Stratford, where his family had continued to live throughout the years he had spent in London, and the move has often been referred to as a "retirement." Shakespeare did not immediately give up playwriting, however: *The Tempest* (1611), *Henry VIII* (c. 1612), and *Two Noble Kinsmen* (c. 1613) all date from after his move to Stratford. By the time he left London Shakespeare was indeed a relatively wealthy man, with substantial investments both in real estate and in the tithes of the town (an arrangement that would be comparable to buying government bonds today).

After 1613 we have no record of any further writing; he died on 23 April 1616, aged 52. In his will, Shakespeare left his extensive property to the sons of his daughter, Susanna (described in her epitaph as

---

1 In his early years in London Shakespeare may well have acquired much of his reading material from Richard Field, a man from Stratford-upon-Avon of about Shakespeare's age who was in the book trade. Field printed Shakespeare's early poems, *Venus and Adonis* and *The Rape of Lucrece* and it is certainly possible that the two men had some understanding by which Shakespeare borrowed some of the books he read, which otherwise might have been prohibitively expensive. (Among the works printed by Field was a multi-volume Thomas North translation of *Plutarch's Lives*, of which Shakespeare made extensive use.) Shakespeare also lodged for a time in London with a French Huguenot family named Montjoy, whose home may have been the source for some of the French books that his plays demonstrate a familiarity with. And he may also have had the use of the libraries of one or more of his aristocratic patrons.

"witty above her sex"). To his wife, he left his "second-best bed"—a bequest which many have found both puzzling and provocative. He was buried as a respectable citizen in the chancel of the parish church, where his gravestone is marked not with a name, but a simple poem:

Good friend, for Jesus' sake forbear
To dig the dust enclosed here.
Blest be the man that spares these stones,
And curst be he that moves my bones.

Shakespeare's work appears to have been extremely well regarded in his lifetime; soon after his death a consensus developed that his work—his plays in particular—constitutes the highest achievement in English literature. In some generations he has been praised most highly for the depth of his characterization, in others for the dense brilliance of his imagery, in others for the extraordinary intellectual suggestiveness of the ideas that his characters express (and occasionally embody). But in every generation since the mid-seventeenth century a consensus has remained that Shakespeare stands without peer among English authors.

In most generations the study of Shakespeare has also helped to shape the development of literary criticism and theory. From John Dryden and Samuel Johnson to Samuel Taylor Coleridge to Northrop Frye, works central to the development of literary theory and criticism have had Shakespeare as their subject. And in the past 50 years Shakespeare has been a vital test case in the development of feminist literary theory, of post-colonial theory, and of political, cultural, and new historicist criticism: just as with each generation people of the theater develop new ways of playing Shakespeare that yield fresh insight, so too do scholars develop new ways of reading texts through reading Shakespeare.

The Merchant of Venice

*T*he *Merchant of Venice* is a play animated by pairs of opposing concepts, among them Jew/Christian, man/woman, fortune/ failure, and love/hate. Not surprisingly, it is the first of these pairings that has received by far the most attention. A merchant is nominally the central character of the play, but for centuries directors, literary scholars, and ordinary playgoers have all tended to see the money-lender Shylock as occupying center stage. That perception, indeed, seems to have been present from the play's earliest days; when Shakespeare's theatrical company first entered the play on the Stationers' Register in 1598, they referred to it as "a book of the Merchaunt of Venyce, or otherwise called the Jewe of Venyce." The play is as intimately bound up as any text in English literature with the history of relations between Christians and Jews (a history characterized by a good deal more persecution of Jews by Christians than many are aware of, even in this post-Holocaust era), as well as with the history of human attitudes toward money.

A play that was used as Nazi propaganda in World War II, *The Merchant of Venice*—uncomfortably listed under "Comedies" in the First Folio—presents a quandary in the twenty-first century. To what extent is *The Merchant of Venice* anti-Semitic? To what extent was Shakespeare anti-Semitic? Given the way in which Shylock is portrayed, the play demands inclusion in any history of the literature of anti-Semitism. Its story turns viciously against "the Jew" in ways that are consistent with a long tradition of anti-Jewish literature. But it is clear too that the story is structured—and that Shylock is given a voice—in ways that leave the play far more open to multiple interpretations than are other anti-Jewish works of the era. That openness should not necessarily be taken as evidence that Shakespeare himself intended the play to be read as a protest against anti-Semitism. Consider, for example, Shylock's famous "Hath not a Jew eyes?" speech:

> Hath not a Jew eyes? Hath not a Jew hands, organs, dimensions, senses, affections, passions? Fed with the same food, hurt with the same weapons, subject to the same diseases, healed by the

same means, warmed and cooled by the same winter and summer as a Christian is? If you prick us do we not bleed?

These lines—perhaps the most frequently quoted of any in the play—are generally read as if they directly confront prejudice against Jews. To be sure, the lines go some distance in humanizing Shylock. Yet it is worth noting that in Shylock's list of questions there is no mention of what humans have come to regard as our "higher" faculties. Shylock does not ask if a Jew possesses higher moral understanding, or imagination, or a capacity for spiritual experience. To the contrary: all the things he alludes to are physical or mental properties that humans are capable of sharing not only with other humans but with a number of other animal species. One could substitute *gorilla* or *chimpanzee* for *Jew* and the passage would make perfect sense. The speech, in other words, need not have done anything to disturb the assumptions of those who saw a Jew as being of a lower order than a Christian—than one who was fully human.

While Shakespeare's text can easily be read as anti-Jewish, it does make other readings possible. As has been repeatedly demonstrated in recent decades, it is even possible to mount productions in which the Christians are presented as the true villains. To be sure, such presentations often create this impression by deviating from Shakespeare's text. In his 2004 film version of the play, for example, director Michael Radford rearranges the plot to open the production with Antonio (Jeremy Irons) humiliating Shylock (Al Pacino) by spitting at him while other Venetian Jews are publicly abused and their holy books are burned. Showing us this episode first (rather than, as in the play, having it recounted to us after it has occurred), is one way in which the film tries to align our sympathies with the oppressed rather than the oppressor. That may be a reading not entirely faithful to Shakespeare's text. But neither is it in complete contradiction to what we find there; again, *The Merchant of Venice* is a text sufficiently open as to make available a multiplicity of possible readings—including readings that may go against the grain of the storyline.

The powerful issue of anti-Semitism—and the powerful presence of Shylock—often overshadow the play's other characters and other lines of story. The titular character is Antonio, a Christian Venetian merchant, and the play is, at least in part, an English playwright's look at life in Renaissance Venice and at early modern commerce. Shakespeare also presents a second, dreamier locale in Belmont, which is controlled, to a large extent, by Portia, an aristocratic woman. This setting contrasts with the ruthless, capricious, and very masculine world of Venetian commerce, but it is itself a place of potent competition. In Belmont, love is a high-stakes game—sometimes literally, as in the test given to Portia's prospective suitors—in which money plays a role at least as often as affection does.

As in so much of Shakespeare, the game of love may be between characters of different genders or of the same gender, and relationships between characters are complicated by power dynamics, by gender expectations, and even by cross-dressing. One particularly ambiguous relationship is that between Antonio and Bassanio, which is sometimes interpreted as an erotic and romantic bond, and sometimes as a strong friendship characterized by the passionate expressions of affection that were expected and valued between male friends during the early modern period. In any case, Antonio and Bassanio's relationship is one of the most intense in the play: as Solanio says of Antonio's feelings toward Bassanio, "I think he only loves the world for him."

To what extent and in what ways is the love between Antonio and Bassanio in tension with that between Bassanio and Portia? How should we read the relationships in each pairing both in terms of love and in terms of money? What commentary does the pairing between Lorenzo and Jessica offer on the broader themes of money and love, Christian and Jew? Even lesser pairings within the play—such as Gobbo and his father, Tubal and Shylock, and Nerissa and Portia—may stimulate a variety of readings. By the time the play reaches its perplexing climax and proceeds to the denouement, we have been introduced to Jews who have become Christians, women who appear to be men, and men whose greatest fortunes hinge not on their commercial successes but on the love of their friends. At an intellectual level, the play has the power to raise an extraordinarily wide range of questions—questions of money and love; of tolerance and intolerance; of justice and mercy; of the ethics of love and the ethics of commerce; of what humans owe to one another; and of the place of money in human society.

Sources

While many stories about contracts between Christian and Jewish merchants circulated throughout the medieval and early modern periods, Shakespeare's primary source appears to be a fourteenth-century Italian novella, *Il Pecorone*, known in English as *The Simpleton*. It recounts the story of Giannetto, a young man who is in love with a woman from Belmont. To win her, he must engage in a contest for which he requires money. He receives the funds from his godfather, who in turn has borrowed the sum from a Jewish moneylender who demands a pound of flesh if the loan is not repaid. The guarantee is invalidated when the woman from Belmont defends true justice in court.

As James Shapiro suggests, the trial scene in *The Merchant of Venice* may have also been influenced by Alexander Silvayn's *The Orator*, a collection of speeches published in an English translation in 1596. Additionally, Shakespeare quite possibly had in mind the recent sensational trial of Elizabeth I's doctor, Roderigo Lopez—a Jew who had converted to Christianity—who was hanged, drawn, and quartered in 1594 for allegedly attempting to poison the queen.

While Shakespeare is repeatedly associated with the "pound of flesh" motif he drew from *Il Pecorone*, neither Shakespeare nor his source can take credit for the gruesome bond. Details in scholarship differ on its origins, and it is unclear at what point the creditor comes to be clearly identified as Jewish. One early extant tale that employs the device, the Old French *Dolopathos* (late twelfth or early thirteenth century), combines numerous Greek and Latin narratives, which had been adapted from Arabic and Persian stories. In each of these versions, a story can be found about a creditor who demands a pound of flesh from a protagonist who is in love with a woman who imposes strange conditions on her suitors.

Jews and Christians in Europe and England

The religious and intellectual traditions of Christianity and Judaism overlap in at least one very important way: what Christians call the "Old Testament," which forms the largest part of the Christian Bible, also contains the works that comprise the Jewish Bible (though reordered and with some additions). How, then, did Jews come to be persecuted with such venom for so many centuries throughout so much of the Christian world?

It is important to be clear, first of all, that enmity among Christians toward Jews does not date from the time of Jesus Christ; early Christians regarded their faith as a branch of Judaism, and Jesus himself was, of course, a Jew. The three earlier gospels attributed the death of Jesus to the Sadducees (a particular group of Jewish priests); it is not until the somewhat later Gospel of John (which dates from the second century CE) that Jews are collectively blamed for killing Christ. In the late fourth and early fifth century the most influential of the "Church fathers," Augustine of Hippo, went further, arguing not only that Jews were collectively responsible for the death of Jesus but that, in perpetuity, all Jews deserved to suffer in punishment for the deed. (Notably, some of Augustine's contemporaries criticized him for being too tolerant toward Jews because he forbade killing them, arguing that, given their importance as witnesses to the Christian revelation and the role they had to play in the end of days, they should be permitted to live.)

The climate for Jews in the Christian world was thus made extremely difficult throughout the medieval period—though the severity of persecution began to increase in the twelfth century. In Europe anti-Semitism at that time received a powerful impetus from the interplay of religious doctrines and economic developments. The European system of feudalism that prevailed from the fifth through to the eleventh century had been based primarily on subsistence agriculture; in most areas there had been little by way of trade and virtually no money based economy. In the eleventh and twelfth centuries—and even earlier in Venice—that began to change; trade began to grow, labor began to be somewhat more specialized, and the seeds of a merchant economy began to be sown throughout Europe. Both merchant ventures and the commercial growing of crops could require substantial amounts of money—and if one did not possess enough to fund one's efforts, one needed to borrow. Such needs placed Christians in a difficult position: economic pressures required that ventures be funded, and funding on any substantial scale could hardly be expected to be forthcoming unless lenders could receive some return on their money. But the Christian church had since the fourth century forbidden the practice of charging interest on any loan.

Whereas one might have expected these economic pressures to have led to a softening of the Church's antipathy toward moneylending, the opposite happened; the third and fourth Lateran Councils (of 1179 and 1215) hardened the Church's position against "usury," which was then defined far more broadly than it is today. Now, the term is applied only to the charging of excessive interest, but in the Middle Ages charging any interest whatsoever was considered usury. So too, in the more wide-ranging definitions, was any form of compensation for lending money; payment of "interest" in the form of goods or services was as strictly forbidden as was the charging of interest in monetary form. Many Christians continued to lend money, often making creative use of elaborate contracts to disguise interest charges, but faced severe penalties if they were caught. The medieval church declared that any Christian who engaged in usury would be excommunicated—a punishment that not only meant spiritual exclusion, since excommunicates could not receive communion or other sacraments, but also carried devastating social consequences.

To try to reconcile the economic need to borrow with the religious prohibition on borrowing the Christians turned to the Jews, who were prohibited by their religion from lending to fellow Jews, but not from lending to "foreigners." In most jurisdictions it became common to prohibit Jews from engaging in a wide variety of occupations, but to permit them and, indeed, to encourage them to lend money. William the Conqueror made a point of bringing Jewish settlers into Britain in order to act as moneylenders—with the clear understanding that the Crown would be a frequent borrower. In northern Italy as in England, Jews were not allowed to own land. They were allowed to lend money, however; Jewish moneylenders were to be found on benches in local grain markets, advancing payment against expected future receipts of the harvest, and, before long, against anticipated future receipts of grain deliveries to distant ports. (The Old Italian *banco* means *bench*; these were the roots of banking, which had developed in something like its modern sense by the late fourteenth century in the northern Italian centers of Siena, Florence, Genoa, and Venice.)

To restrict Jewish people very largely to a necessary occupation that Christianity regarded as villainy may have been an effective way of dealing with Christians' conflicted feelings, and certainly it was an effective means of keeping the wheels of commerce turning. But the almost inevitable by-product was the transference of negative associations linked to the growing moneyed economy onto Jewish people themselves. If harvests failed and loans could not readily be repaid, if the general economy soured, if Christians came to feel that the world was becoming too commercial, too materialistic, there was a convenient scapegoat.

The association between Jews and financial hardship combined with other factors—such as an increase in religious fervor, stirred up by the Crusades—and in the twelfth and thirteenth centuries anti-Semitism took on a new virulence throughout Europe. Christians began to accuse Jews of outrageous crimes such as re-enacting the Crucifixion using Christian victims; murdering Christian children and drinking their blood; and desecrating the host (the bread used in communion, which is spiritually equivalent to the body of Christ). The stereotypes applied to Jews became increasingly frightening and dehumanized: Jews were seen not only as extortionate, wealthy, and motivated by greed but also as cruel, bestial, and motivated by hatred of Christians and Christianity. In 1189 and 1190 Christians killed hundreds of Jews in massacres throughout England; in 1264 Simon de Montfort was among those calling for all Jews in London to be killed.

Initially, the monarchy offered some protection to Jews because the moneylending services they provided (not to mention the disproportionately high taxes they paid) were an important financial contribution to the government. But in 1275 Edward I responded to the tide of anti-Semitism by forbidding Jews from moneylending, thus leaving them little or no means of legal subsistence; in 1290 he went further, expelling all Jews from England. Although some Jews may have remained illegally and some converted to Christianity, most of the Jewish population—which by this point had been reduced to about 2,000, less than half of what it had been 150 years before—left as a result of Edward's edict. From the late thirteenth century until 1656 no Jew could live legally in England.

Even though there were virtually no Jews in England, the figure of the Jew continued to play a prominent role in the English literature of the late medieval and Renaissance periods. In stories of the miracles of the Virgin that were popular currency throughout the late Middle Ages; in Geoffrey Chaucer's "The Prioress's Tale"; in John Mandeville's *Travels* and other widely read travel literature; in Raphael Hollinshed's *Chronicles* and other popular histories; in popular works of prose fiction such as Thomas Nashe's *The Unfortunate Traveller*; in plays such as Christopher Marlowe's *The Jew of Malta*—in English literature as a whole through these centuries, Jews are pilloried, caricatured not just as heartless moneylenders but also as purveyors of blasphemy and sadistic violence.[1] John Foxe, the author of the enormously popular *Actes and Monuments* (1563), described Jews in one of his sermons as "scorpionlike savages, so furiously boiling against the innocent infants of the Christian Gentiles," and railed against the Jews' supposed "heinous abominations, insatiable butcheries, treasons, frenzies, and madness." Similar language is common in other writings of the period.

Edward I may have expelled the Jews centuries earlier, but Christians in England[2] had not ceased to be conflicted about matters of money and religion, and the figure of the imagined Jew provided an outlet for such anxieties. As the level of commerce increased—especially in London, which was becoming a great commercial center—imagined Jews retained a central place in English consciousness (and, surely, in the English unconscious as well). If one were writing about

---

1 Though Jews were vilified in the vast majority of cases where they are represented in the literature of the time, it should be noted that the popular imagination also occasionally offered an alternative point of view. Robert Wilson's *The Three Ladies of London* (1584), for example, presents a scenario strikingly similar to that of *The Merchant of Venice*, except that the roles are reversed: an Italian merchant who has borrowed 2,000 ducats from a Jewish moneylender and then failed to repay the loan (despite having profited from it) is depicted as greedy and mean-spirited, while the Jew is depicted as reasonable and courteous throughout. The play frames the action as portraying behavior untypical of both Christians and Jews (the Judge in the case concludes that "as appears by this, / Jews seek to excel in Christianity, and the Christians in Jewishness"), but the play is nevertheless a far cry from the Jew-hating diatribes that were more common literary fare in the period. Shakespeare was in all probability familiar with Wilson's play.

2 To use the umbrella term "Christians in England" may well be said to represent a distortion as well as an oversimplification; the conflicts between Catholic and Protestant (and among many Protestant groups) are a dominant theme from the early sixteenth century onward. But hostility toward Jews remained one thing that Catholics and Protestants of almost every stripe held broadly in common; for that reason it has been decided not to retell in this context a story that is so well told elsewhere. It may be worth noting, however, that Catholics were among the groups who were viciously discriminated against in 1590s England; that as a consequence many Catholics practiced their faith in secret (much as Jews had done); and that many scholars have suggested that Shakespeare may himself have been raised in a family that secretly practiced Catholicism.

commerce and about money in Shakespeare's England, one would almost always come back to the figure of the Jew.

The Economic Background

The word "merchant" is the root of the word economic historians use to refer to the economic system that prevailed in late sixteenth- and early seventeenth-century Europe: mercantilism. In some respects trade during this period was similar to international trade today: it was conducted in part by individual merchants, in part by companies, and it had begun to be financed largely through the two primary means companies use today to raise capital: borrowing money or selling shares in the company. In other ways, however, international trade in the world of mercantilism was quite different. Insurance did not yet exist; until well into the seventeenth century one could not manage (or, indeed, calculate) financial risk in the way that is done today as a matter of course. Another important difference was that individual merchants or companies from within a country usually did not compete against each other for the same trade as companies do today. Instead, individuals or companies were typically granted monopolies to trade in particular goods in particular areas; in return for the grant of the charter, they paid a fee to the monarch. In England the first of these companies and also the first English joint-stock company was the Company of Merchant Adventurers, chartered in 1551. Over the next sixty years many more were given their charter— among them the Venice Company, the East India Company, and the Virginia Company.

If the possibility of storms and shipwrecks was an ever-present threat to international shipping in the 1590s, the threat of piracy could sometimes be just as great. Another means through which monarchs raised money was the sale of licenses entitling sailors to seize ships of other nations and commandeer their cargo. Cargoes of precious metal were specially prized; even more than is the case today, precious metals such as gold and silver were taken to be the foundation of the world's system of money, trade, and wealth. (The caskets of gold, silver, and lead that feature in the test given to Portia's suitors are one of many respects in which the world of *The Merchant of Venice* reflects the world of the 1590s.) The English were especially adept at "privateering"—to use the more polite word for the state-sanctioned piracy of the time. It was largely due to the success of English privateers off the coasts of Spain and Portugal that Spain, its finances in ruin, abandoned its efforts to invade England. All this is very much a part of the background to *The Merchant of Venice*—and in some instances part of the foreground as well. Notably, when Salarino calls up the image of the ship *Andrew* having been lost, it is generally accepted that the play is referencing the *San Andrés*, a Spanish galleon captured by English ships during a raid on the city of Cadiz in 1596.

* * *

If anti-Semitism was a constant presence in English culture through the late medieval and early modern period, it was especially virulent during times of economic crisis. In England, the 1590s was just such a time. The decade in which the greatest flowering of English poetry and drama began was also a decade of severe economic hardship for the majority of people. In the large sweep of English history, the 1590s lie close to the center of the centuries-long period of transition from the feudalism of the medieval period to the establishment of modern capitalism in the eighteenth and nineteenth centuries. Under the feudalism of the manorial system, the vast majority of the population had worked on land owned by the lord, paying him rent with a portion of the crops produced on the land. The loss of more than half the populace through plague in 1348 helped to set in motion a vast series of changes.[1] Wage labor became common—as did guilds of workers in various trades. Agricultural land began to be consolidated and worked by fewer hands, and displaced workers gravitated more and more to towns; the problem that we now call unemployment was what sixteenth-century writers are referencing when they speak of "vagabonds and beggars." Overall, England was more and more becoming a money economy. Though both prices and wages were set by state-appointed magistrates and were supposed to bear a "reasonable" relation to each other, in practice prices rose faster than

---

1 For reasons that remain unclear, after the Black Death population levels in England did not rebound as they did in other European countries; the population of England and Wales remained relatively steady from the late 1300s until the beginning of the sixteenth century. Modest population growth became the norm from the 1520s onwards, but this growth was frequently interrupted—for example, by widespread disease in the 1550s and widespread harvest failure in the 1590s.

wages throughout the sixteenth century. Those who employed laborers or who lived largely off rents did well—as did many merchants (of which more below). The majority were far less fortunate—particularly when the 1590s brought five years of consecutive failed or disappointing harvests (from 1594–98) that were devastating for agricultural laborers. Less work meant lower wages, and grain shortages sent prices skyrocketing. All of this resulted in the buying power of ordinary laborers being lower in the late 1590s than at any other time in recorded English history. Many craftsmen and farm laborers became more and more desperate; rioting was widespread.

Understandably enough in such circumstances, more and more workers made efforts to establish themselves as something other than wage earners—or, very frequently, as wage earners with another business on the side, becoming clothiers or smiths or small-time traders. All such activity fueled the growth of the money economy, and fueled too dependence on an economy of credit and debt; investments were made by incurring debts, and goods were increasingly sold on credit. The expansion of credit networks was so large, and those networks so fragile, that from the 1580s onwards lawsuits over unpaid debts drove the largest litigation boom in English history. By the 1590s it was not only the great merchants with their argosies who worried about debt, but a wide cross section of the populace. In times of economic downturn, people might not complain about wages being too low, but they would surely complain about the charges levied on debt being too high.

And what were those charges? After 1571 the charging of interest no longer had to be dressed up as some other sort of charge or fee; the Act against Usury made it legal to charge interest, while capping the interest rate at 10 per cent. When Shakespeare wrote *The Merchant of Venice*, usury had for twenty-five years been legally defined not as the charging of interest per se, but as the charging of excessive interest. But the debate over whether usury should be defined this way—and the outrage many still felt at the very idea of earning money from money—remained very much a part of the English landscape, for many yeomen and artisans and laborers as well as for the merchant class.

There was much outrage too during the course of this period over a closely related issue: the penalties incurred if debts were not repaid according to the letter of the bond (the document binding the debtor to the creditor). Very commonly that penalty was double the amount lent; in other words, debtors who were a day late in repaying their loans would suddenly owe twice the amount they had originally borrowed. Given that the terms of most bonds specified repayment in three months rather than a full year, this meant that forfeiture penalties could amount to the equivalent of an annual rate of interest of 400 per cent. The Common Law was so rigid that the penalty could be claimed even in instances where the loan had been partially or even fully repaid: the only proof of repayment Common Law courts accepted was a signed and sealed acquittance (a type of receipt) noting repayment, or else the original bond "cancelled" by its text being crossed out and its seal removed. This meant that friends, relatives, or traders might settle a debt informally and think no more about it for 5, 10, or even 20 years, but when they died their executors or heirs discovered their un-cancelled bonds and put them in suit to claim the penalty. In such a case Common Law procedure did not allow testimony or explanations but looked only at the bond itself for signs of cancelling—which helps explain why Shylock repeatedly tells Antonio to "look to his bond" (3.1.39–41) and refuses to hear Antonio speak (e.g. 3.3.11–13).[1]

The temptation to claim bond penalties, then, was clearly very strong in Elizabethan England (just as it is in the play, where Shylock appears so focused on forfeiture that he charges Antonio no interest at all on his loan). Nor was there any escape of the sort offered by today's procedures for personal bankruptcy, under the terms of which individuals may be relieved of the burden of unsustainable debts. In the late sixteenth century imprisonment was starting to become the most common penalty for non-repayment of a debt. In many cases too,

---

1   This strict "letter of the law" approach upset many debtors, who ran to the Court of Chancery, an alternative to Common-Law courts. The Court of Chancery did not have to follow the Common Law but instead operated according to the principle of equity, meaning it had the flexibility to make rulings that took account of personal circumstances and ethical concerns. This court did offer relief to many debtors, but the discretion it employed could be misused or misapplied, for example if a debtor lied about having repaid a loan while the creditor was alive. *The Merchant of Venice* does not contain any direct references to the kind of equity dispensed in Chancery, but the loud Elizabethan debate about strict liability and equitable discretion or fairness, especially with regard to debt, provides one of the topical backdrops for the action of the play.

lenders were accused of resorting to questionable practices in order to disguise the full financial implications from those contemplating taking out a loan. (One might liken such practices to those followed in the twenty-first century by unscrupulous financial institutions offering sub-prime mortgages to unwary first-time house buyers of limited means.) In this context, the extremity of the terms of Shylock's bond may have been perceived in 1590s England as being far less distant from the actual practices of lenders than it may seem today. More generally, financial hardship combined with fear of debt to make the English climate in the 1590s extremely hostile toward moneylenders, and—the concept of "Jew" having become so closely entwined in the Christian imagination with the concept of "moneylender"—particularly hospitable to anti-Jewish feeling.

* * *

As today, debt in the late sixteenth century was not only a matter of what was owed by individuals; it was also a matter of what was owed by the state. The defeat of the Spanish Armada by Sir Francis Drake (and the weather) in 1588 is fixed in the popular imagination as a great triumph for England—and in a real sense it was. But it is often forgotten that the war dragged on until 1603 (there were Spanish Armadas in 1596, 1597, and 1601 as well as in 1588) and ended in stalemate. Though the cost of war was less ruinous to the English than to the Spanish, it was nonetheless very steep. Elizabeth raised taxes, sold land, and sold monopolies to help pay for the war, but she was also forced to borrow. She may have incurred far less debt than her successor, James I, but her policy of borrowing in England rather than from European moneylenders must have had the effect of reducing the supply of funds available for lending elsewhere. This was one more factor contributing to the economic crisis in general, and to the frustration of borrowers and would-be borrowers in particular.

Jews in Early Modern England and Venice

If the pressures of financing the war effort contributed to public sentiment against moneylenders (and thereby against Jews), so too did war-related efforts to inspire national feeling. As we see reflected in the sentiments expressed in *Henry V* (which Shakespeare wrote at about the same time as he wrote *The Merchant of Venice*), national identity was not yet fully forged during this era. And, as James Shapiro has persuasively argued, one way of identifying "those who were not English [was] by pointing to those who were assuredly not—e.g., the Irish and the Jews," and by caricaturing these groups with exaggerated or imagined features. Jews were said to be characterized by long noses and an unpleasant smell.

But who were the Jews?[1] In the late fifteenth century, around the time that Jews were banished from Spain and from Portugal, many had converted to Christianity. How many converts adopted Christian beliefs, and how many feigned them to avoid persecution and exile? That could never be known with any degree of certainty, but Jews who had converted came to be known as Marranos or Conversos—and the suspicion among Christians persisted that their true beliefs (as well as their true ethnicity) remained Jewish. Throughout the period, such doubts continued to cast a shadow over Jews who had converted to Christianity (a fact that adds additional resonance to Shylock's forced conversion). Venice went so far as to expel most of its Marranos in 1550. This is how the ambassador of the Duke of Ferreira put the matter in a letter written that year:

> Marranos are worse than Jews, because they are neither Christians nor Jews. All the Jews live together in the Ghetto, separated from Christians, but the Marranos have to do with Christians and live in several parts of the city.... Such association is the cause of many errors, especially in making many Christians transgress. Furthermore, the Marranos lend money upon usury, and they may by their familiarity persuade our own people to do the same thing. They are a malevolent, faithless people, up to no good, and they might infect not only the souls of Christians but also their bodies with disease.

In England, the term "Marranos" came to be used as shorthand for "Jews"—especially Spanish Jews—who professed to be Christian

---

1 This question is complicated not least of all by the tenets of Judaism, according to which one cannot cease being a Jew simply by renouncing the faith; Judaism is thus defined not only as a matter of faith but also as a matter of culture and lineage. In Shakespeare's England there were certainly some Jews according to this latter definition, though probably very few.

while secretly practicing Judaism. Though they were far more numerous in popular imagination than they were in fact, paranoia regarding Marranos came to color the common perception of Jews in general, such that Jewishness was associated not only with usury and greed but also, now even more than at other points in English history, with foreignness and duplicity.

The most famous Marrano in Shakespeare's England was the Queen's doctor, Roderigo Lopez, who has often been suggested as a model Shakespeare may have had in mind when he drew the character of Shylock. Raised as a Christian in Portugal, Lopez had become a successful doctor[1] but was driven from the country by the Inquisition's systematic persecution of converted Jews. He settled in London where he again built a successful medical practice, became the Queen's physician, and was granted a monopoly on the importation of two sorts of medicinal herb. In 1594, however, he was accused of conspiring to poison the Queen. Though the evidence was flimsy, he was convicted and executed. According to the Elizabethan historian William Camden, Lopez died "affirming that he loved the Queen as well as he loved Jesus Christ." Camden goes on to say that Lopez's words, "coming from a man of the Jewish profession, moved no small laughter in the standers-by"; Camden, in other words, presumes that, despite having been a practicing Christian all his life, Lopez, as a Jew by birth, must also have been one who secretly professed Judaism.

While openly practicing Jews were simply unable to live in England during Shakespeare's lifetime, in Venice they faced legal discrimination of a different kind. Before 1516, Jews had been banned from staying in the city for more than 15 days a year; by the provisions of a 1516 decree, Jews were "permitted to come and live in Venice." It was a "privilege" that came with severe restrictions attached, however, as outlined in the decree:

> Given the urgent needs of the present times, the said Jews have been permitted to come and live in Venice…. But no godfearing

---

1   Lopez had been accepted as a Christian by the medical school at the University of Coimbra in central Portugal; he graduated in 1540. Portuguese universities, like most others in Europe—several Italian institutions being notable exceptions—did not allow Jews to enroll as students. There was nevertheless a strong Jewish medical tradition across Europe, and it was quite common for members of the nobility (as well as bishops and popes) to have a personal physician of Jewish background.

subject of our state would have wished them, after their arrival, to disperse throughout the city, sharing houses with Christians and going wherever they choose by day and night, perpetrating all those misdemeanors and detestable and abominable acts which are generally known and shameful to describe…. [Therefore], all the Jews who are at present living in different parishes within our city, and all others who may come here, until the law is changed as the times may demand and as shall be deemed expedient, shall be obliged to go at once to dwell together in the houses within the court within the Geto at San Hieronimo, where there is plenty of room for them to live…. Two high walls shall be built to close off the other two sides, which rise above the canals, and all the quays attached to the said houses shall be walled in.

This was the origin of the term *ghetto*. Jews were also restricted from entering professions other than the manufacture of certain items of clothing, the trade in second-hand goods, and various professions related to moneylending. The rate of interest they could charge was controlled—restricted from 1573 until well into the seventeenth century to a maximum of 5 per cent per annum. Later in the century the Pope banned the Talmud (a compendium of teachings central to Jewish law and culture), and in 1571, the Venetian government unsuccessfully attempted to expel Jewish people from Venice.[1] The law, then, was designed to ensure that Jews would contribute commercially to Venice on terms laid down by the city's Christian rulers, while ensuring at the same time that the Jewish presence would have minimal social impact on its Christian residents.

---

1 It may be worth noting here that Venetian law sometimes made distinctions between different types of Jew. When the Venetian statutes of the time refer simply to "Jews" ("Ebrei"), they mean Ashkenazi Jews (sometimes referred to by the Venetians as "Ebrei Tedeschi")— Jews of Germanic or Central European ethnic background. It was this group that suffered the severest persecution. If they were often involved in activities such as moneylending, it was largely because, as in many other jurisdictions in Europe, they had little choice. Jews of Mediterranean ethnic origin (known as Sephardic Jews) were sometimes treated rather less harshly by the authorities—particularly if they were wealthy Sephardic Jews wishing to immigrate to Venice. (Jews had been expelled from Spain in 1492, from Portugal in 1495, and from Naples in 1533.) Even the Sephardic Jews, however, were required in the same way as other Jews to wear a yellow identifying cap, and to live in the Jewish ghetto.

As may readily be surmised from this account of institutionalized discrimination, Antonio's treatment of Shylock would not have been atypical in late sixteenth-century Venice.

Venice and the World of Commerce

In the late sixteenth century Venice was—like London—a great trading city with a population of about 200,000; appropriately enough, *The Merchant of Venice* opens with grand poetic descriptions of the centrality of trade to commerce. Salarino and Solanio depict the exotic and opulent Venice, whose ports are filled with ships heading for the Orient and returning with spices and silks. The firm grip that Venice had held for centuries over trade in the Mediterranean made it an obvious setting for a play concerned with bonds and the hazards of trade. Yet at the time Shakespeare was writing *The Merchant of Venice*, Italy's dominance over trade was beginning to wane, while England—despite its economic hardships—was ascending as a European maritime power. By the 1590s England was asserting itself as a powerful commercial force in the Mediterranean as elsewhere.

While improved foreign relations may have contributed to England's successes in the Mediterranean trade, a crisis in Italian shipping may have also been partially responsible. Well-constructed for trade in the Mediterranean, the Italian ships were ill-suited to the much larger and wilder Atlantic. As nautical improvements and larger ships began to make travel throughout the Atlantic and Indian oceans more feasible in the late sixteenth century, the Italians failed to rebuild in order to keep pace; by the 1590s their merchant fleet was beginning to seem antiquated by comparison with those of the English, Dutch, Portuguese, or Spanish.

Did ambitious investments in new ships come less easily to Venetians in the late sixteenth and early seventeenth centuries than they had in earlier times? That may well have been the case. There was evidently no shortage of available funds to invest. But there seems to have been a trend toward more Venetian investment inland in agricultural ventures. And there also seems to have been a shift in attitudes. Though it dates from some fifteen years after *The Merchant of Venice* was written, a very interesting 1612 report by Sir Dudley Carleton, then the English ambassador, on the state of Venice and of

Venetians may well be of relevance, as he is clearly writing of changes that would have happened over the course of many years. While acknowledging that the Venetians remain skilled in the art of "raising money," Carleton does not speak as well of the prospects for Venetian trade and commerce:

> [Venetians] change their manners, they are grown factious, vindictive, loose, and unthrifty. Their former course of life was merchandising, which is now quite left, and they look to landward, being house and land, furnishing themselves with coach and horses, and giving themselves the good time with more show and gallantry than was wont, ... Their [former habit] ... was to send their sons upon galleys into the Levant to accustom them to navigation and to trade. They now send them to travaile [i.e., to gentlemanly work], and to learn more of the gentleman than the merchant.... In manner of trade the decay is so manifest that all men conclude within twenty years [there will be] not one part left of three....

We cannot know, of course, to what extent Shakespeare may have had knowledge of the trends in behavior and attitude of the merchant class in Venice when he was writing of Antonio. But the picture that *The Merchant of Venice* paints is consistent with those trends. As the play opens the merchant Antonio has gambled his fortune on capricious seas. And he is clearly ambitious in the risks he takes; as a major entrepreneur, he is the owner of "argosies"—merchant ships—that "overpeer the petty traffickers / That curtsy to them, do them reverence." When the play opens, Antonio's companions worry that their friend may be feeling the burden of the risks inherent to his trade. He assures them he has managed his risks ("My ventures are not in one bottom trusted, / Nor to one place") and remains untroubled—so much so that he is willing to go further into debt in order to provide his beloved Bassanio with "the means / To hold a rival place" with Portia's wealthy suitors. In the end, Antonio's confidence is indeed shaken by the disasters that are believed to have befallen him. He seems to be left with no appetite for investing in new merchant ventures; all that he expects to remain of his wealth he directs to be held in trust for Lorenzo and Jessica. And when he is improbably saved from financial ruin ("three of your argosies / Are richly come to harbour suddenly"), we hear nothing of any new ventures; the play's final act is dominated by the ring plot, by sweet music, and by the dalliance of Jessica and Lorenzo, who has become a gentleman of leisure. As we see them at play's end, the Venetians are indeed "giving themselves the good time" in the opulent world of Belmont.

Revenge and Justice

In Renaissance English drama, revenge was an extremely popular theme. Its prevalence reflected the influence of the first-century Roman playwright Seneca, many of whose five-act plays centered on the protagonist's struggle to avenge a wrong—typically through gruesomely violent acts that are wholly out of proportion to the original offense. Seneca's plays depict violent revenge, rather than condoning it; to the contrary, Seneca himself claimed that anger led people into a temporary insanity, from which state they were driven to do danger ous and immoral things.

Revenge came to dominate the English stage after the debut of Thomas Kyd's *The Spanish Tragedy* (c. 1589), a play that did more than any other to set the pattern of the "revenge drama." Kyd's play adopted Seneca's plot structure, his use of rhetorical devices such as stichomythia (the quick exchange of single lines of dialogue between two characters), his incorporation of a ghost who appears to the protagonist early in the play, and the central element of excessive, violent vengeance. *The Spanish Tragedy*, however, differed from its Roman predecessors in that, while Seneca's plays described the action in long speeches, Kyd's enacted the violence onstage. Though early modern revenge tragedies drew heavily on *The Spanish Tragedy* as a model, they differed among themselves in how closely they adhered to it, and in the degree of sophistication with which they explored the psychology of the revenger. Such variation exists within the works of Shakespeare himself: one of his earliest plays, *Titus Andronicus* (c. 1590), displays a relatively straightforward adoption of revenge drama's conventions, while *Hamlet* (c. 1601) is a much more mature, even experimental execution of the form.

The Merchant of Venice is a play about revenge that falls partly outside the tradition of the revenge drama. Like a typical revenger,

Shylock is driven by anger and hatred to exact vengeance even at the expense of his own interests—in his pursuit of the pound of flesh, he refuses repayment three times what he is owed. The penalty he wishes to enforce is, of course, extremely severe in relation to Antonio's crime. Shylock's actions are, however, moderate and rational in contrast with the extreme depictions of madness and grisly bloodbaths that appeared in typical revenge tragedies of the period. Most importantly, while typical revengers have no recourse to the law and take matters into their own hands, in *The Merchant of Venice* revenge is sought by legal means. Though he admits that his demand for the pound of flesh is motivated by "a lodged hate and a certain loathing" he bears toward Antonio, Shylock believes himself to be legally in the right: "If you deny me," he claims, "There is no force in the decrees of Venice." Shylock sees the law as specifying an exact penalty—the pound of flesh for the failure to repay the debt—and he frames the legal obligation in terms of buying and selling: "The pound of flesh which I demand of him / Is dearly bought. 'Tis mine, and I will have it." While typical revengers pursue their vengeance outside the normal social order, Shylock attempts his vengeance through the enforcement of a contract. *The Merchant of Venice* thus dramatizes the violence underlying everyday economic and legal interactions in a way not usually seen in revenge plays.

In the end, the court does not defend the rights Shylock believes himself to possess. Portia, in her lawyer's disguise, argues that, while Shylock has the right to a pound of flesh, he is not entitled to shed any blood—and that if he does he will be punished for an attempt to kill a Venetian Christian. But Portia goes even further, turning the law against Shylock entirely: for his attempt on Antonio's life, he is condemned to lose half his fortune, required to will the rest to the daughter who betrayed him, and forced to convert to Christianity. Though the Christians frequently speak of mercy during the courtroom scene, it may be argued that by the end of the trial they, as much as Shylock, have become seekers of unreasonable revenge—only, in the case of the Christians, revenge appears in the guise of justice, sanctioned by the Venetian court.

It has been suggested that the action at this point in the play is implausible. How can a judge keep discovering provisions that no one else seems to have been aware of? In this respect, though, Shakespeare may again have been writing with more knowledge of the true state of affairs in Venice than he is sometimes given credit for. Among the Venetian documents that have come down to us from the second half of the sixteenth century is a 1580 commentary by Alberto Bolognetti, a papal nuncio, on the degree to which the Venetians "make extensive use of discretion" and are inclined "to punish crime on the strength of conjecture alone." A somewhat earlier commentary on Venice's legal system (*Relatione di Venicia in tre parti*, c. 1569) goes even further:

> Nor are their laws very constant and stable, for they are often altered and fundamentally changed—hence the truth of the saying,
> "Seven days suffice before
> Time obscures a Venetian law."

The law in Venice, then, may well have been fluid and unpredictable—and open to arbitrary interpretation and caprice. The historical record, as much as Shakespeare's play, leaves a great deal of uncertainty as to what constituted justice in late sixteenth-century Venice.

Gender, Love, Marriage, Money

Like several of Shakespeare's other dramas, *The Merchant of Venice* engages with the expectations early modern English culture attached to womanhood—and uses cross-dressing to grant some characters a temporary reprieve from those expectations. Portia and her gentlewoman, Nerissa, defy gender precepts in order to save Bassanio's best friend, Antonio. Disguising themselves as young men—Portia as a young lawyer and Nerissa as "his" clerk—they boldly take control of the male space of the courtroom, where Portia depends on her intellectual and rhetorical skill to argue for Antonio's life.

Cross-dressing was a frequent plot device in English Renaissance drama. In plays of this period, most cross-dressing characters are women disguised as men—a trend complicated by the fact that on the Elizabethan stage female characters were themselves played by convincingly costumed men or boys. Shakespeare incorporated cross-dressing plots into about a fifth of his plays, and cross-dressing heroines feature in many of his comedies; Viola in *Twelfth Night* and Rosalind in *As You Like It* are notable examples. However, the light-hearted treatment of male disguise in such plays belies the fact that outside the theater cross-dressing was illegal as well as morally censured (and associated, both in Venice and in London, with prostitution and other sexual misconduct).

Dressing in disguise enables Portia and Nerissa to play a role in the legal process that was not available to the women in the play's audience. Early modern English women did not have the same rights in a courtroom as men did, though certainly many women were involved in court proceedings. According to the dictates of Elizabethan Common Law, only unmarried women were usually permitted to make legal claims independently of their husbands or male relatives, but in actual practice, it was not at all unusual for women to speak for themselves in court—including the many married women who made legal claims alongside their husbands. Since watching other people's court proceedings was a much more common pastime in early modern London than it is now, many members of *Merchant*'s original audience would have seen women speak knowledgeably and articulately in a court setting. No one, however, would have seen a real-life woman wield the sort of legal authority that Portia displays, as no women were permitted to occupy any official roles in the court. This prohibition reflected common attitudes toward the capacities of women; while the period distinguished all humans from "mere beasts" on account of their reason, women were generally regarded as less rational than men and, by extension, more governed by emotion and physical passions. But in the courtroom scene Portia acts according to reason rather than passion to secure Antonio's life and Shylock's punishment; the persuasive power of her speeches comes not from overflowing emotion but from rhetorical effect, reasoned argument, and knowledge of the law.

Extremely rich and independent as well as intelligent, Portia is nonetheless restricted by norms dictating that obedience to one's father or one's husband should trump an upper-class woman's personal desires. It is not always clear to what extent she employs her wits and her wealth in the service of obedience, and to what extent she uses them to assert her own agency. Compelled by her deceased father to marry the first man to pass the test of the three caskets, does Portia faithfully subject herself to her father's will? Or does the music she selects to be played during Bassanio's test—a song in which each line of the first verse rhymes with "lead," the correct casket—constitute a subtle hint to ensure Bassanio's victory? Does she adopt her lawyer's disguise merely to save her husband's friend, or does her use of the disguise to obtain Bassanio's ring suggest an attempt to secure the upper hand in her marriage? Portia's clever, perhaps subversive compliance contrasts with the overt rebellion of Jessica—another cross-dressing character—who employs a male disguise to expressly disobey Shylock, not only escaping her father's house to marry without his consent but also rejecting his religion and stealing his riches.

The emphasis placed on Portia's wealth—and on Jessica's theft from her father—in *The Merchant of Venice* suggests the degree to which wealthy Elizabethans viewed marriage as a commercial arrangement. The strange game that Portia's father has imposed on her to determine her husband may be rooted in a desire to counter the suitors' intentions of marrying for wealth, but the storyline is equally dependent on Bassanio's borrowing money to make himself seem wealthier than he is in order to woo Portia. "If you do love me, you will find me out," asserts Portia, but the audience may be forgiven for feeling it may not be quite so simple. Bassanio argues that the world is "deceived with ornament"; rejecting the symbols of wealth and of beauty, he chooses the lead casket rather than the silver or the gold—and thereby gains Portia's wealth as well as her beauty.

The final act of *The Merchant of Venice* takes the form of a conventional comedy of love, with the knotted narrative strands wittily untangled so that Antonio is once again wealthy and the three couples' marriages are affirmed. In Act 5 Venice has disappeared; Shylock's misery is forgotten, and the world of commerce is treated as if it were irrelevant to the lovers in dreamy Belmont. But do we forget the world in which money and the love of money seem to be the most powerful engines of human interaction, religious hatred holds sway, and fortunes may be swallowed by the sea or by the caprice of the law? Antonio's survival, Lorenzo and Jessica's promised financial security, and even Portia and Nerissa's trickery regarding their disguised courtroom appearance, are all of course connected to Shylock's ruin in the previous act. For many audiences, the play's seemingly lighthearted resolution does little to cover over the dark events that led to it.

The Text

Like most editions, this one uses the First Quarto of 1600 as its base text. We do not know precisely when the play was written, or when it was first performed, though the First Quarto indicates that the play had been by that time performed with some frequency by The Lord Chamberlain's Men. The play is referred to in a 1598 work by Francis Meres, and it was also entered on the Stationers' Register during that year. The apparent reference to the 1596 raid on Cadiz would seem to preclude dating the play before then; almost all scholars have concluded that it dates from between 1596 and 1598.

The First Quarto does not include a list of characters, or divisions into acts and scenes. The present edition follows convention in taking the act divisions from the 1623 Folio (the first to include them), and adopting the scene divisions that were first incorporated in the eighteenth century.

* * *

In the preparation of this edition, the advice of the following academics has been invaluable: Adrienne Williams Boyarin, University of Victoria; Julia Garrett, University of Wisconsin, Madison; Stephen Guy-Bray, University of British Columbia; Tim Stretton, Saint Mary's University.

THE MERCHANT
OF VENICE

The Merchant of Venice[1]

[THE ACTORS' NAMES[2]

The Duke of Venice.

Morocco, a Prince, and a suitor to Portia.

The Prince of Aragon, suitor also to Portia.

Bassanio, an Italian Lord, suitor likewise to Portia.

Antonio, a merchant of Venice.

Salarino,   } Gentlemen
Solanio,   } of Venice,
Graziano,   } and companions
Lorenzo,   } with Bassanio.

Shylock, the rich Jew and father of Jessica.

Tubal, a Jew, Shylock's friend.

Portia, the rich Italian Lady.

Nerissa, her waiting-gentlewoman.

Jessica, daughter to Shylock.

Gobbo, an old man, father to Lancelot.

Lancelot Gobbo the clown.

Leonardo, Bassanio's servant.

Salerio,[3] a messenger from Venice.

Man, one of Antonio's servants.

Stefano, Portia's messenger.

Balthasar, one of Portia's servants.

Messenger, another of Portia's servants.

Servingman, another of Portia's servants.

Jailor, magnificoes,[4] court officers, attendants, and musicians.]

---

1   *The Merchant of Venice* In the Quarto, the first printed edition of the play, the title page calls the play "The most excellent *Historie of the Merchant of Venice*," though the title appears throughout the play itself as "The comicall History of the Merchant of Venice." The shorter *The Merchant of Venice* appeared in the later Folio edition, printed in 1623.

2   THE ACTORS' NAMES No list of characters appeared in either the First Quarto or First Folio editions; the following is based on that which appeared in the Third Quarto, the first edition to contain such a list.

3   *Salerio* Some scholars consider the names "Salerio" and "Salarino" to refer to the same character, and thus some editions of the play omit the name "Salarino" and replace it with "Salerio." In this edition, both names appear as they do in the First Quarto text.

4   *magnificoes* Important Venetian leaders.

ACT 1, Scene I

(Enter Antonio, Salarino, and Solanio.)

ANTONIO. In sooth,° I know not why I am so   *truth*
    sad.°   *melancholy*
    It wearies me, you say it wearies you;
    But how I caught it, found it, or came by it,
    What stuff 'tis made of, whereof it is born,
5   I am to learn; and such a want-wit sadness makes of me,
    That I have much ado to know myself.[1]
SALARINO. Your mind is tossing on the ocean,
    There where your argosies with portly[2] sail,
    Like signors and rich burghers on the flood,[3]
10   Or as it were the pageants[4] of the sea,
    Do overpeer the petty traffickers[5]
    That curtsy[6] to them, do them reverence,
    As they fly by them with their woven wings.[7]
SOLANIO. Believe me, sir, had I such venture forth,
15   The better part of my affections° would   *emotions*
    Be with my hopes abroad.[8] I should be still°   *unceasingly*
    Plucking the grass[9] to know where sits the wind,
    Peering in maps for ports and piers and roads,°   *anchorages*
    And every object that might make me fear
20   Misfortune to my ventures out of doubt
    Would make me sad.

---

1 *such a ... know myself* Sadness has made it so that I can barely recognize my own self; *want-wit* Person lacking in intelligence.

2 *argosies* Large merchant ships; *portly* Dignified, but also stout, suggesting strength and fullness not just of their build but also, perhaps, of their merchandise.

3 *signors* Gentlemen, likely members of the Venetian governing body known as the Signoria; *burghers* Affluent citizens; *flood* Movement of the tide, also alluding to the sea itself.

4 *pageants* Theatrical performances, especially processions incorporating traveling stages. Pageants were popular both in Shakespeare's London and in Venice.

5 *overpeer* Either to rise above or to look down upon; *petty traffickers* Low-ranking tradesmen, in this case also referring to small watercraft.

6 *curtsy* Act of bending the knees as a sign of respect, here likened to the way that smaller ships might demonstrate deference to larger ships by lowering their topsails.

7 *wings* I.e., sails.

8 *had I ... hopes abroad* If I had made this sort of risky investment, most of my thoughts and feelings would be focused on it.

9 *Plucking the grass* Tossing grass in the air in order to gage wind direction.

SALARINO.   My wind° cooling my broth   *breath*
Would blow me to an ague[1] when I thought
What harm a wind too great might do at sea.
I should not see the sandy hour-glass run   25
But I should think of shallows and of flats,°   *sandbanks*
And see my wealthy Andrew[2] docked in sand,
Vailing her high-top lower than her ribs
To kiss her burial.[3] Should I[4] go to church
And see the holy edifice of stone   30
And not bethink me straight of[5] dangerous rocks,
Which, touching but my gentle vessel's side,
Would scatter all her spices on the stream,
Enrobe the roaring waters with my silks,
And, in a word, but even now worth this,   35
And now worth nothing?[6] Shall I have the thought
To think on this, and shall I lack the thought
That such a thing bechanced, would make me sad?
But tell not me, I know Antonio
Is sad to think upon his merchandise.   40
ANTONIO. Believe me, no. I thank my fortune for it,
My ventures are not in one bottom trusted,[7]
Nor to one place; nor is my whole estate
Upon the fortune of this present year:[8]
Therefore my merchandise makes me not sad.   45
SOLANIO. Why then, you are in love.
ANTONIO.   Fie, fie.
SOLANIO. Not in love neither: Then let us say you are sad
Because you are not merry; and 'twere as easy

---

1   *ague* Fever, especially one that causes shivering.
2   *Andrew* Name of a ship. Almost certainly a reference to the *San Andrés*, a Spanish ship
    captured during the English and Dutch naval expedition to Cadiz in 1596.
3   *Vailing her   burial* Iron bending the ship's sails to kiss the sand where the ship will
    meet its death;   *Vailing* Bending in a sign of deference.
4   *Should I* If I should.
5   *bethink me straight of* Instantly think of.
6   *even now ... worth nothing?* The goods are only valuable to Antonio if his ships survive
    their perilous journeys.
7   *My ventures ... trusted* I have not put all my investments into the hull of one ship.
8   *nor is my ... present year* Neither are all my investments dependent on the outcome of
    this year.

For you to laugh and leap and say you are merry
Because you are not sad. Now, by two-headed Janus,[1]
Nature hath framed strange fellows in her time:
Some that will evermore peep through their eyes[2]
100 And laugh like parrots at a bagpiper,[3]
And other° of such vinegar aspect[4]   *others*
That they'll not show their teeth in way of smile,
Though Nestor[5] swear the jest be laughable.

(*Enter Bassanio, Lorenzo, and Graziano.*)

Here comes Bassanio, your most noble kinsman,
105 Graziano, and Lorenzo. Fare ye well,
We leave you now with better company.
SALARINO. I would have stayed till I had made you merry,
If worthier friends had not prevented me.
ANTONIO. Your worth is very dear in my regard.
110 I take it your own business calls on you,
And you embrace th'occasion° to depart.   *opportunity*
SALARINO. Good morrow, my good lords.
BASSANIO. Good signors both, when shall we laugh? Say, when?
You grow exceeding strange:° must it be so?   *distant*
115 SALARINO. We'll make our leisures to attend on yours.[6]

(*Exeunt Salarino and Solanio.*)

LORENZO. My lord Bassanio, since you have found Antonio,
We two will leave you; but at dinner-time
I pray you have in mind where we must meet.
BASSANIO. I will not fail you.
120 GRAZIANO. You look not well, Signor Antonio;

---

1   *two-headed Janus*   Roman god of beginnings who had two faces, each oriented in a different direction.
2   *peep through their eyes*   Suggestion of the way a person laughing appears to have half-shut eyes.
3   *laugh like ... a bagpiper*   The parrot, associated with foolishness, would "laugh" even at a bagpipe's sound, which was considered melancholy.
4   *vinegar aspect*   Sour expression.
5   *Nestor*   King of Pylos and esteemed oldest Greek general in Homer's *Iliad*, known for his serious demeanor.
6   *We'll make ... on yours*   I.e., we will make sure we are available when you are to spend leisure time together.

You have too much respect upon the world:[1]
They lose it that do buy it with much care.
Believe me, you are marvellously changed.
ANTONIO. I hold the world but as the world, Graziano,
  A stage where every man must play a part,   125
  And mine a sad one.
GRAZIANO.   Let me play the fool:[2]
  With mirth and laughter let old wrinkles come,
  And let my liver rather heat with wine[3]
  Than my heart cool with mortifying[4] groans.
  Why should a man, whose blood is warm within,   130
  Sit like his grandsire cut in alabaster,[5]
  Sleep when he wakes, and creep into the jaundice[6]
  By being peevish? I tell thee what, Antonio—
  I love thee, and 'tis my love that speaks—
  There are a sort of men whose visages°   *faces* 135
  Do cream and mantle[7] like a standing° pond,   *stagnant*
  And do a wilful stillness entertain,
  With purpose to be dressed in an opinion°   *reputation*
  Of wisdom, gravity, profound conceit,[8]
  As who should say,[9] "I am sir Oracle,   140
  And when I ope my lips let no dog bark."[10]
  O my Antonio, I do know of these

---

1 *You have ... the world* You are too involved in worldly concerns. Graziano has not taken Lorenzo's clue that they should leave ("We two will leave you") and continues to engage in conversation.

2 *play the fool* In the Italian tradition of *commedia dell'arte*, a type of improvisational theater, the role of the comic doctor was called Graziano.

3 *liver rather ... with wine* The liver was seen as the seat of passions in the body, and wine as capable of inflaming them.

4 *heart cool* In Aristotelian physiology, the heart was considered capable of producing heat; *mortifying* Penitential; also, resulting in death.

5 *Sit like ... in alabaster* Sit as still as a stone effigy of one's grandfather, an object that would commonly be found at a grave.

6 *jaundice* Disease resulting in yellowing of the skin and considered a consequence of having an excess of yellow bile, one of the four humors. Yellow bile was associated with anger and irritability.

7 *cream and mantle* Become pale, resembling cream floating on the surface of milk.

8 *profound conceit* Deep thought, perhaps relating to understanding of the self.

9 *As who should say* As if to say.

10 *I am ... dog bark* Demand for silence and admiration.

That therefore only are reputed wise
For saying nothing, when I am very sure
145   If they should speak, would almost damn those ears
Which, hearing them, would call their brothers fools.
I'll tell thee more of this another time.
But fish not with this melancholy bait
For this fool gudgeon,[1] this opinion.—
150   Come, good Lorenzo.—Fare ye well awhile;
I'll end my exhortation after dinner.
LORENZO. Well, we will leave you then till dinner-time.
I must be one of these same dumb° wise men,   *mute*
For Graziano never lets me speak.
155 GRAZIANO. Well, keep me company but two years more,
Thou shalt not know the sound of thine own tongue.
ANTONIO. Fare you well. I'll grow a talker for this gear.°   *discourse*
GRAZIANO. Thanks, i'faith, for silence is only commendable
In a neat's tongue dried and a maid not vendible.[2]

(*Exeunt [Graziano and Lorenzo].*)

160 ANTONIO. It is that anything now.[3]
BASSANIO. Graziano speaks an infinite deal of nothing,
more than any man in all Venice. His reasons[4] are as
two grains of wheat hid in two bushels of chaff: you
shall seek all day ere you find them, and when you
165   have them, they are not worth the search.
ANTONIO. Well, tell me now what lady is the same
To whom you swore a secret pilgrimage,
That you today promised to tell me of.
BASSANIO. 'Tis not unknown to you, Antonio,
170   How much I have disabled mine estate
By something showing a more swelling port

---

1 *fish not ... fool gudgeon* Do not fish for the reputation of being wise by pretending to be silent and melancholy. The gudgeon, a fish associated with extreme gullibility, reinforces the foolishness of this pursuit.
2 *neat's tongue dried* Dried ox tongue, also a bawdy reference to impotency; *not vendible* No longer marriageable.
3 *It is ... anything now* Sometimes printed, "Yet is that anything now?"
4 *reasons* Ideas or arguments.

Than my faint means would grant continuance.[1]
Nor do I now make moan° to be abridged°   *lament / truncated*
From such a noble rate;[2] but my chief care
Is to come fairly off from the great debts[3]   175
Wherein my time something too prodigal,
Hath left me gaged.° To you, Antonio,   *bound*
I owe the most in money and in love,
And from your love I have a warranty°   *authorization*
To unburden° all my plots and purposes   *divulge* 180
How to get clear of all the debts I owe.

ANTONIO. I pray you, good Bassanio, let me know it,
And if it stand, as you yourself still do,
Within the eye of honour, be assured
My purse, my person, my extremest means,   185
Lie all unlocked to your occasions.[4]

BASSANIO. In my schooldays, when I had lost one shaft,° *arrow*
I shot his fellow of the selfsame flight[5]
The selfsame way, with more advised° watch   *mindful*
To find the other forth, and by adventuring both   190
I oft found both. I urge this childhood proof
Because what follows is pure innocence.[6]
I owe you much, and, like a wilful youth,
That which I owe is lost; but if you please
To shoot another arrow that self° way   *same* 195
Which you did shoot the first, I do not doubt,
As I will watch the aim, or° to find both,   *either*
Or bring your latter hazard[7] back again
And thankfully rest° debtor for the first.   *remain*

ANTONIO. You know me well, and herein spend but time   200
To wind about my love with circumstance,

---

1 *Than means ... grant continuance* How much I have bankrupted my inheritance through living a lifestyle beyond that which my wealth permits.

2 *noble rate* Luxurious way of life an aristocrat might expect to enjoy.

3 *come ... debts* Clear myself with honor of the debts.

4 *unlocked to your occasions* Accessible for all your needs.

5 *fellow of the selfsame flight* Arrow of the same kind and following the same flight path.

6 *I urge ... innocence* I use this story from my childhood to demonstrate that my argument is sincere; *innocence* Earnestness.

7 *latter hazard* Second stake invested.

And out of° doubt you do me now more wrong   *beyond*
In making question of my uttermost[1]
Than if you had made waste of all I have.
205   Then do but say to me what I should do
That in your knowledge may by me be done,
And I am pressed unto it: therefore speak.
BASSANIO. In Belmont is a lady richly left,[2]
And she is fair and, fairer than that word,
210   Of wondrous virtues. Sometimes[3] from her eyes
I did receive fair speechless messages.
Her name is Portia, nothing undervalued[4]
To Cato's daughter, Brutus' Portia;[5]
Nor is the wide world ignorant of her worth,
215   For the four winds blow in from every coast
Renowned suitors, and her sunny locks
Hang on her temples like a golden fleece,[6]
Which makes her seat of Belmont Colchis' strand,
And many Jasons come in quest of her.
220   O my Antonio, had I but the means
To hold a rival place with one of them,
I have a mind presages° me such thrift°   *foretells / profit*
That I should questionless be fortunate.
ANTONIO. Thou knowst that all my fortunes are at sea,
225   Neither have I money nor commodity°   *merchandise*
To raise a present sum.[7] Therefore go forth—
Try what my credit can in Venice do;
That shall be racked,° even to the uttermost,   *stretched*
To furnish thee to Belmont, to fair Portia.
230   Go presently inquire, and so will I,

---

1 *making question ... my uttermost* Casting doubt on my pledge to do all that I can.
2 *richly left* Possessing a large fortune through inheritance.
3 *Sometimes* At one time, possibly in the past.
4 *nothing undervalued* No less worthy than.
5 *Cato's ... Portia* Wife of Brutus (one of Julius Caesar's assassins) and daughter of Marcus Porcuis Cato, a noble tribune. Shakespeare would soon portray her as a noble character in his *Julius Caesar*.
6 *golden fleece* In Greek mythology, Jason, the leader of the Argonauts, sailed to the shores of Colchis on a quest for the golden fleece.
7 *a present sum* Immediately accessible cash.

Where money is, and I not question make
To have it of my trust or for my sake.[1]

(*Exeunt.*)

ACT 1, Scene 2

(*Enter Portia with her waiting-woman Nerissa.*)

PORTIA. By my troth,[2] Nerissa, my little body is aweary of this
  great world.
NERISSA. You would be,[3] sweet madam, if your miseries were in
  the same abundance as your good fortunes are; and yet, for
  aught I see, they are as sick that surfeit with too much as they   5
  that starve with nothing. It is no mean happiness, therefore,
  to be seated in the mean:[4] superfluity comes sooner by white
  hairs, but competency lives longer.[5]
PORTIA. Good sentences[6] and well pronounced.
NERISSA. They would be better if well followed.   10
PORTIA. If to do were as easy as to know what were good to do,
  chapels had been[7] churches and poor men's cottages princes'
  palaces. It is a good divine[8] that follows his own instructions.
  I can easier teach twenty what were good to be done than to
  be one of the twenty to follow mine own teaching. The brain   15
  may devise laws for the blood, but a hot temper leaps o'er a
  cold decree, such a hare is madness the youth, to skip o'er
  the meshes of good counsel the cripple.[9] But this reasoning is

---

1 *of my ... my sake* On my professional credit or through my personal connections.
2 *troth* Faith.
3 *would be* Would have cause to be.
4 *no mean ... the mean* Nerissa puns dual meanings of the word "mean": "insignificant"
  and "average."
5 *superfluity ... lives longer* A life of overindulgence brings about old age faster than one
  lived in moderation.
6 *sentences* Maxims, though Portia likens following Nerissa's advice to the legal meaning
  of "sentence."
7 *had been* Would have been.
8 *divine* Clergyman.
9 *brain ... blood* While the brain was considered the seat of reason, the blood was believed
  to be the seat of emotion/passion; *a hot temper ... cripple* A passionate constitution
  (imagined as a leaping hare) is not restrained by the wisdom of the aged, here associated
  with cold and infirmity; *meshes* Hunting nets.

not in the fashion to choose me a husband.[1] O me, the word
20 “choose”! I may neither choose who I would, nor refuse who I
dislike, so is the will of a living daughter curbed by the will of
a dead father.[2] Is it not hard, Nerissa, that I cannot choose one
nor refuse none?

NERISSA. Your father was ever virtuous, and holy men at their
25 death have good inspirations; therefore the lottery that he hath
devised in these three chests of gold, silver, and lead, whereof
who chooses his meaning chooses you, will no doubt never be
chosen by any rightly but one who you shall rightly[3] love. But
what warmth is there in your affection towards any of these
30 princely suitors that are already come?

PORTIA. I pray thee over-name them; and as thou namest them,
I will describe them and, according to my description, level at
my affection.[4]

NERISSA. First there is the Neapolitan[5] prince.

35 PORTIA. Ay, that's a colt indeed, for he doth nothing but talk of
his horse, and he makes it a great appropriation to his own
good parts[6] that he can shoe him himself. I am much afeard my
lady his mother played false with a smith.[7]

NERISSA. Then is there the County Palatine.[8]

40 PORTIA. He doth nothing but frown, as who should say “An[9] you
will not have me, choose.” He hears merry tales and smiles not;
I fear he will prove the weeping philosopher when he grows

---

1   *But this ... a husband*   But this rhetoric will not be useful in selecting a husband.

2   *will ... father*   Pun on two meanings of “will”: the self-determination of a daughter is constrained by the legal will, or testament, of a dead father.

3   *virtuous*   Competent, but also alluding to masculine strength; *lottery*   Venture in which participants are rewarded with prizes designated by chance; *rightly but ... shall rightly*   Pun on two meanings of “rightly”: “correctly” and also “truly.”

4   *over-name*   Name in consecutive order; *level at*   Guess; *affection*   Level of appreciation.

5   *Neapolitan*   From Naples, Italy. Neapolitans were known for horsemanship in Shakespeare's time.

6   *colt*   Immature, silly young man; *good parts*   Achievements.

7   *I ... smith*   I (scandalously) suspect that the Neapolitan Prince may have inherited his affinity for horses because he was illegitimately fathered by a blacksmith.

8   *County Palatine*   Someone from a palatinate, or a district with regal privileges.

9   *An*   If.

old, being so full of unmannerly sadness[1] in his youth. I had
rather be married to a death's head[2] with a bone in his mouth
than to either of these. God defend me from these two.   45

NERISSA. How say you by[3] the French lord, Monsieur Le Bon?

PORTIA. God made him, and therefore let him pass for a man.
In truth, I know it is a sin to be a mocker, but he, why, he
hath a horse better than the Neapolitan's, a better bad habit
of frowning than the Count Palatine. He is every man in no   50
man.[4] If a throstle sing, he falls straight a-capering.[5] He will
fence with his own shadow. If I should marry him, I should
marry twenty husbands. If he would despise me, I would
forgive him, for if he love me to madness, I shall never requite
him.   55

NERISSA. What say you then to[6] Falconbridge, the young baron
of England?

PORTIA. You know I say nothing to him, for he understands not
me, nor I him. He hath neither Latin, French, nor Italian,
and you will come into the court and swear that I have a poor   60
pennyworth in the English.[7] He is a proper man's picture,
but, alas, who can converse with a dumbshow?[8] How oddly
he is suited.[9] I think he bought his doublet in Italy, his round
hose in France, his bonnet in Germany, and his behaviour
everywhere.[10]   65

NERISSA. What think you of the Scottish lord, his neighbour?

---

1 *weeping philosopher* Heraclitus of Epheseus, Greek philosopher (sixth–fifth century
   BCE), known for his melancholy and pensiveness; *sadness* Solemnity.
2 *death's head* Image of a skull, representative of death.
3 *by* Concerning.
4 *He ... no man* He fashions an identity by imitating others because he lacks one of his
   own.
5 *throstle* Thrush; *straight* Immediately; *a-capering* Dancing in a playful manner.
6 *What say ... then to* What, then, do you have to say about.
7 *and you ... English* You could testify that I can communicate in English only very
   poorly.
8 *He ... picture* He has the appearance of an attractive man; *dumbshow* Performance
   in which actors communicate with gestures and no words.
9 *suited* Dressed.
10 *I think ... everywhere* A fashion sense made through a combination of clothing from
   different cultures was a stereotype associated with Englishmen; *doublet* Jacket-
   like garment worn by men; *round hose* Short breeches, which were often padded;
   bonnet Hat.

PORTIA. That he hath a neighbourly charity in him, for he
borrowed a box of the ear of the Englishman and swore
he would pay him again when he was able.[1] I think the
70 Frenchman became his surety and sealed under[2] for another.
NERISSA. How like you the young German, the Duke of Saxony's
nephew?
PORTIA. Very vilely in the morning when he is sober, and most
vilely in the afternoon when he is drunk. When he is best, he
75 is a little worse than a man, and when he is worst, he is little
better than a beast. An the worst fall that ever fell, I hope I shall
make shift[3] to go without him.
NERISSA. If he should offer[4] to choose and choose the right
casket, you should refuse to perform your father's will if you
80 should refuse to accept him.
PORTIA. Therefore, for fear of the worst, I pray thee set a deep
glass of Rhenish wine on the contrary casket, for if the devil be
within, and that temptation without, I know he will choose it.[5]
I will do anything, Nerissa, ere I will be married to a sponge.
85 NERISSA. You need not fear, lady, the having any of these lords.
They have acquainted me with their determinations, which is
indeed, to return to their home and to trouble you with no
more suit, unless you may be won by some other sort[6] than
your father's imposition, depending on the caskets.
90 PORTIA. If I live to be as old as Sibylla, I will die as chaste as
Diana,[7] unless I be obtained by the manner of my father's will.
I am glad this parcel of wooers are so reasonable, for there is

---

1 *borrowed ... able* Conflict between the English and the Scots was common at the time
Shakespeare was writing; *pay him again* Repay him.
2 *Frenchman* The Frenchman supporting the Scottish Lord alludes to the ongoing
military alliance between the French and the Scots; *surety* Person who agrees to
be responsible for another person's repayment of a debt; *sealed under* Took on an
agreement that necessitated his personal seal and signature.
3 *An the worst ... fell* If the worst that could happen comes to pass; *make shift* Devise
a way.
4 *offer* Attempt.
5 *Rhenish wine* White wine from Rhineland, a region of Germany; *contrary* Incorrect;
if the devil ... choose it Even if the casket contains the devil, the young German will not
be able to resist the lure of the wine.
6 *determinations* Plans; *suit* Courtship, or undertaking of a quest; *sort* Method.
7 *Sibylla* In Ovid's *Metamorphoses* (see Book 14), a Prophetess given a long life by her
lover Apollo; *Diana* Roman goddess of the hunt and of chastity.

not one among them but I dote on his very absence, and I pray
God grant them a fair[1] departure.

NERISSA. Do you not remember, lady, in your father's time, a   95
Venetian, a scholar and a soldier,[2] that came hither in company
of the Marquis of Montferrat?

PORTIA. Yes, yes, it was Bassanio, as I think, so was he called.

NERISSA. True, madam. He, of all the men that ever my foolish
eyes looked upon, was the best deserving a fair lady.   100

PORTIA. I remember him well, and I remember him worthy of thy
praise.

(*Enter a Servingman.*)

How now, what news?

SERVINGMAN. The four strangers seek for you, madam, to take
their leave; and there is a forerunner[3] come from a fifth, the   105
Prince of Morocco, who brings word the Prince his master will
be here tonight.

PORTIA. If I could bid the fifth welcome with so good heart
as I can bid the other four farewell, I should be glad of
his approach. If he have the condition of a saint and the   110
complexion of a devil, I had rather he should shrive me than
wive[4] me. Come, Nerissa.—Sirrah,[5] go before. Whiles we shut
the gate upon one wooer, another knocks at the door.

(*Exeunt.*)

---

1 *parcel* Collection; *fair* Unimpeded.
2 *scholar and a soldier* With these qualities, Bassanio fits a Renaissance ideal for courtiers.
3 *four* Nerissa has described six suitors; the discrepancy may result from a text revision;
   strangers Outsiders; *forerunner* One who arrives before another, usually delivering a
   message of the latter's imminent arrival.
4 *condition* Temperament; *complexion of a devil* Though complexion could refer
   to character, it could also allude to physical appearance; the devil was traditionally
   depicted as black; *shrive* Hear confession and give absolution; the task of a
   priest; *wive* Marry.
5 *Sirrah* Designation for one who is socially inferior.

ACT 1, Scene 3

(Enter Bassanio with Shylock the Jew.)

SHYLOCK. Three thousand ducats,[1] well.

BASSANIO. Ay, sir, for three months.

SHYLOCK. For three months, well.

BASSANIO. For the which, as I told you, Antonio shall be bound.[2]

5 SHYLOCK. Antonio shall become bound, well.

BASSANIO. May you stead me? Will you pleasure[3] me? Shall I
know your answer?

SHYLOCK. Three thousand ducats for three months, and Antonio
bound.

10 BASSANIO. Your answer to that.

SHYLOCK. Antonio is a good[4] man.

BASSANIO. Have you heard any imputation[5] to the contrary?

SHYLOCK. Ho, no, no, no, no. My meaning in saying he is a
good man is to have you understand me that he is sufficient,

15 yet his means are in supposition.[6] He hath an argosy bound to
Tripolis, another to the Indies; I understand moreover upon
the Rialto, he hath a third at Mexico, a fourth for England,
and other ventures he hath squandered[7] abroad. But ships
are but boards,[8] sailors but men; there be land rats, and water

20 rats, water thieves, and land thieves—I mean pirates—and
then there is the peril of waters, winds and rocks. The man is
notwithstanding sufficient. Three thousand ducats: I think I
may take his bond.

BASSANIO. Be assured[9] you may.

---

1   *ducats*   Italian gold coins that had the equivalent value of about nine shillings. As
Sandra K. Fischer has argued, 3,000 ducats was a considerable sum, worth more than a
diamond and as much as a decent annual income.

2   *bound*   Contractually obligated (to pay back).

3   *stead*   Help; *pleasure*   Accommodate.

4   *good*   Financially stable.

5   *imputation*   Accusation of a fault or crime.

6   *he is sufficient*   Antonio has enough security to risk such a loan;   *in supposition*   Unpredictable.

7   *Tripolis*   Mediterranean port and popular trade destination for Venetian merchants;   *the
Rialto*   Exchange where Venetian merchants did business;   *squandered*   Scattered
widely, but with the negative connation of "unwise" or "reckless."

8   *boards*   I.e., made of wooden planks.

9   *Be assured*   I.e., have faith in Antonio.

JEW. I will be assured I may; and, that I may be assured, I will   25
    bethink me.[1] May I speak with Antonio?

BASSANIO. If it please you to dine with us.

JEW. Yes, to smell pork, to eat of the habitation which your
    prophet the Nazarite conjured the devil into.[2] I will buy
    with you, sell with you, talk with you, walk with you and so   30
    following. But I will not eat with you, drink with you nor pray
    with you. What news on the Rialto? Who is he comes here?

    (*Enter Antonio.*)

BASSANIO. This is Signor Antonio.

JEW. [*Aside.*] How like a fawning publican[3] he looks.
    I hate him for he is a Christian;   35
    But more, for that in low simplicity[4]
    He lends out money gratis,° and brings down   *without interest*
    The rate of usance° here with us in Venice.   *usury, interest*
    If I can catch him once upon the hip,[5]
    I will feed fat the ancient grudge I bear him.   40
    He hates our sacred nation,[6] and he rails,
    Even there where merchants most do congregate,
    On me, my bargains and my well-won thrift,[7]
    Which he calls interest. Cursed be my tribe[8]
    If I forgive him.   45

BASSANIO.   Shylock, do you hear?

SHYLOCK. I am debating of my present store,[9]
    And, by the near guess of my memory,

---

1 *I will be assured* I will have a legal guarantee; *bethink me* Concoct a plan.

2 *to eat ... into* Reference to the events of Matthew 8.29–43, in which Jesus expels evil
   spirits from a man and sends them into a nearby herd of swine; *Nazarite* Person from
   Nazareth, i.e., Jesus.

3 *publican* Tax gatherer, a figure historically held in distaste for supporting the Jews'
   Roman rulers.

4 *low simplicity* Humble naivety.

5 *upon the hip* In a position of disadvantage (a term from wrestling).

6 *our sacred nation* I.e., Jewish people.

7 *thrift* Wealth attained through usury, where "thrift" serves as a sort of euphemism for
   "lending with interest."

8 *my tribe* The Jewish nation. "Tribe" may also refer to the division of ancient Jewish
   people into the twelve tribes of Israel.

9 *I am debating ... store* I am evaluating how much money I have currently available.

I cannot instantly raise up the gross°   *total*
50   Of full three thousand ducats. What of that?
Tubal, a wealthy Hebrew of my tribe,
Will furnish me.[1] But soft,° how many months   *wait*
Do you desire? [*To Antonio.*] Rest you fair, good signor,
Your worship was the last man in our mouths.[2]

55   ANTONIO. Shylock, albeit I neither lend nor borrow
By taking nor by giving of excess,°   *interest*
Yet, to supply the ripe wants[3] of my friend,
I'll break a custom. [*To Bassanio.*] Is he yet possessed
How much ye would?[4]

SHYLOCK.   Ay, ay, three thousand ducats.

60   ANTONIO. And for three months.

SHYLOCK. I had forgot, three months, you told me so.
Well then, your bond; and let me see—but hear you:
Methoughts you said you neither lend nor borrow
Upon advantage.°   *interest*

ANTONIO.   I do never use it.

65   SHYLOCK. When Jacob grazed his uncle Laban's sheep,
This Jacob from our holy Abram[5] was,
(As his wise mother wrought in his behalf)[6]
The third possessor; ay, he was the third.

ANTONIO. And what of him, did he take interest?

70   SHYLOCK. No, not take interest, not as you would say
Directly interest. Mark what Jacob did:[7]
When Laban and himself were compromised°   *agreed*
That all the eanlings which were streaked and pied[8]

---

1   *furnish me* I.e., provide me with the rest.
2   *Your worship ... our mouths* We were just now discussing you.
3   *ripe wants* Pressing requirements.
4   *Is he ... ye would* Has he been informed yet how much you need?
5   *Abram* Abraham, the biblical patriarch who was the father of Isaac and grandfather of
    Jacob, himself the father of twelve sons who formed the tribes of Israel.
6   *wise mother ... his behalf* In Genesis 27, Rebecca helps her son Jacob trick his father into
    giving him the inheritance meant for his older brother.
7   *what Jacob did* Shylock retells the events of Genesis 30.25–43, in which Jacob and his
    father-in-law Laban agree that Jacob will keep as payment all the spotted sheep in Laban's
    flock. By placing spotted branches in sight of the sheep during mating, Jacob causes the
    best sheep to conceive spotted lambs.
8   *eanlings* Young lambs; *streaked and pied* Lightly striped and spotted.

Should fall as Jacob's hire, the ewes, being rank,°   *in heat*
In end of autumn turned to the rams;   75
And when the work of generation° was   *breeding*
Between these wooly breeders in the act,
The skilful shepherd peeled me certain wands,[1]
And, in the doing of the deed of kind,[2]
He stuck them up before the fulsome° ewes,   *lustful*   80
Who, then conceiving, did in eaning°-time   *lambing*
Fall° parti-coloured° lambs, and those were   *Deliver / spotted*
    Jacob's.
This was a way to thrive, and he was blest:
And thrift is blessing, if men steal it not.
ANTONIO. This was a venture, sir, that Jacob served for,[3]   85
    A thing not in his power to bring to pass,
    But swayed and fashioned by the hand of heaven.
    Was this inserted to make interest good?[4]
    Or is your gold and silver ewes and rams?
SHYLOCK. I cannot tell,[5] I make it breed as fast.   90
    But note me, signor.
ANTONIO.   Mark you this, Bassanio,
    The devil can cite Scripture[6] for his purpose.
    An evil soul producing holy witness
    Is like a villain with a smiling cheek,
    A goodly[7] apple, rotten at the heart.   95
    O, what a goodly outside falsehood hath.
SHYLOCK. Three thousand ducats, 'tis a good round sum.
    Three months from twelve, then, let me see the rate.
ANTONIO. Well, Shylock, shall we be beholden to you?
SHYLOCK. Signor Antonio, many a time and oft   100
    In the Rialto you have rated° me   *berated*

---

1   *peeled ... wands*   Pulled the bark off thin branches.
2   *deed of kind*   Mating.
3   *served for*   Assisted in the accomplishment of.
4   *Was this ... interest good?*   Was this scripture injected into our conversation to defend the morality of usury?
5   *I cannot tell*   I do not know or have a comment.
6   *devil can cite Scripture*   Shylock's knowledge of scripture is compared to a passage in Matthew 4.6, in which the devil is also able to quote scripture.
7   *goodly*   Outwardly appealing.

      About my moneys and my usances.
      Still have I borne it with a patient shrug,
      For suffrance° is the badge° of all our tribe.   *endurance / mark*
105   You call me misbeliever, cut-throat dog,
      And spit upon my Jewish gaberdine,[1]
      And all for use[2] of that which is mine own.
      Well, then, it now appears you need my help.
      Go to,[3] then, you come to me and you say,
110   "Shylock, we would have moneys." You say so.
      You, that did void your rheum[4] upon my beard
      And foot° me as you spurn a stranger cur[5]   *kick*
      Over your threshold, moneys is your suit.°   *wish*
      What should I say to you? Should I not say,
115   "Hath a dog money? Is it possible
      A cur can lend three thousand ducats?" Or
      Shall I bend low and in a bondman's key,[6]
      With bated breath and whispering humbleness,
      Say this: "Fair Sir, you spat on me on Wednesday last,
120   You spurned° me such a day another time,   *kicked*
      You called me dog: and, for these courtesies,
      I'll lend you thus much moneys."
      ANTONIO. I am as like° to call thee so again,   *likely*
      To spit on thee again, to spurn thee too.
125   If thou wilt lend this money, lend it not
      As to thy friends, for when did friendship take
      A breed for barren metal[7] of° his friend?   *from*
      But lend it rather to thine enemy,
      Who, if he break,[8] thou mayst with better face
130   Exact the penalty.[9]

---

1   *gaberdine* Loosely worn cape or cloak.
2   *use* Practice of earning through interest.
3   *Go to* Utterance of irritation.
4   *void your rheum* Spit.
5   *stranger cur* Vagrant dog.
6   *bondman's key* Vocal intonation of a serf or slave.
7   *A breed ... barren metal* Process of making metal coins, which should be naturally "barren," generate more money (as in usury).
8   *if he break* If he cannot pay what is owed because he has become bankrupt.
9   *thou ... penalty* Your enforcement of the consequence will seem more justified (since it is not a deal among friends).

SHYLOCK.　　　　Why, look you, how you storm.
　I would be friends with you and have your love,
　Forget the shames that you have stained me with,
　Supply your present wants and take no doit[1]
　Of usance for my moneys, and you'll not hear me.
　This is kind° I offer.　　　　　　　　　　　　*benevolence* 135
BASSANIO.　　　　This were kindness.
SHYLOCK. This kindness will I show.
　Go with me to a notary,° seal me there　　　　　*legal clerk*
　Your single bond,[2] and, in a merry sport,
　If you repay me not on such a day,
　In such a place, such sum, or sums, as are　　　　　　140
　Expressed in the condition,° let the forfeit　　　　　*deal*
　Be nominated° for an equal pound　　　　　　　　*named*
　Of your fair flesh, to be cut off and taken
　In what part of your body pleaseth me.
ANTONIO.　Content, in faith: I'll seal to[3] such a bond　　　145
　And say there is much kindness in the Jew.
BASSANIO.　You shall not seal to such a bond for me;
　I'll rather dwell in my necessity.[4]
ANTONIO.　Why, fear not, man, I will not forfeit it;
　Within these two months, that's a month before　　　150
　This bond expires, I do expect return
　Of thrice three times the value of this bond.[5]
SHYLOCK.　O, father Abram, what these Christians are,
　Whose own hard dealings teaches them suspect
　The thoughts of others. Pray you, tell me this:　　　155
　If he should break his day, what should I gain
　By the exaction of the forfeiture?[6]
　A pound of man's flesh, taken from a man,
　Is not so estimable,° profitable neither,　　　　　*valued*

1　*doit*　Dutch coin worth very little.
2　*single bond*　Legal agreement in which one party agrees to pay a specific amount of
　money to another at a specific time, with no other conditions.
3　*seal to*　Officially agree to, with a signature or personal wax seal.
4　*dwell in my necessity*　Remain in my position of financial insufficiency.
5　*I do ... this bond*　I foresee making a profit worth three times the sum of this bond.
6　*exaction ... forfeiture*　Claiming of the penalty Antonio will owe for failing to repay his
　bond.

160 As flesh of muttons, beeves,° or goats. I say   *cattle*
To buy his favour I extend this friendship;
If he will take it so, if not adieu.
And for my love I pray you, wrong me not.
ANTONIO. Yes, Shylock, I will seal unto this bond.
165 SHYLOCK. Then meet me forthwith at the notary's;
Give him direction for this merry bond,
And I will go and purse the ducats straight,[1]
See to my house, left in the fearful° guard   *questionable*
Of an unthrifty knave,[2] and presently
170 I'll be with you.

    (*Exit.*)

ANTONIO.   Hie° thee, gentle Jew.   *Hurry*
The Hebrew will turn Christian, he grows kind.
BASSANIO. I like not fair terms and a villain's mind.
ANTONIO. Come on, in this there can be no dismay,
My ships come home a month before the day.

    (*Exeunt.*)

ACT 2, SCENE 1

(*Enter [the Prince of] Morocco, a tawny Moor, all in white,[3] and three or four Followers accordingly, with Portia, Nerissa, and their train.*)

MOROCCO. Mislike me not for my complexion,
The shadowed livery of the burnished sun,[4]
To whom I am a neighbour and near bred.[5]
Bring me the fairest creature northward born,

---

1 *purse the ducats straight* Pack the money into a purse right away.
2 *unthrifty knave* Incompetent male employee.
3 *tawny Moor* Dark-skinned person from an area in northwestern Africa; *all in white* The prince's white clothing perhaps alludes to Islamic tradition.
4 *shadowed livery ... burnished sun* I.e., the prince's dark skin, described as the dark-hued attire of someone living in close proximity to the sun.
5 *near bred* Nurtured alongside, referencing the geographical location near the equator where the prince was raised.

Where Phoebus' fire[1] scarce thaws the icicles,   5
And let us make incision[2] for your love,
To prove whose blood is reddest,[3] his or mine.
I tell thee, lady, this aspect[4] of mine
Hath feared° the valiant; by my love I swear,   *terrorized*
The best-regarded virgins of our clime°   *land* 10
Have loved it too. I would not change this hue
Except to steal your thoughts, my gentle queen.
PORTIA. In terms of choice I am not solely led
By nice direction[5] of a maiden's eyes.
Besides, the lott'ry of my destiny   15
Bars me the right of voluntary choosing.
But, if my father had not scanted° me   *limited*
And hedged° me, by his wit, to yield myself   *restricted*
His wife who wins me by that means I told you,
Yourself (renowned prince) then stood as fair[6]   20
As any comer I have looked on yet
For my affection.
MOROCCO.   Even for that I thank you.
Therefore, I pray you, lead me to the caskets
To try my fortune. By this scimitar,[7]
That slew the Sophy° and a Persian prince   *Persian king* 25
That won three fields° of Sultan Suleiman,[8]   *battles*
I would o'erstare° the sternest eyes that look,   *outstare*
Outbrave the heart most daring on the earth,
Pluck the young sucking cubs from the she-bear,
Yea, mock the lion when a° roars for prey,   *he* 30
To win the lady. But, alas the while,

---

1 *Phoebus' fire* The sun. Phoebus was the sun god in classical mythology.
2 *make incision* Cut to draw blood.
3 *whose blood is reddest* Having redder blood would suggest that one was more courageous and masculine.
4 *aspect* Appearance or facial expression.
5 *nice direction* Cautious aim.
6 *fair* Fairly considered, but also a play on the difference in their skin coloring.
7 *scimitar* Sword with a large curved blade.
8 *Sultan Suleiman* Turkish sultan who ruled over the Ottoman Empire from 1520 to 1566.

If Hercules and Lichas[1] play at dice
Which is the better man, the greater throw
May turn by fortune[2] from the weaker hand.
35 So is Alcides beaten by his rage,
And so may I, blind Fortune[3] leading me,
Miss that which one unworthier may attain,
And die with grieving.
PORTIA.   You must take your chance;
And either not attempt to choose at all,
40 Or swear, before you choose, if you choose wrong
Never to speak to lady afterward
In way of marriage, therefore be advised.
MOROCCO. Nor will not.[4] Come, bring me unto my chance.
PORTIA. First, forward to the temple;[5] after dinner
45 Your hazard° shall be made.   *attempt*
MOROCCO.   Good fortune, then,
To make me blest[6] or cursed'st among men.

(*Exeunt.*)

ACT 2, SCENE 2

(*Enter [Lancelot Gobbo] the Clown, alone.*)

CLOWN.[7] Certainly, my conscience will serve me[8] to run from
this Jew, my master. The fiend[9] is at mine elbow and tempts

---

1 *Hercules* Heroic figure of ancient Greek mythology, also known as Alcides or Heracles, and celebrated for his phenomenal strength; *Lichas* Hercules' servant, who, at the request of Hercules' wife Deianira, delivered him the shirt of Nessus, which was poisoned. It is this incident, and Hercules' enraged state after wearing the shirt of Nessus, that the prince seems to be incorporating into his story of a game of dice.
2 *May ... fortune* May derive as a result of chance.
3 *blind Fortune* During the Renaissance Fortune was personified as a blind goddess, her blindness representing the unknown consequences over which she presides.
4 *Nor will not* I.e., I agree to never marry if I choose wrongly.
5 *temple* Church, in which they will take the oath.
6 *blest* I.e., most blessed.
7 *CLOWN* Comic role that was a staple in many Elizabethan plays.
8 *serve me* I.e., allow me to run away. Lancelot's portrayal of being torn between conscience and devil parodies the popular depiction of good and evil battling over a mortal soul.
9 *fiend* Devil.

me, saying to me, "Gobbo, Lancelot Gobbo, good Lancelot,"
or "Good Gobbo," or "Good Lancelot Gobbo, use your legs,
take the start,[1] run away." My conscience says, "No; take heed,   5
honest Lancelot, take heed, honest Gobbo," or, as aforesaid,
"Honest Lancelot Gobbo, do not run, scorn running with
thy heels." Well, the most courageous fiend bids me pack.[2]
"*Fia*,"[3] says the fiend, "away," says the fiend, "for the heavens,
rouse up a brave mind," says the fiend, "and run." Well, my   10
conscience, hanging about the neck of my heart,[4] says very
wisely to me: "My honest friend, Lancelot," being an honest
man's son, or rather an honest woman's son, for indeed my
father did something smack, something grow to[5]—he had
a kind of taste—well, my conscience says, "Lancelot, budge   15
not." "Budge," says the fiend. "Budge not," says my conscience.
"Conscience," say I, "you counsel well. Fiend," say I, "you
counsel well." To be ruled by my conscience, I should stay with
the Jew my master, who (God bless the mark) is a kind of devil;
and, to run away from the Jew, I should be ruled by the fiend,   20
who, saving your reverence,[6] is the devil himself. Certainly the
Jew is the very devil incarnation,[7] and, in my conscience, my
conscience is but a kind of hard conscience, to offer to counsel
me to stay with the Jew. The fiend gives the more friendly
counsel: I will run, fiend, my heels are at your commandment;   25
I will run.

(*Enter Old Gobbo with a basket.*)

---

1 *take the start* Make a move.
2 *pack* Leave.
3 *Fia* Italian: away.
4 *hanging about ... my heart* Lancelot's imagined conscience clings around his heart like a controlling necklace.
5 *honest friend ... honest man* Lancelot plays on two senses of honest, meaning either "righteous" or "chaste"; *did something smack* Had some of the flavor or scent of, i.e., his father was somewhat honest; *something grow to* Expand, suggesting an erect penis.
6 *God bless the mark* Apologetic verbalization intended to soften the offense after bringing up something indecent or indelicate; *saving your reverence* Another apologetic remark.
7 *devil incarnation* Comic malapropism (misuse of a word), as Lancelot means "incarnate."

GOBBO. Master[1] young-man, you, I pray you, which is the way to
  Master Jew's?

CLOWN. [*Aside.*] O, heavens, this is my true-begotten father, who,
30 being more than sand-blind, high-gravel blind,[2] knows me not.
  I will try confusions[3] with him.

GOBBO. Master young gentleman, I pray you, which is the way to
  Master Jew's?

CLOWN. Turn up on your right hand at the next turning, but, at
35 the next turning of all, on your left. Marry,[4] at the very next
  turning, turn of no hand, but turn down indirectly to the Jew's
  house.

GOBBO. By God's sonties, 'twill be a hard way to hit.[5] Can you
  tell me whether one Lancelot, that dwells with him, dwell with
40 him or no?

CLOWN. Talk you of young Master Lancelot? [*Aside.*] Mark me
  now, now will I raise the waters.[6] [*To Gobbo.*] Talk you of
  young Master[7] Lancelot?

GOBBO. No master,[8] sir, but a poor man's son. His father, though
45 I say't, is an honest, exceeding poor man, and, God be thanked,
  well to live.[9]

CLOWN. Well, let his father be what 'a will, we talk of young
  Master Lancelot.

GOBBO. Your worship's friend and Lancelot, sir.

50 CLOWN. But, I pray you, ergo,[10] old man, ergo, I beseech you, talk
  you of young Master Lancelot.

GOBBO. Of Lancelot, ant[11] please your mastership.

---

1 *Master* Title given only to those of the gentry class. Gobbo has poor vision and can't see
  that it is his son—not a member of the gentry—to whom he is speaking.

2 *sand-blind* Poorly sighted; *high-gravel blind* Lancelot conceives of this term to
  describe a level of blindness between sand-blind and stone (completely) blind.

3 *confusions* Lancelot means "conclusions," or experiments, though his efforts will soon
  cause confusions as well.

4 *Marry* By Virgin Mary, a common oath.

5 *sonties* Saints; *hit* Find.

6 *raise the waters* Incite tears (possibly as a result of causing more confusion).

7 *Master* Lancelot calls himself "Master" to elevate his own status.

8 *No master* Old Gobbo reinforces Lancelot's lack of social status.

9 *well to live* Living comfortably, though perhaps this statement, made just after
  reinforcing their poverty, is a sign of Gobbo's confusion.

10 *ergo* Latin: therefore, a term frequently used in logical arguments.

11 *ant* If it.

CLOWN. Ergo, Master Lancelot. Talk not of Master Lancelot, father, for the young gentleman, according to Fates and Destinies and such odd sayings, the Sisters Three and such branches of learning, is indeed deceased,[1] or, as you would say in plain terms, gone to heaven.   55

GOBBO. Marry, God forbid, the boy was the very staff of my age, my very prop.

CLOWN. [*Aside.*] Do I look like a cudgel, or a hovel post,[2] a staff,   60
or a prop? [*To Gobbo.*] Do you know me, Father?

GOBBO. Alack the day, I know you not, young gentleman! But I pray you tell me, is my boy—God rest his soul—alive, or dead?

CLOWN. Do you not know me, father?

GOBBO. Alack, sir, I am sand-blind, I know you not.   65

CLOWN. Nay, indeed, if you had your eyes you might fail of the knowing me: it is a wise father that knows his own child.[3] Well, old man, I will tell you news of your son. [*Kneels.*] Give me your blessing, truth will come to light, murder cannot be hid long; a man's son may, but in the end truth will out.   70

GOBBO. Pray you, sir, stand up. I am sure you are not Lancelot my boy.

CLOWN. Pray you, let's have no more fooling, about it, but give me your blessing. I am Lancelot, your boy that was, your son that is, your child that shall be.[4]   75

GOBBO. I cannot think[5] you are my son.

CLOWN. I know not what I shall think[6] of that. But I am Lancelot, the Jew's man, and I am sure Margery your wife is my mother.

---

1 *father* Common address to an older man; *Sisters Three* Three fates of Greek mythology, depicted as three women who produce and determine the length of the thread that represents the lives of humans; *deceased* Lancelot heightens the confusion, reasoning that since someone named Lancelot and also possessing the title "master" does not exist, he should be considered dead.

2 *hovel post* Post used to support a door or hut.

3 *father ... child* Typical of Lancelot throughout this scene, he shows off his knowledge of proverbs and mixes them up in the process. In this case, the original proverb declares that "it is a wise child that knows his own father."

4 *your boy ... shall be* Awkward rephrasing of the *Gloria Patri* from the *Book of Common Prayer*: "As it was in the beginning, is now, and ever shall be."

5 *I cannot think* I cannot be sure.

6 *think* Contemplate.

80 GOBBO. Her name is Margery indeed. I'll be sworn, if thou be
Lancelot, thou art mine own flesh and blood: Lord worshipped
might he be, what a beard[1] hast thou got! Thou hast got more
hair on thy chin than Dobbin, my fill-horse,[2] has on his tail.

CLOWN. It should seem, then, that Dobbin's tail grows
85   backward.[3] I am sure he had more hair of his tail than I have of
my face[4] when I last saw him.

GOBBO. Lord, how art thou changed: how dost thou and thy
master agree?[5] I have brought him a present; how 'gree you[6]
now?

90 CLOWN. Well, well: but, for mine own part, as I have set up my
rest to run away, so I will not rest till I have run some ground.[7]
My master's a very Jew.[8] Give him a present? Give him a
halter![9] I am famished in his service. You may tell[10] every finger
I have with my ribs. Father, I am glad you are come. Give me
95   your present to one Master Bassanio, who indeed gives rare
new liveries:[11] if I serve not him, I will run as far as God has any
ground. O, rare fortune, here comes the man. To him, Father,
for I am a Jew if I serve the Jew any longer.[12]

(*Enter Bassanio with a follower or two [including Leonardo].*)

BASSANIO. [*Addressing one of his followers.*] You may do so, but let
100   it be so hasted that supper be ready at the farthest by five of the
clock. See these letters delivered, put the liveries to making and
desire Graziano to come anon to my lodging.

---

1   *thou* Familiar address that Gobbo uses for Lancelot now that he has accepted that he
is his son (he has been using the more formal "you" until now);   *what a beard* Gobbo
has confused the back of Lancelot's head with his face.

2   *fill-horse* Cart horse.

3   *grows backward* Grows from long to short.

4   *of his tail* In his tail;   *of my face* On my face.

5   *how dost ... master agree* How do you and your master get along?

6   *how 'gree you* Do you think this will contribute to your relationship?

7   *set up my rest* Decided to take the risk;   *run some ground* Covered some area.

8   *very* True;   *Jew* Jewish person but also meaning a usurer or someone artful and
scheming.

9   *halter* Hangman's noose.

10 *tell* Count.

11 *rare new liveries* Lavish servants' uniforms.

12 *I am ... any longer* I.e., I am a villain if I work for the Jew any longer.

[Exit one of the followers.]

CLOWN. To him, Father.

GOBBO. God bless your worship.

BASSANIO. Gramercy.[1] Wouldst thou aught with me?   105

GOBBO. Here's my son, sir, a poor boy—[2]

CLOWN. Not a poor boy, sir, but the rich Jew's man that would,
    sir, as my father shall specify—

GOBBO. He hath a great infection,[3] sir, as one would say, to
    serve—   110

CLOWN. Indeed the short and the long is, I serve the Jew, and
    have a desire, as my father shall specify—

GOBBO. His master and he (saving your worship's reverence) are
    scarce cater-cousins—[4]

CLOWN. To be brief, the very truth is that the Jew, having done   115
    me wrong, doth cause me, as my father—being, I hope, an old
    man—shall frutify[5] unto you—

GOBBO. I have here a dish of doves that I would bestow upon
    your worship, and my suit is—

CLOWN. In very brief, the suit is impertinent[6] to myself, as your   120
    worship shall know by this honest old man, and though I say
    it, though old man, yet poor man my father.

BASSANIO. One speak for both. What would you?

CLOWN. Serve you, sir.

GOBBO. That is the very defect[7] of the matter, sir.   125

BASSANIO. I know thee well. Thou hast obtained thy suit.
    Shylock thy master spoke with me this day
    And hath preferred° thee, if it be preferment   *recommended*
    To leave a rich Jew's service, to become
    The follower of so poor a gentleman.   130

---

1   *Gramercy*   Much thanks.
2   *poor boy*   Gobbo may mean "unlucky," but his son interprets the meaning as "financially
    poor" in his next line.
3   *infection*   Gobbo, in his first of several malapropisms, means "affection," or desire to
    serve.
4   *scarce*   Hardly; *cater-cousins*   Dear friends.
5   *frutify*   Lancelot, who contributes several of his own malapropisms to the conversation,
    means "certify," though he confuses it with "fructify," or bloom.
6   *impertinent*   Lancelot means "pertinent."
7   *defect*   Gobbo means "effect," or intent.

CLOWN. The old proverb is very well parted between my master
  Shylock and you, sir: you have the grace of God, sir, and he
  hath enough.[1]
BASSANIO. Thou speak'st it well. Go, father, with thy son.
135 Take leave of thy old master and enquire
  My lodging out. [*To one of his followers.*] Give him a livery
  More guarded[2] than his fellows': see it done.
CLOWN. Father, in. I cannot get a service, no, I have ne'er a
  tongue in my head![3] [*Studying the palm of his hand.*] Well: if
140 any man in Italy have a fairer table, which doth offer to swear
  upon a book, I shall have good fortune.[4] Go to, here's a simple
  line of life; here's a small trifle of wives.[5] Alas, fifteen wives is
  nothing: eleven widows and nine maids is a simple coming in
  for one man, and then to scape drowning thrice, and to be in
145 peril of my life with the edge of a feather-bed.[6] Here are simple
  scapes.[7] Well, if Fortune be a woman, she's a good wench for
  this gear.[8] Father, come; I'll take my leave of the Jew in the
  twinkling.

  (*Exit Clown [with his father].*)

BASSANIO. I pray thee, good Leonardo, think on this:
150 These things being bought and orderly bestowed,[9]

---

1 *parted* Distributed; *you have ... hath enough* Echo of the proverbial saying "The Grace of God is gear enough," adapted from 2 Corinthians 12.9.
2 *guarded* Ornamented with braided trim.
3 *I cannot ... head* Ironic exclamation now that he has indeed achieved his goal of employment with Bassanio (though this is despite of his dubious powers of speech).
4 *if any ... good fortune* I.e., If any man in Italy can swear on the Bible with a better palm than mine, I do not know him; *table* Area between the main lines in the palm of the hand, used to read fortunes.
5 *simple* Common, spoken here with irony; *line of life* Circular line beginning at the base of the thumb that is thought to foretell the length and character of one's life; *wives* The number of wives in a man's future was thought to be signified by long, deep lines found between the ball of the thumb and the life line.
6 *coming in* Income, but there is also a sexual insinuation; *edge ... feather-bed* Danger posed by the marriage bed.
7 *scapes* Either adventurous exploits or misdeeds, both of which Lancelot seems to expect after interpreting his palm.
8 *if Fortune ... this gear* Proverbial Fortune was pictured as a woman who was both fickle and in support of fools; *gear* Function.
9 *bought and orderly bestowed* Arranged and stored, perhaps on a ship (for the trip to Belmont).

Return in haste, for I do feast tonight
My best esteemed acquaintance. Hie thee, go.
LEONARDO. My best endeavours shall be done herein.

(*Enter Graziano.*)

GRAZIANO. Where's your master?
LEONARDO.   Yonder, sir, he walks.

(*Exit.*)

GRAZIANO. Signor Bassanio!   155
BASSANIO. Graziano!
GRAZIANO. I have suit to you.[1]
BASSANIO. You have obtained it.
GRAZIANO. You must not deny me; I must go with you to
    Belmont.   160
BASSANIO. Why then, you must. But hear thee, Graziano,
    Thou art too wild, too rude and bold of voice:
    Parts that become thee happily enough
    And in such eyes as ours appear not faults.
    But where thou are not known, why, there they show   165
    Something too liberal.[2] Pray thee, take pain
    To allay with some cold drops of modesty
    Thy skipping spirit,[3] lest through thy wild behaviour
    I be misconstered° in the place I go to   *misconstrued*
    And lose my hopes.   170
GRAZIANO.   Signor Bassanio, hear me:
    If I do not put on a sober habit,[4]
    Talk with respect, and swear but now and then,
    Wear prayer-books in my pocket,[5] look demurely,
    Nay more, while grace is saying,° hood mine eyes   *being said*
    Thus with my hat,[6] and sigh and say "amen,"   175
    Use all the observance of civility,

---

1 *I have ... to you*   I have something to request of you.
2 *too liberal*   Boisterous or unruly.
3 *allay with ... skipping spirit*   Use moderation to restrain your excessive liveliness.
4 *sober habit*   Serious attitude and attire.
5 *Wear ... my pocket*   Adopt the custom of keeping a Bible or prayer book on my person.
6 *hood mine ... my hat*   Shield my eyes with my hat (in order to appear reverent).

Like one well studied in a sad ostent[1]
To please his grandam,[2] never trust me more.
BASSANIO. Well, we shall see your bearing.°   *manner*
180 GRAZIANO. Nay, but I bar tonight; you shall not gauge me
By what we do tonight.[3]
BASSANIO.   No, that were pity.
I would entreat you rather to put on
Your boldest suit of mirth,[4] for we have friends
That purpose merriment. But fare you well;
185 I have some business.
GRAZIANO. And I must to Lorenzo and the rest,
But we will visit you at supper-time.

(*Exeunt.*)

ACT 2, SCENE 3

(*Enter Jessica and the Clown.*)

JESSICA. I am sorry thou wilt leave my father so.
Our house is hell and thou, a merry devil,
Didst rob it of some taste° of tediousness.   *amount*
But fare thee well; there is a ducat for thee.
5 And, Lancelot, soon at supper shall thou see
Lorenzo, who is thy new master's guest.
Give him this letter, do it secretly,
And so farewell. I would not have my father
See me in talk with thee.
10 CLOWN. Adieu. Tears exhibit[5] my tongue, most beautiful pagan,
most sweet Jew! If a Christian do not play the knave and get

---

1   *sad ostent*   Sober appearance.
2   *grandam*   Grandmother or elderly woman.
3   *Nay, but ... do tonight*   But you cannot judge how I will behave in Belmont by how I act
    tonight.
4   *suit of mirth*   Playful outfit, referring to behavior but also echoing Graziano's dress-
    related language.
5   *exhibit*   Lancelot means "inhibit," though this mistake lends another meaning, that his
    tears will communicate feelings in ways his words do not.

thee, I am much deceived.¹ But adieu; these foolish drops do
something drown my manly spirit.² Adieu!

[*Exit.*]

JESSICA. Farewell, good Lancelot.
  Alack, what heinous sin is it in me   5
  To be ashamed to be my father's child!
  But, though I am a daughter to his blood,
  I am not to his manners.° O, Lorenzo,   *disposition*
  If thou keep promise I shall end this strife,³
  Become a Christian, and thy loving wife.   10

  (*Exit.*)

ACT 2, SCENE 4

(*Enter Graziano, Lorenzo, Salarino, and Solanio.*)

LORENZO. Nay, we will slink away in supper-time,
  Disguise us at my lodging, and return, all in an hour.
GRAZIANO. We have not made good preparation.
SALARINO. We have not spoke us yet of torch-bearers.⁴
SOLANIO. 'Tis vile unless it may be quaintly ordered,   5
  And better in my mind not undertook.⁵
LORENZO. 'Tis now but four of clock; we have two hours
  To furnish us.⁶

  (*Enter Lancelot [carrying a letter].*)

Friend Lancelot, what's the news?

---

1 *If a ... deceived* Some scholars have argued that this line implies Jessica was fathered
  illegitimately by a Christian, though it also seems to reference Jessica's relationship
  with Lorenzo; *play the knave* Take on the character of an artful scoundrel; *get*
  thee Procure you in marriage and as a sexual partner (or, possibly, father you).
2 *these foolish ... spirit* These tears, in their femininity, threaten my masculine image.
3 *strife* Discord, with an especially personal sense for Jessica, who feels torn between her
  Jewish father and Christian lover. Her marriage to Lorenzo and joining of his family will
  end this conflict because it will make her Christian.
4 *not spoke ... yet of* Not yet enlisted; *torch-bearers* Part of the entourage that
  accompanied masquers, which also included a herald to introduce them and musicians
  to help them make a festive entrance.
5 *'Tis vile ... undertook* If we cannot execute our masquing plans with appropriate skill
  and flair (because we have so little time), it would be better not to do anything.
6 *furnish us* Prepare ourselves and obtain what we need.

10 CLOWN. An it shall please you to break up this, it shall seem to
signify.[1]
LORENZO. I know the hand; in faith, 'tis a fair hand,
And whiter than the paper it writ on
Is the fair hand that writ.[2]
GRAZIANO. Love, news in faith.
15 CLOWN. By your leave,[3] sir.
LORENZO. Whither goest thou?
CLOWN. Marry, sir, to bid my old master, the Jew, to sup tonight
with my new master, the Christian.
LORENZO. Hold here, take this.[4] Tell gentle Jessica
20 I will not fail her; speak it privately.
Go, gentlemen, will you prepare you for this masque tonight?
I am provided of a torch-bearer.

(*Exit Clown.*)

SALARINO. Ay, marry, I'll be gone about it straight.
SOLANIO. And so will I.
25 LORENZO. Meet me and Graziano at Graziano's lodging some
hour[5] hence.
SALARINO. 'Tis good we do so.

[*Exit Salarino and Solanio.*]

GRAZIANO. Was not that letter from fair Jessica?
LORENZO. I must needs tell thee all. She hath directed
30 How I shall take her from her father's house,
What gold and jewels she is furnished with,
What page's suit she hath in readiness.
If e'er the Jew her father come to heaven,
It will be for his gentle[6] daughter's sake;
35 And never dare misfortune cross her foot

---

1 *break up this* Break the seal on the letter he has given Lorenzo; *seem to signify* Give
you some meaning.
2 *a fair hand ... that writ* Lorenzo puns on two meanings of "fair hand": first "skillful
handwriting," and second referring to Jessica's pale-colored hand, with the suggestion
that its whiteness makes it beautiful.
3 *By your leave* Excuse me (an apologetic announcement of departure).
4 *take this* Take this tip for your services.
5 *some hour* About an hour.
6 *gentle* Pun on "Gentile."

Unless she° do it under this excuse: *misfortune*
That she is issue to a faithless Jew.[1]
Come, go with me, peruse this as thou goest.
Fair Jessica shall be my torch-bearer.

   (*Exeunt.*)

ACT 2, Scene 5

(*Enter [Shylock the] Jew and his man that was, the Clown.*)

JEW. Well, thou shalt see, thy eyes shall be thy judge,
  The difference of old Shylock and Bassanio.
  [*Calling his daughter.*] What, Jessica!—Thou shalt not
    gormandize,[2]
  As thou hast done with me.—What, Jessica!—
  And sleep, and snore, and rend apparel out.[3]   5
  —Why, Jessica, I say!
CLOWN.   Why, Jessica!
SHYLOCK. Who bids thee call? I do not bid thee call.
CLOWN. Your worship was wont to tell me I could do nothing
  without bidding.

   (*Enter Jessica.*)

JESSICA. Call you? What is your will?
JEW. I am bid forth[4] to supper, Jessica.   10
  There are my keys. But wherefore should I go?
  I am not bid for love; they flatter me,
  But yet I'll go in hate, to feed upon
  The prodigal Christian. Jessica, my girl,
  Look to my house. I am right loath[5] to go;   15
  There is some ill a-brewing towards my rest,[6]
  For I did dream of money-bags[7] tonight.°   *last night*

---

1 *she is faithless Jew* Jessica is the child of a Jew; *faithless* Non-Christian but also
  untrustworthy.
2 *gormandize* Eat voraciously.
3 *rend apparel out* Destroy clothes through excessive wear.
4 *bid forth* Invited.
5 *Look to* Watch over; *right loath* Very hesitant.
6 *towards my rest* Making threat to my sense of peace.
7 *dream of money-bags* A bad portent, since objects in dreams were thought to represent
  opposite meanings.

CLOWN. I beseech you, sir, go. My young master doth expect
    your reproach.[1]
20 JEW. So do I his.
CLOWN. And they have conspired together. I will not say you
    shall see a masque, but, if you do, then it was not for nothing
    that my nose fell a-bleeding on Black Monday[2] last, at six
    o'clock i'th' morning, falling out that year on Ash Wednesday
25   was four year in th'afternoon.
   JEW. What, are there masques? Hear you me, Jessica,
    Lock up my doors, and when you hear the drum
    And the vile squealing of the wry-necked fife,[3]
    Clamber not you up to the casements° then,   *windows*
30   Nor thrust your head into the public street
    To gaze on Christian fools with varnished faces;[4]
    But stop my house's ears—I mean my casements—
    Let not the sound of shallow foppery enter
    My sober house. By Jacob's staff,[5] I swear,
35   I have no mind of feasting forth tonight.
    But I will go. Go you before me, sirrah:
    Say I will come.
   CLOWN.   I will go before, sir.
    [*Aside to Jessica.*] Mistress, look out at window for all this,[6]
    There will come a Christian by
40   Will be worth a Jewess' eye.[7]

    [*Exit.*]

---

1 *reproach* Lancelot means "approach," though again he could be considered correct in
    that the Christians often reproach, or disparage, Shylock. This is the meaning Shylock
    appropriates.
2 *Black Monday* Day after Easter Sunday, meaning it cannot fall on Ash Wednesday and
    so Lancelot's talk is nonsensical.
3 *wry-necked fife* Flute-like instrument played in such a way that the musician must tilt
    his head to the side.
4 *varnished faces* Distorted painted masks.
5 *Jacob's staff* Oath referencing the biblical patriarch Jacob's beginning as a poor man
    with a staff his only belonging (See Genesis 32.10).
6 *for all this* I.e., despite what your father has instructed.
7 *Jewess' eye* Proverbial phrase indicating something of value.

JEW. What says that fool of Hagar's offspring,[1] ha?

JESSICA. His words were "Farewell, mistress," nothing else.

JEW. The patch° is kind enough, but a huge feeder,   *fool*

    Snail-slow in profit,[2] and he sleeps by day

    More than the wildcat. Drones[3] hive not with me,   45

    Therefore I part with him, and part with him

    To one that I would have him help to waste

    His borrowed purse. Well, Jessica, go in;

    Perhaps I will return immediately.

    Do as I bid you; shut doors after you. "Fast bind, fast find."[4]   50

    A proverb never stale in thrifty mind.

    (*Exit.*)

JESSICA. Farewell, and if my fortune be not crossed,°   *impeded*

    I have a father, you a daughter, lost.

    (*Exit.*)

ACT 2, SCENE 6

(*Enter the masquers Graziano and Salarino.*)

GRAZIANO. This is the penthouse[5] under which Lorenzo

    Desired us to make stand.

SALARINO. His hour[6] is almost past.

GRAZIANO. And it is marvel he outdwells his hour,

    For lovers ever run before the clock.   5

SALARINO. O, ten times faster Venus' pigeons[7] fly

    To seal love's bonds[8] new made than they are wont

    To keep obliged faith[9] unforfeited!°   *unbroken*

---

1 *Hagar's offspring* Reference to Ishmael, the son of Abraham and his gentile attendant Hagar; Ishmael would be outcast along with his mother after the birth of Isaac.

2 *profit* Progress in learning.

3 *wildcat* I.e., nocturnal animal; *Drones* Male bees whose only work is to mate with the queen.

4 *Fast ... find* Things that are kept securely can be recovered quickly and easily.

5 *penthouse* Sheltered area under the protruding roof of a house's upper story.

6 *hour* I.e., the hour at which he wanted us to meet him.

7 *Venus' pigeons* Doves that pull Venus' chariot.

8 *seal love's bonds* Become sexually intimate.

9 *obliged faith* I.e., faithfulness between married or engaged lovers.

GRAZIANO. That ever holds:[1] who riseth from a feast,
10   With that keen appetite that he sits down?
     Where is the horse that doth untread° again   *retrace*
     His tedious measures° with the unbated fire[2]   *footfalls*
     That he did pace them first? All things that are,
     Are with more spirit chased than enjoyed.
15   How like a younger[3] or a prodigal,
     The scarfed bark[4] puts from her native bay,
     Hugged and embraced by the strumpet wind![5]
     How like the prodigal doth she return,
     With overweathered ribs[6] and ragged sails,
20   Lean, rent° and beggared° by the   *torn / impoverished*
     strumpet wind!

    (*Enter Lorenzo.*)

SALARINO. Here comes Lorenzo; more of this hereafter.
LORENZO. Sweet friends, your patience for my long abode.°   *delay*
     Not I but my affairs have made you wait.
     When you shall please to play the thieves for wives,
25   I'll watch as long for you then: approach;
     Here dwells my father Jew. Ho! who's within?

    ([*Enter*] *Jessica above.*)

JESSICA. Who are you? Tell me for more certainty,
     Albeit I'll swear that I do know your tongue.
LORENZO. Lorenzo, and thy love.
30 JESSICA. Lorenzo certain, and my love indeed,
     For who love I so much? And now, who knows
     But you, Lorenzo, whether I am yours?
LORENZO. Heaven and thy thoughts are witness that thou art.

---

1   *ever holds*   Is always proven true.
2   *unbated fire*   Unrestrained eagerness.
3   *younger*   Reference to the Parable of the Prodigal Son from Luke 15.11–13, the story of a younger son who abandons his father and squanders his inheritance, then returns home.
4   *scarfed bark*   Ship adorned with streamers or flags.
5   *strumpet wind*   Fickle, unpredictable wind that, like a prostitute, imparts favors in an unpredictable, impersonal manner.
6   *overweathered ribs*   Wooden planks (on the ship) that have been ravaged by weather.

JESSICA. Here, catch this casket; it is worth the pains.
  I am glad 'tis night you do not look on me,   35
  For I am much ashamed of my exchange.[1]
  But love is blind, and lovers cannot see
  The pretty° follies that themselves commit,   *crafty*
  For, if they could, Cupid[2] himself would blush
  To see me thus transformed to a boy.   40
LORENZO. Descend, for you must be my torch-bearer.
JESSICA. What, must I hold a candle to[3] my shames?
  They, in themselves, good sooth, are too too light.[4]
  Why, 'tis an office of discovery,[5] love,
  And I should be obscured.   45
LORENZO.   So are you, sweet,
  Even in the lovely garnish° of a boy. But come at once, *clothing*
  For the close° night doth play the runaway,[6]   *furtive*
  And we are stayed for° at Bassanio's feast.   *awaited*
JESSICA. I will make fast the doors and gild[7] myself
  With some more ducats, and be with you straight.   50

    [*Exit.*]

GRAZIANO. Now, by my hood,[8] a gentle, and no Jew.
LORENZO. Beshrew me[9] but I love her heartily,
  For she is wise, if I can judge of her,
  And fair she is, if that mine eyes be true,
  And true she is, as she hath proved herself: 55
  And therefore like herself, wise, fair and true,
  Shall she be placed in my constant soul.

    (*Enter Jessica.*)

---

1 *exchange* Change in attire, i.e., Jessica's disguise as a boy.
2 *Cupid* Venus' blind son.
3 *hold a candle to* Illuminate or bear witness to.
4 *light* Clear but also morally light, or indecent.
5 *office of discovery* Duty (as torch-bearer) to cast light on the situation.
6 *doth play the runaway* Is slipping away quickly.
7 *gild* Decorate with gold.
8 *by my hood* An oath; possibly also a punning reference to Graziano's masquer's dress.
9 *Beshrew me* Let evil come to me.

What, art thou come? On, gentleman,[1] away,
Our masquing mates by this time for us stay.

[*Exeunt everyone but Graziano.*]

(*Enter Antonio.*)

60 ANTONIO. Who's there?
GRAZIANO. Signor Antonio?
ANTONIO. Fie, fie, Graziano. Where are all the rest?
'Tis nine o'clock; our friends all stay for you.
No masque tonight, the wind is come about.[2]
65 Bassanio presently will go aboard;
I have sent twenty out to seek for you.
GRAZIANO. I am glad on't. I desire no more delight
Than to be under sail and gone tonight.

(*Exeunt.*)

ACT 2, SCENE 7

(*Enter Portia [and Nerissa] with Morocco and both their trains.*)

PORTIA. Go, draw aside the curtains and discover°   *reveal*
The several° caskets to this noble prince.   *various*
Now make your choice.
MOROCCO. This first of gold, who this inscription bears:
5   "Who chooseth me shall gain what many men desire."
The second, silver, which this promise carries:
"Who chooseth me shall get as much as he deserves."
The third, dull[3] lead, with warning all as blunt:
"Who chooseth me must give and hazard all he hath."
10   How shall I know if I do choose the right?
PORTIA. The one of them contains my picture, prince.
If you choose that, then I am yours withal.[4]
MOROCCO. Some god direct my judgment! Let me see.
I will survey th'inscriptions back again.

---

1   *gentleman* I.e., Jessica in her boy's disguise.
2   *come about* Changed course.
3   *dull* Tiresome, but also unsharpened or blunt.
4   *withal* Along with it.

What says this leaden casket?   15
"Who chooseth me must give and hazard all he hath."
"Must give," for what? For lead, hazard for lead?
This casket threatens: men that hazard all
Do it in hope of fair advantages.
A golden mind stoops not to shows of dross;[1]   20
I'll then nor give nor hazard aught for lead.
What says the silver with her virgin hue?[2]
"Who chooseth me shall get as much as he deserves."
"As much as he deserves." Pause there, Morocco,
And weigh thy value with an even hand.[3]   25
If thou be'st rated by thy estimation[4]
Thou dost deserve enough; and yet, enough
May not extend so far as to the lady.
And yet, to be afeard of my deserving
Were but a weak disabling° of myself.   *disparagement*   30
As much as I deserve: why, that's the lady.
I do in birth deserve her, and in fortunes,
In graces and in qualities of breeding.
But more than these, in love I do deserve,[5]
What if I strayed no farther, but chose here?   35
Let's see once more this saying graved in gold:
"Who chooseth me shall gain what many men desire."
Why, that's the lady, all the world desires her.
From the four corners of the earth they come
To kiss this shrine, this mortal breathing saint.[6]   40
The Hyrcanian deserts[7] and the vasty wilds
Of wide Arabia are as throughfares[8] now
For princes to come view fair Portia.

---

1 *dross* Worthless material, as in the material discarded in the process of melting metals.
2 *virgin hue* Silver's pure color is likened to the moon and Diana, its virgin goddess.
3 *even hand* Impartial judgment.
4 *thy estimation* Your own assessment.
5 *But more ... deserve* In addition to all these credentials, I deserve her because I offer her love.
6 *shrine* Place of interment for the remains of a saint; *mortal breathing saint* I.e., living saint.
7 *Hyrcanian deserts* Persian region associated with wildness, located south of the Caspian sea.
8 *throughfares* Roads (made by the high volume of suitors traveling them).

The watery kingdom,¹ whose ambitious head
45   Spits in the face of heaven, is no bar
To stop the foreign spirits,² but they come,
As o'er a brook, to see fair Portia.
One of these three contains her heavenly picture.
Is't like that lead contains her? 'Twere damnation
50   To think so base³ a thought; it were too gross
To rib her cerecloth⁴ in the obscure° grave.   *darkened*
Or shall I think in silver she's immured,°   *contained*
Being ten times undervalued to tried⁵ gold?
O, sinful thought, never so rich a gem
55   Was set in worse than gold. They have in England
A coin that bears the figure of an angel⁶
Stamped in gold: but that's insculped upon.⁷
But here, an angel in a golden bed⁸
Lies all within. Deliver me the key.
60   Here do I choose, and thrive I as I may.
PORTIA. There, take it, prince, and if my form lie there,
Then I am yours!

[*He opens the gold casket.*]

MOROCCO. O, hell! What have we here, a carrion death,⁹
Within whose empty eye there is a written scroll.
65   I'll read the writing.
        All that glisters is not gold,
        Often have you heard that told.

---

1   *watery kingdom* Sea.
2   *whose ambitious ... spirits* Whose wild ruler Poseidon, in causing huge waves and much turbulence, is still unable to slow the many adventurous men seeking out Portia in Belmont.
3   *base* Shameful, but also a reference to lead's lowly position as a base metal.
4   *rib* Enclose, as if with ribs; *cerecloth* Burial wrapping made of waxed cloth.
5   *ten times undervalued* Silver was ten times less valuable than gold; *tried* Examined to determine its value.
6   *coin that ... an angel* Coin depicting the archangel Michael battling a dragon, worth ten shillings.
7   *but that's insculped upon* But it is only etched on the coin's surface.
8   *angel ... bed* I.e., Portia's image interred in the gold casket.
9   *carrion death* Skull.

> *Many a man his life hath sold*
> *But° my outside to behold.*   Only
> *Gilded timber do worms infold.*   70
> *Had you been as wise as bold,*
> *Young in limbs, in judgment old,*
> *Your answer had not been inscrolled,*
> *Fare you well, your suit is cold.*

Cold indeed, and labour lost,   75
Then farewell, heat, and welcome frost.[1]
Portia, adieu. I have too grieved a heart
To take a tedious leave: thus losers part.°   depart

(*Exit.*)

PORTIA. A gentle riddance. Draw the curtains, go.
Let all of his complexion choose me so.   80

(*Exeunt.*)

ACT 2, SCENE 8

(*Enter Salarino and Solanio.*)

SALARINO. Why, man, I saw Bassanio under sail.[2]
  With him is Graziano gone along,
  And in their ship I am sure Lorenzo is not.
SOLANIO. The villain Jew with outcries raised° the Duke,   woke
  Who went with him to search Bassanio's ship.   5
SALARINO. He came too late, the ship was under sail.
  But there the Duke was given to understand
  That in a gondola[3] were seen together
  Lorenzo and his amorous Jessica.
  Besides, Antonio certified° the Duke   assured 10
  They were not with Bassanio in his ship.

---

1 *farewell ... welcome frost* Goodbye to passion, since in making this choice Morocco
   must now uphold his agreement to never marry.
2 *under sail* Ready to embark on the journey.
3 *gondola* Passenger boat used for traversing the canals. It would be difficult to sight
   Jessica and Lorenzo because gondolas were covered, obscuring the identities of passengers.

SOLANIO. I never heard a passion so confused,[1]
  So strange, outrageous, and so variable
  As the dog Jew did utter in the streets:
15 "My daughter! O, my ducats! O, my daughter!
  Fled with a Christian, O, my Christian ducats.
  Justice, the law, my ducats, and my daughter!
  A sealed bag, two sealed bags of ducats,
  Of double ducats,[2] stol'n from me by my daughter!
20 And jewels, two stones, two rich and precious stones,[3]
  Stol'n by my daughter! Justice! Find the girl;
  She hath the stones upon her, and the ducats."
SALARINO. Why, all the boys in Venice follow him,
  Crying "His stones, his daughter and his ducats!"
25 SOLANIO. Let good Antonio look he keep his day,[4]
  Or he shall pay for this.
SALARINO.   Marry, well remembered.
  I reasoned° with a Frenchman yesterday   *conversed*
  Who told me, in the narrow seas that part
  The French and English,[5] there miscarried°   *shipwrecked*
30 A vessel of our country richly fraught.
  I thought upon Antonio when he told me,
  And wished in silence that it were not his.
SOLANIO. You were best to tell Antonio what you hear.
  Yet do not suddenly, for it may grieve him.
35 SALARINO. A kinder gentleman treads not the earth.
  I saw Bassanio and Antonio part;
  Bassanio told him he would make some speed
  Of his return. He answered, "Do not so,
  Slubber not[6] business for my sake, Bassanio,
40 But stay the very riping of the time;[7]

---

1 *passion* Intense outburst; *confused* Combining many elements.
2 *double ducats* Coins possessing twice the value of a ducat.
3 *jewels, two ... precious stones* While Shylock is mourning the actual jewels his daughter has stolen, there is also a sexual meaning attached to both "jewels," a possible reference to Jessica's now lost virginity, and "stones," which could mean "testicles."
4 *look ... his day* Make certain he repays his loan according to the deadline.
5 *narrow seas ... and English* The English Channel.
6 *Slubber not* Do not act in sloppy haste.
7 *But stay ... the time* Stay until you have accomplished your goal in Belmont.

And for° the Jew's bond, which he hath of me,   *as for*
Let it not enter in your mind of love.[1]
Be merry, and employ your chiefest thoughts
To courtship, and such fair ostents° of love   *exhibitions*
As shall conveniently become you there."   45
And even there,[2] his eye being big with tears,
Turning his face, he put his hand behind him,
And, with affection wondrous sensible,[3]
He wrung Bassanio's hand, and so they parted.
SOLANIO. I think he only loves the world for him.[4]   50
I pray thee, let us go and find him out,
And quicken his embraced heaviness [5]
With some delight or other.
SALARINO.   Do we so.

        (*Exeunt.*)

ACT 2, SCENE 9

(*Enter Nerissa and a Servitor.*)

NERISSA. Quick, quick, I pray thee, draw the curtain straight;
    The Prince of Arragon hath ta'en his oath,
    And comes to his election° presently.   *decision*

        (*Enter [the Prince of] Arragon, his train, and Portia.*)

PORTIA. Behold, there stand the caskets, noble prince.
    If you choose that wherein I am contained,   5
    Straight shall our nuptial rites be solemnized.
    But if you fail, without more speech, my lord,
    You must be gone from hence immediately.
ARRAGON. I am enjoined° by oath to observe three things: *obligated*
    First, never to unfold to anyone   10
    Which casket 'twas I chose; next, if I fail

---

1 *Let it ... of love*   Do not let it distract you in your thoughts of love.
2 *even there*   In that instant.
3 *affection wondrous sensible*   Noticeably passionate emotion.
4 *he ... him*   I.e., Bassanio is Antonio's source of happiness in the world.
5 *quicken ... heaviness*   Lift some of the melancholy Antonio has taken on.

Of the right casket, never in my life
To woo a maid in way of marriage;
Lastly, if I do fail in fortune of my choice,
15   Immediately to leave you and be gone.
PORTIA. To these injunctions everyone doth swear
That comes to hazard for my worthless self.
ARRAGON. And so have I addressed me.[1] Fortune now
To my heart's hope: gold, silver, and base lead.
20   "Who chooseth me must give and hazard all he hath."
You shall look fairer e'er I give or hazard.
What says the golden chest? Ha, let me see:
"Who chooseth me shall gain what many men desire."
"What many men desire": that many may be meant
25   By the fool multitude[2] that choose by show,
Not learning more than the fond° eye doth teach,   *foolish*
Which pries not to th'interior, but like the martlet[3]
Builds in the weather on the outward wall,
Even in the force and road of casualty.[4]
30   I will not choose what many men desire,
Because I will not jump° with common spirits   *concur*
And rank me with the barbarous multitudes.
Why then, to thee, thou silver treasure house:
Tell me once more what title thou dost bear:
35   "Who chooseth me shall get as much as he deserves."
And well said too; for who shall go about[5]
To cozen° Fortune and be honourable   *dupe*
Without the stamp of merit? Let none presume
To wear an undeserved dignity.
40   O, that estates, degrees, and offices[6]
Were not derived° corruptly, and that clear honour   *acquired*
Were purchased° by the merit of the wearer!   *achieved*

---

1 *addressed me* Made myself ready.
2 *that many ... fool multitude* The "many" might indicate the unintelligent masses.
3 *martlet* Swift, a bird similar to a swallow, known for building nests on exterior walls.
4 *Builds ... casualty* Builds its nest in an unsafe location, making it vulnerable to the strength and random effects of misfortune.
5 *go about* Try.
6 *estates, degrees, and offices* Social rankings.

How many then should cover that stand bare?[1]
How many be commanded that command?
How much low peasantry would then be gleaned[2]   45
From the true seed of honour?[3] And how much honour
Picked from the chaff[4] and ruin of the times
To be new varnished?[5] Well, but to my choice.
"Who chooseth me shall get as much as he deserves."
I will assume desert;[6] give me a key for this,   50
And instantly unlock my fortunes here.

    [*He opens the silver casket.*]

PORTIA. Too long a pause for that which you find there.
ARRAGON. What's here? The portrait of a blinking idiot
  Presenting me a schedule!° I will read it.   *scroll*
  How much unlike art thou to Portia!   55
  How much unlike my hopes and my deservings.
  "Who chooseth me shall have as much as he deserves?"
  Do I deserve no more than a fool's head?
  Is that my prize? Are my deserts no better?
PORTIA. To offend and judge are distinct offices,   60
  And of opposed natures.[7]
ARRAGON.   What is here?
    The fire seven times tried[8] *this;*
    Seven times tried that judgment is,
    That did never choose amiss.
    Some there be that shadows° kiss;   *apparitions* 65
    Such have but a shadow's bliss.
    There be fools alive iwis°   *surely*

---

1 *cover that stand bare* Keep their heads covered rather than removing their hats as a sign
   of deference to those with higher authority or status.
2 *gleaned* Collected; especially in the sense of stripping a field of grain after the reapers
   have left.
3 *true seed of honour* I.e., individuals descended from nobility.
4 *chaff* Waste; but also, continuing the metaphor of grain picking, husks divided from
   the grain and discarded.
5 *new varnished* Renewed and returned to former prominence.
6 *assume desert* Formally accept the honor that I deserve.
7 *To offend ... opposed natures* I.e., you cannot serve as a judge in review of your own case,
   or possibly, I cannot comment myself since this outcome concerns me too.
8 *tried* Tested or refined.

> *Silvered o'er,*[1] *and so was this.*
> *Take what wife you will to bed,*
> 70   *I will ever be your head.*
> *So be gone: you are sped.*°   *finished*
> Still more fool I shall appear
> By the time I linger here.
> With one fool's head I came to woo,
> 75   But I go away with two.
> Sweet, adieu. I'll keep my oath,
> Patiently to bear my wroth.[2]

      [Exeunt with his train.]

PORTIA. Thus hath the candle singed the moth.
  O, these deliberate[3] fools when they do choose,
80   They have the wisdom by their wit to lose.
NERISSA. The ancient saying is no heresy:
  "Hanging and wiving goes by destiny."
PORTIA. Come, draw the curtain, Nerissa.

      (Enter Messenger.)

MESSENGER. Where is my lady?
PORTIA.   Here. What would my lord?[4]
85 MESSENGER. Madam, there is alighted at your gate
  A young Venetian, one that comes before
  To signify th'approaching of his lord,
  From whom he bringeth sensible regreets:[5]
  To wit, besides commends and courteous breath,°   *conversation*
90   Gifts of rich value. Yet I have not seen
  So likely° an ambassador of love.   *promising*
  A day in April never came so sweet
  To show how costly° summer was at hand,   *extravagant*
  As this forespurrer[6] comes before his lord.

---

1 *Silvered o'er* Covered in silver, suggesting a superficial exterior hiding a lack of value underneath.
2 *wroth* Woe or anger.
3 *deliberate* Thoughtful or cunning.
4 *my lord* Playful counter to the way the messenger addresses her.
5 *sensible regreets* Material greetings in the form of gifts.
6 *forespurrer* Messenger who arrives ahead of the party on horseback.

PORTIA. No more, I pray thee; I am half afeard   95
Thou wilt say anon he is some kin to thee,
Thou spend'st such high day wit¹ in praising him.
Come, come, Nerissa, for I long to see
Quick Cupid's post° that comes so mannerly.   *messenger*
NERISSA. Bassanio, lord, love, if thy will it be.   100

(*Exeunt.*)

ACT 3, SCENE 1

(*Enter Solanio and Salarino.*)

SOLANIO. Now what news on the Rialto?
SALARINO. Why yet it lives there unchecked,² that Antonio hath a
ship of rich lading wracked on the narrow seas; the Goodwins I
think they call the place, a very dangerous flat, and fatal, where
the carcasses of many a tall ship lie buried, as they say, if my   5
gossip Report³ be an honest woman of her word.
SOLANIO. I would she were as lying a gossip in that as ever
knapped ginger, or made her neighbours believe she wept for
the death of a third husband.⁴ But it is true, without any slips
of prolixity, or crossing the plain highway of talk,⁵ that the   10
good Antonio, the honest Antonio   O, that I had a title good
enough to keep his name company.
SALARINO. Come, the full stop.⁶
SOLANIO. Ha, what sayest thou? Why, the end is, he hath lost a
ship.   15

---

1   *high day wit*   Fancy language used for holidays.
2   *yet it ... unchecked*   An unconfirmed story continues to circulate.
3   *Goodwins*   Treacherous area off the Kentish coast where ships were often lost in the
    shallow banks;   *tall*   Grand;   *gossip*   Person, usually female, who can be counted
    upon to spread rumors;   *Report*   Rumor or hearsay, here used as a name or person-
    ification.
4   *knapped ginger*   Gnawed on ginger, the sharply flavored plant, suggesting the gossip's
    love for ruminating on a salacious story;   *made her ... third husband*   Put on an
    appearance of mourning, perhaps covering excitement over an improved financial
    situation.
5   *slips of prolixity*   Indulgences of excessive, possibly untruthful, wordiness;   *crossing the
    ... of talk*   Departing from the simple truth.
6   *Come, the full stop*   Get to the end of your story.

SALARINO. I would it might prove the end of his losses.

SOLANIO. Let me say "amen" betimes, lest the devil cross[1] my prayer, for here he comes in the likeness of a Jew. How now, Shylock, what news among the merchants?

(*Enter Shylock.*)

20 SHYLOCK. You knew, none so well, none so well as you, of my daughter's flight.

SALARINO. That's certain; I, for my part, knew the tailor that made the wings she flew withal.[2]

SOLANIO. And Shylock, for his own part, knew the bird was 25 fledge, and then it is the complexion of them all to leave the dam.[3]

JEW. She is damned for it.

SALARINO. That's certain, if the devil may be her judge.

JEW. My own flesh and blood to rebel!

30 SOLANIO. Out upon it, old carrion, rebels it at these years?[4]

JEW. I say my daughter is my flesh and blood.

SALARINO. There is more difference between thy flesh and hers than between jet and ivory, more between your bloods than there is between red wine and Rhenish.[5] But tell us, do you 35 hear whether Antonio have had any loss at sea or no?

JEW. There I have another bad match: a bankrupt, a prodigal, who dare scarce show his head on the Rialto, a beggar, that was used to come so smug upon the mart.[6] Let him look to his bond. He was wont to call me usurer; let him look to his bond. 40 He was wont to lend money for a Christian courtesy; let him look to his bond.

SALARINO. Why, I am sure if he forfeit, thou wilt not take his flesh. What's that good for?

---

1   *betimes* I.e., while it is not yet too late;   *cross* Obstruct.
2   *the wings ... flew withal* The costume with which she achieved her escape.
3   *fledge* Prepared to fly;   *dam* Mother.
4   *carrion* Decaying flesh;   *rebels it at these years* Does flesh as old as yours behave scandalously? Solanio twists Shylock's use of "flesh and blood" to mean not his child but Shylock's own body.
5   *red wine and Rhenish* I.e., between white Rhenish wine, which is purer and more valued, and red wine.
6   *match* Bargain;   *smug* Neat or trim;   *mart* Marketplace.

JEW. To bait[1] fish withal; if it will feed nothing else, it will feed
   my revenge. He hath disgraced me and hindered me half a   45
   million,[2] laughed at my losses, mocked at my gains, scorned
   my nation, thwarted my bargains, cooled my friends, heated
   mine enemies, and what's his reason? I am a Jew: Hath not a
   Jew eyes? Hath not a Jew hands, organs, dimensions, senses,
   affections,[3] passions? Fed with the same food, hurt with the   50
   same weapons, subject to the same diseases, healed by the same
   means, warmed and cooled by the same winter and summer as
   a Christian is? If you prick us do we not bleed? If you tickle us
   do we not laugh? If you poison us do we not die? And if you
   wrong us shall we not revenge? If we are like you in the rest, we 55
   will resemble you in that. If a Jew wrong a Christian, what is
   his humility?[4] Revenge! If a Christian wrong a Jew, what should
   his sufferance[5] be by Christian example? Why, revenge! The
   villainy you teach me I will execute, and it shall go hard but I
   will better the instruction.[6]   60

   (*Enter a man from Antonio.*)

SERVANT. Gentlemen, my master Antonio is at his house and
   desires to speak with you both.
SALARINO. We have been up and down to seek him.

   (*Enter Tubal.*)

SOLANIO. Here comes another of the tribe; a third cannot be
   matched,[7] unless the devil himself turn Jew.   65

   (*Exeunt Gentlemen.*)

SHYLOCK. How now, Tubal, what news from Genoa? Hast thou
   found my daughter?

---

1 *bait* Employ as bait for.
2 *hindered ... a million* Kept me from profiting half a million ducats.
3 *dimensions* Measurable physical attributes; *affections* Though not always distinguished from passions in the period, affections were generally experiences of exterior
   sensory stimuli, while passions involved inner emotions.
4 *what is his humility* In what kind and meek manner does he (as a Christian) respond?
   Shylock is being sarcastic here.
5 *sufferance* Patient tolerance of a hardship.
6 *it shall ... the instruction* It will be challenging, but I will try to do even better than I
   have been taught.
7 *cannot be matched* Cannot match them.

TUBAL. I often came where I did hear of her, but cannot find her.

SHYLOCK. Why, there, there, there, there! A diamond gone cost
70   me two thousand ducats in Frankfurt.[1] The curse[2] never fell
upon our nation till now; I never felt it till now. Two thousand
ducats in that, and other precious, precious jewels; I would my
daughter were dead at my foot, and the jewels in her ear; would
she were hearsed[3] at my foot, and the ducats in her coffin. No
75   news of them? Why so? And I know not what's spent in the
search. Why, thou loss upon loss! The thief gone with so much,
and so much to find the thief, and no satisfaction, no revenge,
nor no ill luck stirring but what lights a[4] my shoulders, no sighs
but a my breathing, no tears but a my shedding.

80 TUBAL. Yes, other men have ill luck too. Antonio, as I heard in
   Genoa—

SHYLOCK. What, what, what? Ill luck, ill luck?

TUBAL. Hath an argosy cast away coming from Tripolis.

SHYLOCK. I thank God, I thank God! Is it true, is it true?

85 TUBAL. I spoke with some of the sailors that escaped the wreck.

SHYLOCK. I thank thee, good Tubal: good news, good news! Ha,
   ha, heard in Genoa!

TUBAL. Your daughter spent in Genoa, as I heard, one night
   fourscore[5] ducats.

90 SHYLOCK. Thou stick'st a dagger in me; I shall never see my gold
   again. Fourscore ducats at a sitting? Fourscore ducats!

TUBAL. There came divers of Antonio's creditors in my company
   to Venice, that swear he cannot choose but break.[6]

SHYLOCK. I am very glad of it. I'll plague him; I'll torture him. I
95   am glad of it.

TUBAL. One of them showed me a ring that he had of your
   daughter for a monkey.

---

1   *Frankfurt* German city on the Main river, home to much commercial activity and a
    jewelry fair.
2   *curse* Possibly the curse said to afflict the people of Israel for their role in Christ's
    crucifixion (Matthew 27.24–25).
3   *hearsed* In a coffin.
4   *lights a* Lands on.
5   *fourscore* Eighty.
6   *break* Go bankrupt.

SHYLOCK. Out upon her! Thou torturest me, Tubal. It was my
    turquoise: I had it of Leah[1] when I was a bachelor. I would not
    have given it for a wilderness of monkeys.   100
TUBAL. But Antonio is certainly undone.
SHYLOCK. Nay, that's true; that's very true. Go, Tubal, fee me an
    officer; bespeak him a fortnight before.[2] I will have the heart of
    him if he forfeit, for, were he out of Venice, I can make what
    merchandise I will:[3] go, Tubal, and meet me at our synagogue.   105
    Go, good Tubal, at our synagogue, Tubal.

    (*Exeunt.*)

ACT 3, SCENE 2

(*Enter Bassanio, Portia, [Nerissa,] Graziano, and all their trains.*)

PORTIA. I pray you tarry. Pause a day or two,
    Before you hazard, for in choosing wrong
    I lose your company; therefore, forbear awhile.[4]
    There's something tells me (but it is not love)[5]
    I would not lose you, and, you know yourself,   5
    Hate counsels not in such a quality;
    But, lest you should not understand me well—
    And yet, a maiden hath no tongue but thought[6]—
    I would detain you here some month or two
    Before you venture for me. I could teach you   10
    How to choose right, but then I am forsworn.[7]
    So will I never be, so may you miss me.

---

1   *turquoise* Blue or green-colored stone that was popular as an engagement ring and
highly valued because of the difficulty of acquiring it;   *Leah* Shylock's wife and also
the name of Jacob's first wife, who he is tricked into marrying by her father Laban
(Genesis 29.25).

2   *fee me ... before* Employ the services of a bailiff, a fortnight before Antonio's date of
repayment (in order to arrest him).

3   *I can ... I will* I can engage in whatever business deals I like.

4   *forbear awhile* Hold back on making a decision for some time.

5   *it is not love* This appears to be a denial that Portia loves Bassanio; however, by line 6,
she implies she must love him, and in lines 16–18, she fully confesses she loves him.

6   *a maiden ... thought* A maiden is barred from speaking her true feelings and thoughts
out loud.

7   *I am forsworn* I would break the oath I took (to follow my father's wishes).

But if you do,[1] you'll make me wish a sin,
That I had been forsworn: beshrew your eyes,
15   They have o'erlooked° me and divided me: *bewitched*
One half of me is yours, the other half yours,
Mine own, I would say: but, if mine, then yours,
And so, all yours. O, these naughty° times   *wicked*
Puts bars between the owners and their rights:[2]
20   And so, though yours, not yours, prove it so,[3]
Let Fortune go to hell for it, not I.
I speak too long, but 'tis to peise[4] the time,
To eke° it and to draw it out in length,   *stretch*
To stay° you from election.   *stop*
BASSANIO.   Let me choose,
25   For, as I am, I live upon the rack.[5]
PORTIA.   Upon the rack, Bassanio? Then confess
What treason[6] there is mingled in your love.
BASSANIO.   None but that ugly treason of mistrust,°   *worry*
Which makes me fear th'enjoying of my love.
30   There may as well be amity and life[7]
'Tween snow and fire, as treason and my love.
PORTIA.   Ay, but I fear you speak upon the rack,
Where men enforced do speak anything.
BASSANIO.   Promise me life and I'll confess the truth.
35   PORTIA.   Well then, confess and live.[8]
BASSANIO.   Confess and love
Had been the very sum of my confession.
O happy torment, when my torturer

---

1   *if you do*   If you are unsuccessful at winning me.
2   *Puts bars ... their rights*   Social and legal customs create barriers not only between Bassanio and Portia should he choose wrong but between Portia's feelings and her ability to express them freely.
3   *prove it so*   If it comes to pass in that way.
4   *peise*   Slow down by adding extra weight.
5   *live upon the rack*   Am tormented as though being tortured upon the rack (an instrument that was used to force confessions from its victims by stretching them).
6   *treason*   Considered the worst political crime, treason might also apply to the topic of love because of its implications of disloyalty.
7   *amity and life*   Camaraderie and a living bond.
8   *confess and live*   The common expression Portia and Bassanio invert here is "Confess and be hanged."

Doth teach me answers for deliverance:
But let me to my fortune and the caskets.
PORTIA. Away, then, I am locked in one of them: 40
If you do love me, you will find me out.[1]
Nerissa and the rest, stand all aloof.[2]
Let music sound while he doth make his choice;
Then, if he lose, he makes a swan-like end,[3]
Fading[4] in music. That the comparison   45
May stand more proper,[5] my eye shall be the stream
And wat'ry death-bed for him.[6] He may win,
And what is music then? Then music is
Even as the flourish,[7] when true subjects bow
To a new crowned monarch. Such it is,   50
As are those dulcet sounds in break of day,
That creep into the dreaming bridegroom's ear
And summon him to marriage.[8] Now he goes
With no less presence,[9] but with much more love,
Than young Alcides, when he did redeem   55
The virgin tribute paid by howling Troy
To the sea monster. I stand for sacrifice.[10]
The rest, aloof, are the Dardanian° wives,   *Trojan*
With bleared° visages come forth to view   *tear-stained*
The issue of th'exploit.[11] Go, Hercules,   60

---

1 *find me out* Both find my picture within the casket and find where my true allegiance
   lies.
2 *aloof* Separated by some distance.
3 *a swan-like end* Swans were thought to sing at their own deaths.
4 *Fading* Lessening in strength, with a possible sexual implication of dwindling in size.
5 *stand more proper* Be fitting, with an added possible sexual innuendo attached to the
   verb "stand."
6 *my eye ... him* My tearful eyes will act as a watery grave for him if his attempt results
   in "death" or failure, but Portia's description of accommodating her lover within a wet
   environment continues the pattern of sexual innuendo. "Eye" could be slang for "vagina."
7 *flourish* Trumpet music that accentuates moments of ceremony for a monarch.
8 *dulcet sounds ... to marriage* Reference to the tradition of accompanying a bridegroom
   with music from his waking moment on the morning of his wedding all the way to the
   ceremony.
9 *presence* Noble comportment.
10 *young Alcides ... sea monster* As recounted in Ovid's *Metamorphosis* (Book 11), Hercules
   rescued the Trojan king Laomedon's daughter, Hesione, when she was sacrificed to a sea
   monster; *I stand for sacrifice* I will play the sacrificed virgin's role.
11 *issue of th'exploit* Conclusion of the undertaking.

Live thou,[1] I live. With much, much more dismay°   *fear*
I view the fight, than thou that mak'st the fray.

([*Musicians play*] *a song the whilst Bassanio comments on the caskets to himself.*)

[SINGER.[2]] *Tell me where is fancy[3] bred,*
  Or° in the heart, or in the head,   *Either*
65   *How begot, how nourished?[4]*
[ALL.] *Reply, reply.*
[SINGER.] *It is engendered in the eye,[5]*
  With gazing fed,[6] and fancy dies:
  In the cradle[7] where it lies
70   *Let us all ring fancy's knell.*
  I'll begin it.
  Ding, dong, bell.
[ALL.] *Ding, dong, bell.*

BASSANIO. So may the outward shows be least themselves,
75   The world is still deceived with ornament.
In law, what plea so tainted and corrupt,
But, being seasoned[8] with a gracious voice,
Obscures the show of evil? In religion
What damned error but some sober brow
80   Will bless it and approve it with a text,[9]
Hiding the grossness with fair ornament?
There is no vice so simple° but assumes   *undiluted*
Some mark of virtue on his outward parts.
How many cowards, whose hearts are all as false

---

1 *Live thou* If you live.
2 *SINGER* Though a specific singer is not identified, one of the players sings most of the song, with all of them joining in for the refrain.
3 *fancy* Love, but with a frivolous connotation—not serious or true love.
4 *nourished* This would be pronounced "nourishèd" to rhyme with "bred" and "head." Some critics have suggested that the triple rhyme with "lead" conveys a hint to the listener as to which casket to choose.
5 *engendered in the eye* Eyes were considered a site of entrance for and beginning of attraction.
6 *With gazing fed* I.e., satiated by looking.
7 *cradle* Referring either to the eyes or to the state of infancy.
8 *seasoned* Made more pleasant, as when one seasons food with spices.
9 *approve ... a text* Use a biblical reference to justify it.

As stairs of sand, wear yet upon their chins 85
The beards of Hercules and frowning Mars,[1]
Who, inward searched, have livers white as milk;[2]
And these assume but valour's excrement[3]
To render them redoubted.° Look on beauty, *feared*
And you shall see 'tis purchased by the weight,[4] 90
Which therein works a miracle in nature,
Making them lightest[5] that wear most of it:
So are those crisped° snaky golden locks, *curly*
Which maketh such wanton gambols with the wind
Upon supposed fairness, often known 95
To be the dowry of a second head,
The skull that bred them in the sepulchre.[6]
Thus, ornament is but the guiled° shore *perilous*
To a most dangerous sea; the beauteous scarf
Veiling an Indian beauty;[7] in a word, 100
The seeming truth, which cunning times put on
To entrap the wisest. Therefore, then, thou gaudy gold,
Hard food for Midas,[8] I will none of thee;
Nor none of thee, thou pale and common drudge
'Tween man and man. [9] But thou, thou meagre lead, 105
Which rather threaten'st than dost promise aught,
Thy paleness moves me more than eloquence,
And here choose I; joy be the consequence.
PORTIA. How all the other passions fleet to air,

---

1 *Mars* Roman god of war.
2 *inward searched* Probed by a surgeon; *livers white as milk* A liver (which was according to Elizabethan custom the seat of courage) containing pale or milk-colored blood belonged to a weak and cowardly person.
3 *valour's excrement* I.e., their beards, figured as a sign of bravery but also in this case a waste product sprouting from the face.
4 *purchased by the weight* Bought by the ounce in the form of cosmetics, which were sold this way.
5 *lightest* Most indecent.
6 *the dowry ... sepulchre* Wig made from the hair of someone who has died.
7 *Indian beauty* Someone with dark skin, considered unattractive in Elizabethan England.
8 *Hard food for Midas* Midas, the King of Phrygia, found he could no longer eat after Bacchus granted his wish that everything he touched would turn to gold.
9 *pale and ... and man* I.e., silver, portrayed as a lowly laborer because of its everyday purpose as currency.

110 As° doubtful thoughts, and rash embraced despair: *Such as*
And shuddering fear, and green-eyed jealousy.
O, love, be moderate, allay thy ecstasy,
In measure rain thy joy, scant this excess,
I feel too much thy blessing; make it less
115 For fear I surfeit.
BASSANIO. [*Unlocks the leaden casket.*] What find I here?
Fair Portia's counterfeit.° What demigod *portrait*
Hath come so near creation?[1] Move these eyes?
Or whether riding on the balls of mine
120 Seem they in motion? Here are severed lips
Parted with sugar breath, so sweet a bar
Should sunder such sweet friends.[2] Here, in her hairs,
The painter plays the spider and hath woven
A golden mesh t'entrap the hearts of men
125 Faster[3] than gnats in cobwebs. But her eyes!
How could he see to do them? Having made one,
Methinks it should have power to steal both his
And leave itself unfurnished.[4] Yet look how far
The substance[5] of my praise doth wrong this shadow° *likeness*
130 In underprizing it,[6] so far this shadow
Doth limp behind the substance. Here's the scroll,
The continent° and summary of my fortune. *container*
You that choose not by the view
Chance as fair and choose as true.
135 *Since this fortune falls to you,*
Be content and seek no new.
If you be well pleased with this
And hold your fortune for your bliss,
Turn you where your lady is,
140 *And claim her with a loving kiss.*

---

1 *What demigod ... creation* Bassanio suggests that the portrait's painter is like a creator
since the painting has been made to look so much like its inspiration,
2 *so sweet ... friends* Portia's breath separates her lips from one another the way a barrier
can come between friends.
3 *Faster* More steadfastly.
4 *unfurnished* Without a partner.
5 *The substance* I.e., Portia, the one portrayed in the portrait.
6 *underprizing it* Diminishing its value.

A gentle scroll. Fair lady, by your leave,
I come by note[1] to give and to receive.
Like one of two contending in a prize°   *contest*
That thinks he hath done well in people's eyes:
Hearing applause and universal shout,   145
Giddy in spirit, still gazing in a doubt
Whether those peals of praise be his or no,
So, thrice-fair lady, stand I even so,
As doubtful whether what I see be true,
Until confirmed, signed, ratified by you.   150
PORTIA. You see me, Lord Bassanio, where I stand,
Such as I am. Though for myself alone
I would not be ambitious in my wish
To wish myself much better, yet, for you,
I would be trebled twenty times myself,   155
A thousand times more fair, ten thousand times
More rich, that only to stand high in your account
I might in virtues, beauties, livings,[2] friends
Exceed account.[3] But the full sum of me
Is sum of something: which to term in gross,[4]   160
Is an unlessoned girl, unschooled, unpractised.
Happy in this, she is not yet so old
But she may learn; happier than this,
She is not bred so dull but she can learn.
Happiest of all is that her gentle spirit   165
Commits itself to yours to be directed,
As from her lord, her governor, her king.
Myself, and what is mine, to you and yours
Is now converted. But now[5] I was the lord
Of this fair mansion, master of my servants,   170
Queen o'er myself; and even now, but now
This house, these servants and this same myself,
Are yours, my lord's. I give them with this ring

---

1   *by note*   As directed by the written words on the scroll.
2   *livings*   Belongings or property.
3   *Exceed account*   Surpass calculation.
4   *term in gross*   Convey in a complete or general sense.
5   *But now*   Just a short time ago.

Which, when you part from, lose or give away,
175 Let it presage the ruin of your love,
And be my vantage to exclaim on[1] you.

[*She gives Bassanio a ring.*]

BASSANIO. Madam, you have bereft me of all words.
Only my blood[2] speaks to you in my veins,
And there is such confusion in my powers,°   *faculties*
180 As, after some oration fairly spoke
By a beloved prince, there doth appear
Among the buzzing pleased multitude.
Where every something,[3] being blent together,
Turns to a wild of nothing,[4] save of joy,
185 Expressed and not expressed. But when this ring
Parts from this finger, then parts life from hence;
O, then be bold to say, "Bassanio's dead."
NERISSA. My lord and lady, it is now our time,
That have stood by and seen our wishes prosper,
190 To cry "Good joy, good joy, my Lord and Lady!"
GRAZIANO. My lord Bassanio, and my gentle lady,
I wish you all the joy that you can wish,
For I am sure you can wish none from me:[5]
And when your honours mean to solemnize
195 The bargain of your faith: I do beseech you
Even at that time I may be married too.
BASSANIO. With all my heart, so[6] thou canst get a wife.
GRAZIANO. I thank your lordship; you have got me one.
My eyes, my lord, can look as swift as yours.
200 You saw the mistress; I beheld the maid.[7]

---

1   *vantage to exclaim on*   Opportunity to reprimand.
2   *blood*   Passion, but also Bassanio's aristocratic ancestry.
3   *every something*   Every component.
4   *wild of nothing*   Indecipherable clamor.
5   *I am ... from me*   I am sure you do not need any more wishes of happiness to add to your already abundant supply; or, I'm sure that wishing you happiness will not impede my own prospects for happiness.
6   *so*   So long as.
7   *maid*   I.e., Nerissa. "Maid" designates her status as an unmarried woman and as a lady-in-waiting, a position of high class rather than that of a common servant.

You loved, I loved, for intermission[1]
No more pertains to me, my lord, than you.
Your fortune stood upon the caskets there,
And so did mine too as the matter falls.[2]
For wooing here until I sweat again,[3]   205
And swearing till until my very roof[4] was dry
With oaths of love, at last, if promise last,
I got a promise of this fair one here
To have her love: provided that your fortune
Achieved her mistress.   210

PORTIA.   Is this true, Nerissa?
NERISSA. Madam, it is, so you stand pleased withal.[5]
BASSANIO. And do you, Graziano, mean good faith?[6]
GRAZIANO. Yes, faith,[7] my lord.
BASSANIO. Our feast shall be much honoured in your marriage.
GRAZIANO. We'll play° with them the first boy for a   *wager* 215
    thousand ducats.
NERISSA. What and stake down?[8]
GRAZIANO. No, we shall ne'er win at that sport and stake down.
    But who comes here? Lorenzo and his infidel!°   *non-Christian*
    What, and my old Venetian friend Salerio?

(*Enter Lorenzo, Jessica and Salerio, a messenger from Venice.*)

BASSANIO. Lorenzo and Salerio, welcome hither,   220
    If that the youth of my new interest here[9]
    Have power to bid you welcome. By your leave,
    I bid my very° friends and countrymen,   *true*
    Sweet Portia, welcome.
PORTIA. So do I, my lord. They are entirely welcome.   225

---

1 *intermission* Period of interruption.
2 *as the matter falls* So it transpires.
3 *sweat again* Sweated again and again.
4 *my very roof* Roof of my mouth.
5 *so you ... withal* As long as you are happy with this outcome.
6 *do you ... good faith* Do you plan to be true to your word?
7 *faith* Short version of the oath "in faith," or "in truth."
8 *stake down* Place money on this wager, though Graziano twists this into a joke about
   his inability to win this child-producing bet with his "stake" not erect.
9 *If that ... interest here* If my recent appointment as leader of this household.

LORENZO. I thank your honour. For my part, my lord,
My purpose was not to have seen you here,
But, meeting with Salerio by the way,
He did entreat me, past all saying nay,[1]
230   To come with him along.
SALERIO.   I did, my lord,
And I have reason for it. Signor Antonio
Commends him[2] to you.

[*He presents Bassanio with a letter.*]

BASSANIO.   Ere I ope his letter,
I pray you tell me how my good friend doth.
SALERIO. Not sick, my lord, unless it be in mind,[3]
235   Nor well, unless in mind.[4] His letter there
Will show you his estate.°   *condition*

([*Bassanio*] *opens the letter.*)

GRAZIANO. Nerissa, cheer yond stranger;[5] bid her welcome.
Your hand, Salerio, what's the news from Venice?
How doth that royal° merchant, good Antonio?   *magnificent*
240   I know he will be glad of our success:
We are the Jasons; we have won the fleece.
SALERIO. I would you had won the fleece that he hath lost.
PORTIA. There are some shrewd° contents in yond same   *wicked*
      paper
That steals the colour from Bassanio's cheek:
245   Some dear friend dead, else nothing in the world
Could turn so much the constitution
Of any constant° man. What, worse and worse?   *stable*
With leave, Bassanio I am half yourself,
And I must freely have the half of anything
250   That this same paper brings you.

---

1   *past all ... nay*   Exceeding all my protests.
2   *Commends him*   Sends his best wishes.
3   *unless ... in mind*   Unless his woeful situation has made him mentally sick with grief and worry.
4   *unless in mind*   Unless his mind is strong enough to survive this trial.
5   *stranger*   Person not considered a member of Venetian society.

BASSANIO.   O, sweet Portia,
   Here are a few of the unpleasant'st words
   That ever blotted paper. Gentle lady,
   When I did first impart my love to you,
   I freely told you all the wealth I had
   Ran in my veins, I was a gentleman   255
   And then I told you true. And yet, dear lady,
   Rating° myself at nothing, you shall see   *Assessing*
   How much I was a braggart. When I told you
   My state was nothing,[1] I should then have told you
   That I was worse than nothing; for, indeed,   260
   I have engaged[2] myself to a dear friend,
   Engaged my friend to his mere° enemy,   *utmost*
   To feed my means. Here is a letter, lady,
   The paper as the body[3] of my friend,
   And every word in it a gaping wound   265
   Issuing life blood. But is it true, Salerio?
   Hath all his ventures failed? What, not one hit,[4]
   From Tripolis, from Mexico and England,
   From Lisbon, Barbary and India,
   And not one vessel scape° the dreadful touch   *escape* 270
   Of merchant-marring[5] rocks?
SALERIO.   Not one, my lord.
   Besides, it should appear that if he had
   The present° money to discharge[6] the Jew   *accessible*
   He would not take it. Never did I know
   A creature that did bear the shape of man   275
   So keen° and greedy to confound° a man.   *ferocious / ruin*
   He plies the Duke at morning and at night,
   And doth impeach the freedom of the state[7]
   If they deny him justice. Twenty merchants,

---

1 *state was nothing* Estate was valueless.
2 *engaged* Bound by a pledge of friendship.
3 *The paper ... the body* I.e., the torn paper resembles Antonio's ruined body.
4 *hit* Favorable outcome.
5 *merchant-marring* Merchant ship–damaging.
6 *discharge* Straighten out his debt with.
7 *doth impeach ... the state* Challenges the state of Venice's protection of its citizens' freedom.

280   The Duke himself and the magnificoes
      Of greatest port¹ have all persuaded° with him,   *reasoned*
      But none can drive him from the envious° plea   *malicious*
      Of forfeiture, of justice and his bond.
      JESSICA. When I was with him, I have heard him swear
285   To Tubal and to Chus,² his countrymen
      That he would rather have Antonio's flesh
      Than twenty times the value of the sum
      That he did owe him; and I know, my lord,
      If law, authority and power deny not,³
290   It will go hard with poor Antonio.
      PORTIA. Is it your dear friend that is thus in trouble?
      BASSANIO. The dearest friend to me, the kindest man,
      The best conditioned⁴ and unwearied spirit
      In doing courtesies; and one in whom
295   The ancient Roman honour⁵ more appears
      Than any that draws breath in Italy.
      PORTIA. What sum owes he the Jew?
      BASSANIO. For me three thousand ducats.
      PORTIA. What, no more? Pay him six thousand and deface⁶ the bond.
300   Double six thousand, and then treble that,
      Before a friend of this description
      Shall lose a hair through Bassanio's fault.
      First go with me to church and call me wife,
      And then away to Venice to your friend,
305   For never shall you lie by Portia's side
      With an unquiet soul. You shall have gold
      To pay the petty debt twenty times over.
      When it is paid, bring your true friend along;
      My maid Nerissa and myself meantime

---

1 *port* High distinction.
2 *Tubal and to Chus* Tubal and Cush are the sons of Noah's sons, Ham and Japheth, as told in Genesis 10. "Cush" is spelled "Chus" in the Bishop's Bible, an English translation with which Shakespeare was familiar.
3 *If law ... deny not* If the authorities do not stop Shylock through legal means.
4 *best conditioned* With the best disposition.
5 *ancient Roman honour* Ideals of Roman honor were used as a model for noble behavior in Shakespeare's era.
6 *deface* Dissolve.

Will live as maids and widows. Come away,   310
For you shall hence upon your wedding day.
Bid your friends welcome, show a merry cheer;°   *demeanor*
Since you are dear bought, I will love you dear.[1]
But let me hear the letter of your friend.

BASSANIO. [*Reads.*] *Sweet Bassanio, my ships have all miscarried,*   315
my creditors grow cruel, my estate is very low, my bond to the Jew
is forfeit, and, since, in paying it, it is impossible I should live, all
debts are cleared between you and I if I might but see you at my
death. Notwithstanding, use your pleasure;[2] if your love do not
persuade you to come, let not my letter.   320

PORTIA. O, love! Dispatch all business and be gone.[3]

BASSANIO. Since I have your good leave to go away,
I will make haste. But, till I come again,
No bed shall e'er be guilty of my stay,
Nor rest be interposer[4] 'twixt us twain.   325

(*Exeunt.*)

ACT 3, SCENE 3

(*Enter [Shylock] the Jew, Solanio, Antonio, and the Gaoler.*)

JEW. Gaoler, look to him. Tell not me of mercy.
This is the fool that lent out money gratis.
Gaoler, look to him.

ANTONIO.   Hear me yet, good Shylock.

JEW. I'll have my bond. Speak not against my bond;
I have sworn an oath that I will have my bond.   5
Thou call'dst me dog before thou hadst a cause,
But, since I am a dog, beware my fangs,
The Duke shall grant me justice. I do wonder,
Thou naughty° gaoler, that thou art so fond   *wicked*
To come abroad with[5] him at his request.   10

---

1 *dear bought* Attained at great cost (to Antonio, and possibly also to Portia); *love you*
   dear Love you profoundly.
2 *use your pleasure* Do as you feel is fit.
3 *Dispatch all ... be gone* I.e., quickly make your preparations to leave.
4 *rest be interposer* Sleep or rest interrupt my mission.
5 *come abroad with* Chaperone outside the jail.

ANTONIO. I pray thee, hear me speak.
JEW. I'll have my bond. I will not hear thee speak.
   I'll have my bond, and therefore speak no more.
   I'll not be made a soft and dull-eyed[1] fool,
15 To shake the head, relent, and sigh and yield
   To Christian intercessors. Follow not,
   I'll have no speaking; I will have my bond.

   (*Exit.*)

SOLANIO. It is the most impenetrable cur[2]
   That ever kept° with men.   *consorted*
ANTONIO.   Let him alone.
20 I'll follow him no more with bootless° prayers.   *ineffectual*
   He seeks my life. His reason well I know:
   I oft delivered from his forfeitures°   *penalties*
   Many that have at times made moan to me;
   Therefore he hates me.
25 SOLANIO. I am sure the Duke will never grant
   This forfeiture to hold.
ANTONIO. The Duke cannot deny the course of law;
   For the commodity[3] that strangers have
   With us in Venice, if it be denied,
30 Will much impeach the justice of the state,
   Since that the trade and profit of the city
   Consisteth of all nations.[4] Therefore, go;
   These griefs and losses have so bated[5] me
   That I shall hardly spare a pound of flesh
35 Tomorrow to my bloody creditor.
   Well, gaoler, on, pray God Bassanio come
   To see me pay his debt, and then I care not.

   (*Exeunt.*)

---

1 *dull-eyed* Easily deluded.
2 *impenetrable cur* Dog who is invulnerable to the interference of human wisdom.
3 *commodity* Privileges of trade.
4 *Will much ... all nations* Will threaten the reputation of Venice as a city with a commitment to justice, which enables people from many places to participate in trade activities, trusting that their interests will be protected.
5 *bated* Weakened or shrunk.

ACT 3, Scene 4

(*Enter Portia, Nerissa, Lorenzo, Jessica and [Balthasar,] a man of Portia's.*)

LORENZO. Madam, although I speak it in your presence,
   You have a noble and a true conceit°   *understanding*
   Of godlike amity,[1] which appears most strongly
   In bearing thus the absence of your lord.
   But, if you knew to whom you show this honour,   5
   How true a gentleman you send relief,
   How dear a lover° of my lord, your husband,   *friend*
   I know you would be prouder of the work
   Than customary bounty can enforce you.[2]
PORTIA. I never did repent for doing good,   10
   Nor shall not now; for in companions
   That do converse and waste° the time together,   *spend*
   Whose souls do bear an equal yoke of love,[3]
   There must be needs° a like proportion   *consequently*
   Of lineaments,[4] of manners and of spirit;   15
   Which makes me think that this Antonio,
   Being the bosom lover[5] of my lord,
   Must needs be like my lord. If it be so,
   How little is the cost I have bestowed
   In purchasing the semblance of my soul;[6]   20
   From out the state of hellish cruelty.
   This comes too near the praising of myself;
   Therefore, no more of it. Hear other things:
   Lorenzo, I commit into your hands
   The husbandry and manage[7] of my house,   25
   Until my lord's return. For mine own part,
   I have toward heaven breathed a secret vow,

---

1 *godlike amity* Ideal love between friends.
2 *Than customary ... enforce you* Than habitual benevolence would oblige you to give.
3 *equal yoke of love* Reciprocal bond of love (like the yoke that bonds a team of oxen together).
4 *lineaments* Physical traits.
5 *bosom lover* Beloved friend.
6 *semblance of my soul* Likeness of my own soul (through his resemblance to Bassanio).
7 *husbandry and manage* Administration and keeping.

To live in prayer and contemplation,
Only attended by Nerissa here,
30   Until her husband and my lord's return.
There is a monastery two miles off,
And there we will abide. I do desire you
Not to deny this imposition,[1]
To which my love and some necessity
35   Now lays upon you.
LORENZO.   Madam, with all my heart,
I shall obey you in all fair commands.
PORTIA. My people[2] do already know my mind
And will acknowledge you and Jessica
In place of Lord Bassanio and myself.
40   So fare you well till we shall meet again.
LORENZO. Fair thoughts and happy hours attend on you.
JESSICA. I wish your ladyship all heart's content.
PORTIA. I thank you for your wish, and am well pleased
To wish it back on you. Fare you well, Jessica.

(*Exeunt* [*Jessica and Lorenzo*].)

45   Now, Balthasar, as I have ever found thee honest true,
So let me find thee still. Take this same letter,
And use thou all th'endeavour of a man,[3]
In speed to Padua.[4] See thou render this
Into my cousin's hand, Doctor Bellario;
50   And look what[5] notes and garments he doth give thee,
Bring them, I pray thee, with imagined speed[6]
Unto the traject,[7] to the common ferry,

---

1   *deny this imposition*   Decline this request.
2   *My people*   I.e., my household workers.
3   *th'endeavour of a man*   All the energy a man can exert.
4   *Padua*   The Quarto and Folio texts both give the location as Mantua, but this appears to be a compositor's or Shakespeare's own error. Bellario is later revealed to live in Padua, an Italian city that was home to a renowned law school (see 4.1.108, 118; 5.1.268). Most modern editions modify the text here.
5   *look what*   Also whatever.
6   *imagined speed*   All the speed that can be imagined.
7   *traject*   Ferry, from Italian: *traghetto*.

Which trades to[1] Venice. Waste no time in words
But get thee gone; I shall be there before thee.

BALTHASAR. Madam, I go, with all convenient° speed.   *suitable* 55

   [*Exit.*]

PORTIA. Come on, Nerissa; I have work in hand
That you yet know not of. We'll see our husbands,
Before they think of us.

NERISSA.   Shall they see us?

PORTIA. They shall, Nerissa, but in such a habit
That they shall think we are accomplished   60
With what we lack.[2] I'll hold thee any wager,
When we are both accoutred° like young men,   *dressed*
I'll prove the prettier[3] fellow of the two,
And wear my dagger with the braver[4] grace,
And speak between the change of man and boy   65
With a reed voice,[5] and turn two mincing° steps   *delicate*
Into a manly stride, and speak of frays[6]
Like a fine bragging youth, and tell quaint[7] lies
How honourable ladies sought my love,
Which I denying, they fell sick and died.   70
I could not do withal;[8] then I'll repent,
And wish, for all that, that I had not killed them.
And twenty of these puny lies I'll tell,
The men shall swear I have discontinued school
Above a twelvemonth.[9] I have within my mind   75
A thousand raw° tricks of these bragging jacks°   *juvenile / rascals*
Which I will practise.

---

1 *trades to* Travels to and from.
2 *accomplished ... we lack* Endowed with something that we do not have; a bawdy joke
   about the male disguises they will adopt.
3 *prettier* More adept.
4 *braver* More polished and showy.
5 *speak ... reed voice* Affect the squeaky voice of an adolescent male.
6 *frays* Brawls, but also seductions.
7 *quaint* Cleverly intricate, with a possible sexual innuendo (female genitalia).
8 *I could ... withal* I could do nothing about it.
9 *I have ... twelvemonth* I have been out of school for more than a year.

NERISSA.   Why, shall we turn to¹ men?
PORTIA. Fie, what a question's that,
 If thou wert near a lewd interpreter.
80 But come, I'll tell thee all my whole device°   *plan*
 When I am in my coach, which stays for us
 At the park gate; and therefore haste away,
 For we must measure° twenty miles today.   *journey*

 (*Exeunt.*)

ACT 3, SCENE 5

(*Enter [Lancelot the] Clown and Jessica.*)

CLOWN. Yes, truly, for, look you, the sins of the father are to be
 laid upon the children; therefore, I promise you, I fear you.² I
 was always plain with you, and so now I speak my agitation of
 the matter.³ Therefore be a good cheer, for, truly, I think you
5 are damned. There is but one hope in it that can do you any
 good, and that is but a kind of bastard hope neither.⁴
JESSICA. And what hope is that, I pray thee?
CLOWN. Marry, you may partly hope that your father got⁵ you
 not, that you are not the Jew's daughter.
10 JESSICA. That were a kind of bastard hope indeed, so the sins of
 my mother should be visited upon me.
 CLOWN. Truly, then, I fear you are damned both by father
 and mother: thus, when I shun Scylla your father, I fall into
 Charybdis⁶ your mother; well, you are gone both ways.

---

1 *turn to* Change into, but Portia suggests a more bawdy understanding of the term,
 playing on the sense of "turn" meaning to turn toward a sexual partner.
2 *fear you* Fear for you.
3 *agitation ... matter* Lancelot means "cogitation," or his thinking on the issue, though
 "agitation" is also fitting.
4 *bastard hope* Improbable or false hope, though as the conversation continues, the other
 meaning of "bastard" comes into play with the suggestion that Jessica's mother was
 unfaithful; *neither* Truly.
5 *got* Begot.
6 *Scylla ... Charybdis* In classical mythology, Scylla and Charybdis are a pair of sea
 monsters (or, in some versions, a rock and a whirlpool) located on opposite sides of
 a strait such that avoiding one forces one to pass dangerously close to the other. See
 Homer's *Odyssey*, Book 12, and Ovid's *Metamorphoses*, Book 13; *fall into* This phrase
 carries its literal meaning but also a suggestion of sexual penetration.

JESSICA. I shall be saved by my husband, he hath made me a   15
Christian!¹

CLOWN. Truly, the more to blame he; we were Christians enow
before, in as many as could well live one by another.² This
making of Christians will raise the price of hogs: if we grow all
to be pork eaters, we shall not shortly have a rasher on the coals   20
for money.³

(*Enter Lorenzo.*)

JESSICA. I'll tell my husband, Lancelot, what you say. Here he
comes.

LORENZO. I shall grow jealous of you shortly, Lancelot, if you
thus get my wife into corners.⁴   25

JESSICA. Nay, you need not fear us, Lorenzo, Lancelot and I are
out.⁵ He tells me flatly there's no mercy for me in heaven,
because I am a Jew's daughter; and he says you are no good
member of the commonwealth,⁶ for, in converting Jews to
Christians you raise the price of pork.   30

LORENZO. I shall answer that better to the commonwealth than
you can the getting up of the Negro's belly:⁷ the Moor is with
child by you, Lancelot.

CLOWN. It is much that the Moor should be more than reason;
but if she be less than an honest woman, she is indeed more   35
than I took her for.⁸

LORENZO. How every fool can play upon the word, I think the
best grace of wit will shortly turn into silence, and discourse

---

1 *saved by ... Christian* Lorenzo's Christian faith is strong enough to extend salvation to
his newly converted wife, reinforced in Corinthians 7.14: "For the unbelieving husband
is sanctified by the wife, and the unbelieving wife is sanctified by the husband."

2 *enow* Enough; *one by another* Beside each other, but also making a living off each
other.

3 *rasher* Piece of bacon; *for money* Available at any cost.

4 *into corners* Into private, secretive spaces.

5 *are out* Have fallen out (after a disagreement).

6 *the commonwealth* Society.

7 *getting up ... belly* Impregnating one of the household women who is of African descent,
a lineage for which both designations of "Negro" and "Moor" were used at the time.

8 *more than reason* Larger (and further along) than she ought to be; *but if ... her for* If
she were found to be less than completely trustworthy, that would make her still better
than what I presumed her to be.

grow commendable in none only but parrots.[1] Go in, sirrah;
40   bid them prepare for dinner!
CLOWN. That is done, sir: they have all stomachs.[2]
LORENZO. Goodly Lord, what a wit-snapper are you, then bid
   them prepare dinner.
CLOWN. That is done too, sir; only "cover" is the word.
45 LORENZO. Will you cover[3] then, sir?
CLOWN. Not so, sir, neither; I know my duty.
LORENZO. Yet more quarrelling with occasion,[4] wilt thou
   show the whole wealth of thy wit in an instant? I pray thee,
   understand a plain man in his plain meaning: go to thy fellows,
50   bid them cover the table, serve in the meat,[5] and we will come
   in to dinner.
CLOWN. For the table, sir, it shall be served in; for the meat, sir, it
   shall be covered; for your coming in to dinner, sir, why, let it be
   as humours and conceits[6] shall govern.

   (*Exit.*)

55 LORENZO. O, dear discretion,° how his words are   *discrimination*
   suited.[7]
   The fool hath planted in his memory
   An army of good words, and I do know
   A many fools that stand in better place,[8]
   Garnished[9] like him, that for a tricksy word
60   Defy the matter. How cheer'st thou,[10] Jessica?

---

1 *best grace* Most agreeable element;   *discourse ... parrots* Speech will be favored only
  in parrots, known for speaking nonsense.
2 *stomachs* Appetites.
3 *cover* Prepare the table with a tablecloth, though in the following line Lancelot suggests
  Lorenzo might mean "cover one's head," recalling the custom of taking off a hat in front
  of superiors.
4 *Yet more ... occasion* Still taking every chance to quibble on the meaning of words.
5 *meat* All the food being served.
6 *covered* Presented in covered dishes;   *humours and conceits* Impulses and whimsies.
7 *suited* Applicable to the situation.
8 *stand in better place* Have a higher social rank or post of employment.
9 *Garnished* Equipped (with clothing or with language).
10 *for a tricksy ... the matter* Muddle the meaning in the pursuit of elaborate word-
  ing;   *How cheer'st thou* How are you.

And now, good sweet, say thy opinion:
How dost thou like the Lord Bassanio's wife?
JESSICA. Past all expressing. It is very meet°   *fitting*
  The Lord Bassanio live an upright life,
  For, having such a blessing in his lady,   65
  He finds the joys of heaven here on earth,
  And, if on earth he do not merit it,[1]
  In reason he should never come to heaven.[2]
  Why, if two gods should play some heavenly match
  And on the wager lay[3] two earthly women,   70
  And Portia one: there must be something else
  Pawned° with the other, for the poor rude world   *Staked*
  Hath not her fellow.
LORENZO.   Even such a husband
  Hast thou of me, as she is for wife.
JESSICA. Nay, but ask my opinion too of that!   75
LORENZO. I will anon; first let us go to dinner.
JESSICA. Nay, let me praise you while I have a stomach.[4]
LORENZO. No, pray thee, let it serve for table talk,
  Then how so mere[5] thou speak'st, 'mong other things
  I shall digest[6] it.   80
JESSICA.   Well, I'll set you forth.[7]

    (*Exeunt.*)

---

1 *merit it* "Meane It" in the First Quarto. Most modern editions emend the phrase,
which probably results from a compositor's misreading of the handwriting.

2 *He finds ... to heaven* Because Bassanio has already received a heavenly reward on earth
in the form of Portia, he should take care to live a life of Christian humility, or he will
not also receive rewards after his death.

3 *lay* Stake, but also with a sexual connotation.

4 *stomach* Appetite or inclination.

5 *how so mere* Howsoever.

6 *digest* Swallow, but also think over or tolerate.

7 *set you forth* Declare my praises for you, and also present you as for a feast.

ACT 4, Scene 1

(*Enter the Duke,*[1] *the Magnificoes, Antonio, Bassanio, [Salerio]*
and Graziano [with a number of attendants and court officials].)

DUKE. What, is Antonio here?
ANTONIO. Ready,[2] so please your grace.
DUKE. I am sorry for thee. Thou art come to answer°   *face*
   A stony adversary, an inhumane wretch,
5 Uncapable of pity, void and empty
   From any dram[3] of mercy.
ANTONIO.   I have heard
   Your grace hath ta'en great pains to qualify°   *moderate*
   His rigorous course; but, since he stands obdurate,
   And that no lawful means can carry me
10 Out of his envy's° reach, I do oppose   *malice's*
   My patience to his fury, and am armed
   To suffer with a quietness of spirit,
   The very tyranny and rage of his.
DUKE. Go one and call the Jew into the court.
15 SALERIO. He is ready at the door; he comes, my lord.

   (*Enter Shylock.*)

DUKE. Make room, and let him stand before our face.
   Shylock, the world thinks, and I think so too,
   That thou but leadest this fashion[4] of thy malice
   To the last hour[5] of act, and then 'tis thought
20 Thou'lt show thy mercy and remorse° more   *pity*
    strange°   *remarkable*
   Than is thy strange° apparent° cruelty;   *abnormal / evident*
   And where thou now exacts the penalty,
   Which is a pound of this poor merchant's flesh,
   Thou wilt not only loose° the forfeiture,   *waive*

---

1 *Duke* Though it makes dramatic sense to have one authority figure officiating during the courtroom scene, Venetian legal proceedings at this time were no longer led by the Duke but were instead presided over by forty judges.
2 *Ready* I'm here.
3 *dram* Miniscule amount.
4 *thou but ... fashion* You are just performing this outward expression.
5 *To the last hour* Until the final moment.

But, touched with humane gentleness and love: 25
Forgive a moiety° of the principal,[1]   *portion*
Glancing an eye of pity on his losses
That have of late so huddled on his back,
Enough to press a royal merchant down,
And pluck commiseration of his state   30
From brassy[2] bosoms and rough hearts of flint,
From stubborn Turks, and Tartars,[3] never trained
To offices of tender courtesy.
We all expect a gentle answer, Jew.

JEW. I have possessed° your grace of what I purpose,   *notified* 35
And by our holy Sabbath have I sworn
To have the due and forfeit of my bond.
If you deny it, let the danger light[4]
Upon your charter and your city's freedom.[5]
You'll ask me why I rather choose to have   40
A weight of carrion flesh than to receive
Three thousand ducats. I'll not answer that:
But say it is my humour. Is it answered?
What if my house be troubled with a rat,
And I be pleased to give ten thousand ducats   45
To have it baned?° What, are you answered yet?   *poisoned*
Some men there are love not a gaping pig:[6]
Some that are mad if they behold a cat:
And others, when the bagpipe sings i'th' nose,[7]
Cannot contain their urine: for affection,   50
Mistress of passion, sways it to the mood
Of what it likes or loathes. Now, for your answer:

---

1 *principal* Initial amount borrowed.
2 *brassy* Hard and unyielding.
3 *Turks* The Turks had a reputation for ferocity among their Christian enemies;
  Tartars People from Central Asia who, under the leadership of Genghis Khan, invaded
  much of Eurasia.
4 *let the danger light* Let the threat descend.
5 *your charter ... freedom* Shylock revisits the threat to Venice's international reputation
  mentioned earlier, but this description also presents an English conception of a political
  order that derives freedom from a monarch's charter, rather than reflecting Venice's
  independent status.
6 *gaping pig* Roasted pig with its mouth open.
7 *i'th' nose* In the flat, droning voice of a bagpipe.

As there is no firm reason to be rendered
Why he cannot abide a gaping pig,
55   Why he a harmless necessary cat,
Why he a woollen bagpipe, but of force[1]
Must yield to such inevitable shame
As to offend himself being offended;
So can I give no reason, nor I will not,
60   More than a lodged° hate and a certain°   *deep-rooted / unfaltering*
      loathing
I bear Antonio, that I follow thus
A losing° suit against him! Are you answered?   *profitless*
BASSANIO. This is no answer, thou unfeeling man,
To excuse the current° of thy cruelty!   *momentum*
65   JEW. I am not bound to please thee with my answers!
BASSANIO. Do all men kill the things they do not love?
JEW. Hates any man the thing he would not kill?
BASSANIO. Every offence is not a hate at first!
JEW. What wouldst thou have a serpent sting thee twice?
70   ANTONIO. I pray you, think you question with the Jew.
You may as well go stand upon the beach
And bid the main flood bate his usual height;[2]
You may as well use question[3] with the wolf
Why he hath made the ewe bleat for the lamb;
75   You may as well forbid the mountain of pines
To wag[4] their high tops, and to make no noise
When they are fretten[5] with the gusts of heaven;
You may as well do anything most hard
As seek to soften that than which what's harder:
80   His Jewish heart. Therefore, I do beseech you,
Make no more offers, use no farther means,
But with all brief and plain conveniency[6]
Let me have judgment, and the Jew his will.

---

1   *woollen* Probably refers to the bagpipe's wrappings, which were normally made of wool
    fabric;   *of force* Forced into action by an irrational impulse.
2   *main flood ... height* High tide lessen its height.
3   *use question* Start a debate.
4   *wag* Wave or quiver.
5   *fretten* Fretted or agitated.
6   *brief ... conveniency* Quick decorum.

BASSANIO. For thy three thousand ducats here is six!
JEW. If every ducat in six thousand ducats   85
    Were in six parts, and every part a ducat,
    I would not draw¹ them; I would have my bond!
DUKE. How shalt thou hope for mercy, rendering none?²
JEW. What judgment shall I dread, doing no wrong?
    You have among you many a purchased slave,³   90
    Which, like your asses, and your dogs and mules,
    You use in abject° and in slavish parts,°   *miserable / duties*
    Because you bought them. Shall I say to you,
    Let them be free, marry them to your heirs.
    Why sweat they under burdens? Let their beds   95
    Be made as soft as yours, and let their palates
    Be seasoned with such viands,° you will answer: *foods*
    The slaves are ours, so do I answer you.
    The pound of flesh which I demand of him
    Is dearly bought; 'tis mine, and I will have it.   100
    If you deny me, fie upon your law:
    There is no force in the decrees of Venice.
    I stand for judgment: answer, shall I have it?
DUKE. Upon my power I may dismiss this court,
    Unless Bellario, a learned doctor,⁴   105
    Whom I have sent for to determine this,⁵
    Come here today.
SALERIO.   My lord, here stays without⁶
    A messenger with letters from the doctor,
    New come from Padua.
DUKE. Bring us the letters. Call the messenger.   110

    [*Exit Salerio.*]

---

1 *draw* Receive or take.
2 *How shalt ... none* Echo of the Christian philosophy emphasized in James 2.13: "For he shall have judgment without mercy, that hath showed no mercy."
3 *many a purchased slave* Slavery was practiced in Italian cities like Venice as well as in England and the rest of Europe at this time.
4 *doctor* Scholar who has studied the law.
5 *determine this* Evaluate and resolve this case.
6 *stays without* Is waiting outside.

BASSANIO. Good cheer, Antonio! What, man, courage yet:
The Jew shall have my flesh, blood, bones and all,
Ere thou shalt lose for me one drop of blood!
ANTONIO. I am a tainted wether[1] of the flock,
115 Meetest[2] for death; the weakest kind of fruit
Drops earliest to the ground, and so let me.
You cannot better be employed, Bassanio,
Than to live still and write mine epitaph.

(*Enter [Salerio and] Nerissa [in the disguise of a lawyer's clerk].*)

DUKE. Came you from Padua from Bellario?
120 NERISSA. From both, my lord. [*Presenting a letter to the Duke.*]
Bellario greets your grace.
BASSANIO. Why dost thou whet thy knife so earnestly?
JEW. To cut the forfeiture from that bankrupt there.
GRAZIANO. Not on thy sole, but on thy soul,[3] harsh Jew,
125 Thou mak'st thy knife keen.° But no metal can,   *sharp*
No, not the hangman's° axe, bear half the keenness   *executioner's*
Of thy sharp envy. Can no prayers pierce thee?
JEW. No, none that thou hast wit enough to make.
GRAZIANO. O, be thou damned, inexecrable[4] dog,
130 And for thy life let justice be accused;[5]
Thou almost mak'st me waver in my faith,
To hold opinion with Pythagoras[6]
That souls of animals infuse themselves
Into the trunks° of men. Thy currish[7] spirit   *bodies*
135 Governed a wolf, who hanged for human slaughter,[8]

---

1 *tainted wether* Sickly castrated ram.
2 *Meetest* Most appropriate.
3 *thy sole ... thy soul* While Shylock is using the sole of his shoe to whet his knife, Graziano makes a pun suggestive of the spiritual toll Shylock's actions will take.
4 *inexecrable* Impossible to curse or loathe too much. The word has also been interpreted as a misspelling of "inexorable."
5 *for thy ... accused* Let justice itself be condemned for the fact that you continue to live.
6 *Pythagoras* Greek philosopher who claimed that human souls could be reincarnated in animal bodies—and that animal souls could be reincarnated as human.
7 *currish* Resembling a mongrel dog, but also loathsome.
8 *wolf* Animal frequently used to represent usurers; *hanged for ... slaughter* In Shakespeare's time, predators such as wolves were sometimes tried and executed in the same way as human criminals.

Even from the gallows did his fell° soul fleet,[1]   *vicious*
And whilst thou layest in thy unhallowed dam;
Infused itself in thee; for thy desires
Are wolfish, bloody, starved and ravenous.

JEW. Till thou canst rail[2] the seal from off my bond,   140
Thou but offend'st thy lungs to speak so loud.
Repair thy wit, good youth, or it will fall[3]
To cureless ruin. I stand here for law.

DUKE. This letter from Bellario doth commend
A young and learned doctor to our court.   145
Where is he?

NERISSA.   He attendeth here hard by[4]
To know your answer whether you'll admit him.

DUKE. With all my heart. Some three or four of you
Go give him courteous conduct to this place.

  [*Exeunt several attendants.*]

Meantime the court shall hear Bellario's letter.   150
[*Reads.*] *Your grace shall understand that at the receipt of your*
letter I am very sick, but, in the instant that your messenger
came, in loving visitation[5] was with me a young doctor of
Rome: his name is Balthasar. I acquainted him with the cause
in controversy between the Jew and Antonio the merchant. We   155
turned o'er many books together; he is furnished with my opinion,
which, bettered with his own learning, the greatness whereof I
cannot enough commend, comes with him at my importunity[6] to
fill up your grace's request in my stead. I beseech you, let his lack
of years be no impediment to let him lack[7] a reverend estimation,   160
for I never knew so young a body with so old a head. I leave him
to your gracious acceptance, whose trial shall better publish his
commendation.[8]

---

1 *fleet* Flit (out of the body).
2 *rail* Scorn with derisive language.
3 *fall* Collapse as a house would.
4 *attendeth ... hard by* He is waiting nearby.
5 *in loving visitation* Enjoying a visit between friends.
6 *importunity* Persistent urging.
7 *let him lack* Keep him from receiving.
8 *whose trial ... commendation* Whose actions when put to the test will better demonstrate his skills than I could in words.

ACT 4, SCENE I

(*Enter Portia [disguised as] Balthasar [with several attendants].*)

DUKE. You hear the learned Bellario what he writes,
165   And here, I take it, is the doctor come.
Give me your hand, come you from old Bellario?
PORTIA. I did, my lord.
DUKE.   You are welcome: take your place.
Are you acquainted with the difference°   *disagreement*
That holds this present question in the Court?
170 PORTIA. I am informed throughly° of the cause.   *thoroughly*
Which is the merchant here, and which the Jew?
DUKE. Antonio and old Shylock, both stand forth.
PORTIA. Is your name Shylock?
JEW.   Shylock is my name.
PORTIA. Of a strange nature is the suit you follow,
175   Yet in such rule[1] that the Venetian law
Cannot impugn you[2] as you do proceed.
[*To Antonio.*] You stand within his danger,[3] do you not?
ANTONIO. Ay, so he says.
PORTIA.   Do you confess the bond?[4]
ANTONIO. I do.
PORTIA.   Then must the Jew be merciful.
180 SHYLOCK. On what compulsion must I?[5] Tell me that.
PORTIA. The quality of mercy is not strained:[6]
It droppeth as the gentle rain from heaven[7]
Upon the place beneath. It is twice blest:
It blesseth him that gives and him that takes.
185   'Tis mightiest in the mightiest; it becomes°   *benefits*

---

1 *in such rule* In accordance with the rules.
2 *impugn you* Deny or counter your case.
3 *stand ... danger* Are in the path of his power to destroy you.
4 *confess the bond* Uphold the legitimacy of the deal.
5 *Then must ... must I* Portia means that Shylock must be swayed by moral obligation,
    while Shylock interprets "must" to mean he is being legally coerced.
6 *mercy* Debates on opposing interests of justice and mercy were frequent in the
    Renaissance and hail back to Seneca; Shakespeare takes up the debate in many plays, but
    perhaps most explicitly here and in *Measure for Measure*; *not strained* Not imposed
    through force.
7 *It droppeth ... heaven* Echoes Ecclesiasticus 35.19: "Oh how fair a thing is mercy in time
    of anguish and trouble. It is like a cloud of rain that cometh in the time of a drought."

The thronèd monarch better than his crown.
His sceptre shows the force of temporal[1] power,
The attribute to awe and majesty,
Wherein doth sit the dread and fear of kings.
But mercy is above this sceptred sway;   190
It is enthroned in the hearts of kings,
It is an attribute to God himself,
And earthly power doth then show likest God's
When mercy seasons° justice. Therefore, Jew,   *moderates*
Though justice be thy plea, consider this: 195
That in the course of justice none of us
Should see salvation.[2] We do pray for mercy,
And that same prayer[3] doth teach us all to render
The deeds of mercy. I have spoke thus much
To mitigate the justice of thy plea,[4]   200
Which, if thou follow, this strict court of Venice
Must needs give sentence 'gainst the merchant there.
SHYLOCK. My deeds upon my head,[5] I crave the law,
    The penalty and forfeit of my bond.
PORTIA. Is he not able to discharge the money?   205
BASSANIO. Yes, here I tender it for him in the court,
    Yea, twice the sum. If that will not suffice,
    I will be bound to pay it ten times o'er,
    On forfeit of my hands, my head, my heart.
    If this will not suffice, it must appear   210
    That malice bears down[6] truth.° And I beseech you,   *wisdom*
    Wrest once the law to your authority;[7]
    To do a great right, do a little wrong
    And curb this cruel devil of his will.

---

1 *temporal* Secular or worldly.
2 *salvation* Deliverance, through God's mercy and Christ's sacrifice, to an everlasting life, a Christian concept meant to contrast with Shylock's adherence to the law.
3 *that same prayer* The Lord's Prayer (Matthew 6.9–13), a model of the Christian understanding of mercy.
4 *mitigate ... plea* Soften your call for strict adherence to the deal.
5 *My deeds ... head* I take responsibility for what I do.
6 *bears down* Overpowers.
7 *Wrest once ... authority* Just this once assert your authority over the law.

215 PORTIA. It must not be: there is no power in Venice
Can alter a decree established.
'Twill be recorded for a precedent,
And many an error by the same example
Will rush into the state.[1] It cannot be.
220 SHYLOCK. A Daniel[2] come to judgment; yea, a Daniel.
O, wise young judge, how do I honour thee.
PORTIA. I pray you, let me look upon the bond.
SHYLOCK. Here 'tis, most reverend doctor; here it is.
PORTIA. Shylock, there's thrice[3] thy money offered thee.
225 SHYLOCK. An oath, an oath, I have an oath in heaven!
Shall I lay perjury upon my soul?
No not for Venice.
PORTIA.   Why, this bond is forfeit,
And lawfully by this the Jew may claim
A pound of flesh, to be by him cut off
230 Nearest the merchant's heart. Be merciful:
Take thrice thy money; bid me tear the bond.
SHYLOCK. When it is paid according to the tenor.[4]
It doth appear you are a worthy judge,
You know the law; your exposition
235 Hath been most sound. I charge you by the law,
Whereof you are a well-deserving pillar,[5]
Proceed to judgment. By my soul I swear,
There is no power in the tongue of man
To alter me. I stay[6] here on my bond.
240 ANTONIO. Most heartily I do beseech the court
To give the judgment.

---

1   'Twill be ... the state   It will set a legal precedent for future cases, leading to political and
    legal problems for Venice in the future.
2   Daniel   Old Testament prophet and, in the story of Susannah and the elders in the
    Apocrypha, a wise young man who comes to Susannah's aid and outwits the elders who
    persecute her.
3   thrice   Bassanio just offered twice the sum, not thrice; editors have suggested that this
    could be Shakespeare's inconsistency, a misreading by the compositor, or Portia herself
    choosing to increase the offer.
4   tenor   Conditions set out in the bond.
5   well-deserving pillar   I.e., strong supporter.
6   stay   Remain firmly insistent.

PORTIA.   Why then, thus it is:
  You must prepare your bosom for his knife.
SHYLOCK. O noble judge! O excellent young man!
PORTIA. For the intent and purpose of the law
  Hath full relation to[1] the penalty,   245
  Which here appeareth due upon° the bond.   *because of*
JEW. 'Tis very true. O wise and upright judge,
  How much more elder art thou than thy looks!
PORTIA. Therefore lay bare your bosom.
JEW.   Ay, his breast.
  So says the bond, doth it not, noble judge?   250
  Nearest his heart, those are the very words.
PORTIA. It is so. Are there balance[2] here to weigh the flesh?
JEW. I have them ready.
PORTIA. Have by some surgeon, Shylock, on your charge,[3]
  To stop his wounds, lest he do bleed to death.   255
JEW. Is it so nominated° in the bond?   *specified*
PORTIA. It is not so expressed, but what of that?
  'Twere good you do so much for charity.
JEW. I cannot find it; 'tis not in the bond.
PORTIA. You, merchant, have you anything to say?   260
ANTONIO. But little. I am armed[4] and well prepared.
  Give me your hand, Bassanio. Fare you well,
  Grieve not that I am fall'n to this for you:
  For herein Fortune shows herself more kind
  Than is her custom. It is still° her use°   *usually / habit* 265
  To let the wretched man outlive his wealth,
  To view with hollow eye and wrinkled brow,
  An age of poverty, from which lingering penance
  Of such misery doth she cut me off.
  Commend me to your honourable wife;   270
  Tell her the process of[5] Antonio's end,

---

1 *Hath full relation to* Fully supports.
2 *balance* Scales for measuring the pound of flesh, but also perhaps serving a further symbolic purpose, as the figure of Justice was pictured carrying a set of scales.
3 *Have by* Have waiting nearby; *on your charge* At your expense.
4 *armed* Mentally and spiritually braced.
5 *process of* Both account of and legal proceedings that resulted in.

Say how I loved you, speak me fair[1] in death,
And, when the tale is told, bid her be judge
Whether Bassanio had not once a love.[2]
275 Repent but you[3] that you shall lose your friend,
And he repents not that he pays your debt.
For if the Jew do cut but deep enough
I'll pay it instantly with all my heart.
BASSANIO. Antonio, I am married to a wife
280 Which is as dear to me as life itself;
But life itself, my wife and all the world
Are not with me esteemed above thy life.
I would lose all, ay, sacrifice them all
Here to this devil, to deliver you.
285 PORTIA. Your wife would give you little thanks for that
If she were by to hear you make the offer.
GRAZIANO. I have a wife who I protest I love.
I would she were in heaven, so she could
Entreat some power to change this currish Jew.
290 NERISSA. 'Tis well you offer it behind her back,
The wish would make else an unquiet house.
JEW. These be the Christian husbands, I have a daughter:
Would any of the stock of Barabas[4]
Had been her husband rather than a Christian.
295 We trifle° time; I pray thee, pursue[5] sentence.   *waste*
PORTIA. A pound of that same merchant's flesh is thine;
The court awards it, and the law doth give it.
JEW. Most rightful judge.
PORTIA. And you must cut this flesh from off his breast;
300 The law allows it, and the court awards it.
JEW. Most learned judge! A sentence! Come, prepare.

---

1 *speak me fair* Speak well of me.
2 *love* True friend.
3 *Repent but you* Regret you only.
4 *stock of Barabas* Descendants of Barabas, the criminal who was chosen over Jesus to be
   spared crucifixion (Luke 23.18). Barabas is also the name of the conniving, murdering
   Jewish protagonist in Christopher Marlowe's *The Jew of Malta* (c. 1590).
5 *pursue* Continue with.

PORTIA. Tarry a little, there is something else.
This bond doth give thee here no jot[1] of blood:
The words expressly are a pound of flesh:
Take then thy bond: take thou thy pound of flesh.   305
But in the cutting it, if thou dost shed
One drop of Christian blood, thy lands and goods
Are by the laws of Venice confiscate
Unto the state of Venice.
GRAZIANO.   O upright judge,
Mark, Jew, O learned judge.   310
SHYLOCK. Is that the law?
PORTIA.   Thyself shalt see the act,[2]
For, as thou urgest justice, be assured
Thou shalt have justice more than thou desir'st.
GRAZIANO. O learned judge! Mark, Jew: a learned judge.
JEW. I take his offer, then; pay the bond thrice   315
And let the Christian go.
BASSANIO.   Here is the money.
PORTIA. Soft, the Jew shall have all justice.[3] Soft, no haste,
He shall have nothing but the penalty.
GRAZIANO. O, Jew, an upright judge, a learned judge!
PORTIA. Therefore, prepare thee to cut off the flesh.   320
Shed thou no blood, nor cut thou less nor more
But just a pound of flesh. If thou tak'st more
Or less than a just pound, be it but so much
As makes it light or heavy in the substance[4]
Or the division of the twentieth part   325
Of one poor scruple:[5] nay, if the scale do turn
But in the estimation of a hair,[6]
Thou diest, and all thy goods are confiscate.
GRAZIANO. A second Daniel, a Daniel, Jew!
Now, infidel, I have you on the hip.   330

---

1 *no jot* No miniscule amount.
2 *shalt see the act* Will see the law put into practice.
3 *all justice* All the justice dictated by the law, and nothing else.
4 *substance* Gross weight.
5 *scruple* Apothecary's measure made up of twenty grains; hence a twentieth is one grain, a very small amount.
6 *if the ... a hair* If the scale measures a weight that is off by as much as a hair.

PORTIA. Why doth the Jew pause? Take thy forfeiture.

JEW. Give me my principal, and let me go.

BASSANIO. I have it ready for thee; here it is.

PORTIA. He hath refused it in the open court;

335   He shall have merely[1] justice and his bond.

GRAZIANO. A Daniel still, say I, a second Daniel!

  I thank thee, Jew, for teaching me that word.

SHYLOCK. Shall I not have barely my principal?

PORTIA. Thou shalt have nothing but the forfeiture,

340   To be so taken at thy peril, Jew.

SHYLOCK. Why then, the devil give him good of it!

  I'll stay no longer question.[2]

PORTIA.   Tarry, Jew,

  The law hath yet another hold on you.

  It is enacted in the laws of Venice,

345   If it be proved against an alien

  That by direct, or indirect, attempts

  He seek the life of any citizen,

  The party 'gainst the which he doth contrive°   *plot*

  Shall seize one-half his goods. The other half

350   Comes to the privy coffer of the state,[3]

  And the offender's life lies in the mercy

  Of the Duke only, 'gainst all other voice.[4]

  In which predicament I say thou stand'st,

  For it appears by manifest proceeding

355   That indirectly, and directly too,

  Thou hast contrived against the very life

  Of the defendant, and thou hast incurred

  The danger formerly by me rehearsed.[5]

  Down, therefore, and beg mercy of the Duke.

360 GRAZIANO. Beg that thou mayst have leave to hang thyself,

  And yet, thy wealth being forfeit to the state,

---

1   *merely*   Fully and exclusively.

2   *I'll stay ... question*   I'll persist in my suit no further.

3   *privy ... state*   Private treasury of the state, to which fines would be paid in Shakespeare's England.

4   *'gainst ... voice*   With no chance of appeal.

5   *danger ... me rehearsed*   Legal penalties I have explained to you.

Thou hast not left the value of a cord;
Therefore thou must be hanged at the state's charge.°   *expense*
DUKE. That thou shalt see the difference of our[1] spirit,
I pardon thee thy life before thou ask it.   365
For half thy wealth, it is Antonio's;
The other half comes to the general state,
Which humbleness may drive unto a fine.[2]
PORTIA. Ay, for the state, not for Antonio.[3]
SHYLOCK. Nay, take my life and all, pardon not that.   370
You take my house when you do take the prop
That doth sustain my house. You take my life
When you do take the means whereby I live.
PORTIA. What mercy can you render him, Antonio?
GRAZIANO. A halter[4] gratis, nothing else, for God's sake!   375
ANTONIO. So please my lord the Duke, and all the Court
To quit the fine for one-half of his goods,[5]
I am content, so he will let me have
The other half in use,[6] to render it
Upon his death unto the gentleman   380
That lately stole his daughter.
Two things provided more: that for this favour
He presently become a Christian;[7]
The other, that he do record a gift
Here in the court of all he dies possessed[8]   385
Unto his son Lorenzo and his daughter.

---

1   *our*   I.e., the Duke and the Christian leaders of Venice.
2   *Which humbleness ... a fine*   If you behave with humility I may be convinced to give you a fine rather than making you forfeit half of your goods.
3   *Ay ... Antonio*   Yes, consider a fine for the half of Shylock's goods that are to be remitted to the state rather than Antonio's half.
4   *halter*   Noose for hanging.
5   *quit the ... his goods*   Set aside the fee that would take half of Shylock's assets.
6   *in use*   In trust, possibly with the suggestion that Antonio will use the funds until Shylock's death.
7   *become a Christian*   Jews in Italy were usually made to give up their assets upon conversion to Christianity as a penalty for the offences they were supposed to have committed through the practice of usury.
8   *record ... possessed*   Make a document that bestows upon his death the remainder of his wealth.

DUKE. He shall do this, or else I do recant
　The pardon that I late pronounced here.
PORTIA. Art thou contented, Jew? What dost thou say?
390 SHYLOCK. I am content.
PORTIA.　　　　　　　Clerk, draw a deed of gift.
SHYLOCK. I pray you, give me leave to go from hence.
　I am not well. Send the deed after me
　And I will sign it.
DUKE.　　　　　Get thee gone, but do it.
GRAZIANO. In christening shalt thou have two godfathers.[1]
395　Had I been judge, thou shouldst have had ten more,[2]
　To bring thee to the gallows, not to the font.[3]

　(*Exit [Shylock].*)

DUKE. Sir, I entreat you home[4] with me to dinner.
PORTIA. I humbly do desire, your grace, of pardon;
　I must away this night toward Padua,
400　And it is meet I presently set forth.[5]
DUKE. I am sorry that your leisure serves you not.
　Antonio, gratify° this gentleman,　　　　　　　　　　*reward*
　For in my mind you are much bound to him.

　(*Exeunt Duke and his train.*)

BASSANIO. Most worthy gentleman, I and my friend
405　Have, by your wisdom, been this day acquitted
　Of grievous penalties, in lieu whereof[6]
　Three thousand ducats due unto the Jew
　We freely cope your courteous pains withal.[7]
ANTONIO. And stand indebted, over and above,
410　In love and service to you evermore.

1　*two godfathers*　I.e., Antonio and the Duke.
2　*ten more*　To complete a set of twelve jurors, who were commonly called "godfathers in law."
3　*font*　Vessel used to hold water for baptism.
4　*entreat you home*　Urge you to accept an invitation to my home.
5　*meet I ... set forth*　Fitting that I leave right away.
6　*in lieu whereof*　In return for which.
7　*cope your ... withal*　Repay or remunerate you.

PORTIA. He is well paid that is well satisfied,
 And I, delivering° you, am satisfied,   *saving*
 And therein do account myself well paid;
 My mind was never yet more mercenary.[1]
 I pray you, know me[2] when we meet again.   415
 I wish you well, and so I take my leave.
BASSANIO. Dear sir, of force[3] I must attempt° you further.   *implore*
 Take some remembrance of us as a tribute,
 Not as fee. Grant me two things, I pray you:
 Not to deny me, and to pardon me.[4]   420
PORTIA. You press me far,[5] and therefore I will yield.
 Give me your gloves; I'll wear them for your sake,
 And, for your love,[6] I'll take this ring from you.
 Do not draw back your hand; I'll take no more,
 And you, in love, shall not deny me this.   425
BASSANIO. This ring good sir? Alas, it is a trifle,
 I will not shame myself to give you this!
PORTIA. I will have nothing else but only this,
 And now, methinks, I have a mind to it.
BASSANIO. There's more depends on this than on the value.[7]   430
 The dearest ring in Venice will I give you,
 And find it out by proclamation;[8]
 Only for this, I pray you, pardon me.
PORTIA. I see, sir, you are liberal in offers.
 You taught me first to beg, and now, methinks,   435
 You teach me how a beggar should be answered.
BASSANIO. Good sir, this ring was given me by my wife,
 And when she put it on she made me vow
 That I should neither sell, nor give, nor lose it.

---

1 *was never … mercenary* Has never been very concerned with making money.
2 *know me* Recognize me but also with the added carnal sense of the word, both ironic jokes as Portia talks to her husband while in disguise.
3 *of force* By necessity.
4 *pardon me* Forgive me (for this persistence).
5 *press me far* Push your appeal very strongly, but with a further sexual meaning of pressing down a sexual partner.
6 *for your love* For the sake of friendship and gratitude.
7 *There's more … the value* There is more hinging on this ring than its material value.
8 *by proclamation* By popular approval.

440 PORTIA. That scuse serves[1] many men to save their gifts!
    An if your wife be not a mad woman,
    And know how well I have deserved this ring,
    She would not hold out enemy[2] for ever
    For giving it to me. Well, peace be with you.

    (*Exeunt [Portia and Nerissa].*)

445 ANTONIO. My lord Bassanio, let him have the ring.
    Let his deservings and my love withal
    Be valued 'gainst your wife's commandement.
    BASSANIO. Go, Graziano, run and overtake him;
    Give him the ring, and bring him, if thou canst,
450 Unto Antonio's house. Away, make haste.

    (*Exit Graziano.*)

    Come, you and I will thither presently,
    And in the morning early will we both
    Fly° toward Belmont. Come, Antonio.   *Hurry*

    (*Exeunt.*)

ACT 4, SCENE 2

    (*Enter [Portia and] Nerissa [both still disguised].*)

PORTIA. Enquire the Jew's house out, give him this deed,[3]
    And let him sign it. We'll away tonight,
    And be a day before our husbands home.
    This deed will be well welcome to Lorenzo!

    (*Enter Graziano.*)

5 GRAZIANO. Fair sir, you are well o'erta'en.[4]
    My lord Bassanio, upon more advice,[5]

---

1 *scuse serves* Excuse allows.
2 *hold out enemy* Carry on an animosity with you.
3 *deed* Deed of gift.
4 *you are ... o'erta'en* I am pleased that I have caught up with you.
5 *upon more advice* After further consideration.

Hath sent you here this ring and doth entreat
Your company at dinner.
PORTIA.   That cannot be.
His ring I do accept most thankfully,
And so, I pray you, tell him. Furthermore,   10
I pray you, show my youth old Shylock's house.
GRAZIANO. That will I do.
NERISSA.   Sir, I would speak with you.
[*To Portia.*] I'll see if I can get my husband's ring,
Which I did make him swear to keep for ever.
PORTIA. [*To Nerissa.*] Thou mayst, I warrant. We shall have old[1]   15
    swearing,
That they did give the rings away to men,
But we'll outface[2] them and outswear them too.
Away, make haste, thou knowst where I will tarry.
NERISSA. Come, good sir, will you show me to this house?

(*Exeunt.*)

ACT 5, SCENE 1

(*Enter Lorenzo and Jessica.*)

LORENZO. The moon shines bright. In such a night as this,
When the sweet wind did gently kiss the trees,
And they did make no noise, in such a night
Troilus, methinks, mounted the Trojan walls
And sighed his soul toward the Grecian tents,   5
Where Cressid lay that night.[3]
JESSICA.   In such a night
Did Thisbe fearfully o'ertrip the dew,

---

1   *old* Profuse.
2   *outface* Audaciously challenge.
3   *Troilus ... that night* In Chaucer's *Troilus and Crisyede*, Trojan prince Troilus imagines
    his lover Cressida pining for him by moonlight in the nearby Greek encampment. In
    these and the following lines, Lorenzo and Jessica reference lovers who mainly appear
    in classical texts by Ovid and Virgil, though medieval influences—and especially the
    influence of Chaucer—are also evident in their conversation.

And saw the lion's shadow ere himself,
And ran dismayed° away.[1]   *frightened*

LORENZO.   In such a night
10   Stood Dido with a willow[2] in her hand
Upon the wild sea banks and waft° her love   *beckoned*
To come again to Carthage.

JESSICA.   In such a night
Medea[3] gathered the enchanted herbs
That did renew old Aeson.

LORENZO.   In such a night
15   Did Jessica steal from[4] the wealthy Jew,
And with an unthrift° love did run from Venice   *prodigal*
As far as Belmont.

JESSICA.   In such a night
Did young Lorenzo swear he loved her well,
Stealing her soul with many vows of faith,
20   And ne'er a true one.

LORENZO.   In such a night
Did pretty Jessica, like a little shrew,
Slander her love, and he forgave it her.

JESSICA. I would out-night[5] you did nobody come;
But, hark, I hear the footing° of a man.   *footsteps*

     (*Enter a Messenger.*)

25 LORENZO. Who comes so fast in silence of the night?
MESSENGER. A friend.
LORENZO. A friend, what friend? Your name, I pray you, friend?
MESSENGER. Stefano is my name, and I bring word
My mistress will, before the break of day,

---

1   *Thisbe ... dismayed away* Thisbe was prevented from meeting her lover Pyramus when a lion startled her and caused her to drop her cloak as she fled, resulting in a tragic misunderstanding when Pyramus came upon it. This tale is dramatized by the mechanicals in *A Midsummer Night's Dream*;   *saw the ... himself* Saw the shadow of the lion before she saw the creature itself.

2   *Dido* Queen of Carthage who loved and was forsaken by Aeneas;   *willow* Common symbol of forsaken love.

3   *Medea* Beloved of Jason, Medea was a sorceress who made a concoction of herbs to heal and regenerate Jason's father Aeson.

4   *steal from* Flee from and also take from.

5   *out-night* Outdo you in the game we've made of referencing nights.

Be here at Belmont. She doth stray about   30
By holy crosses,[1] where she kneels and prays
For happy wedlock hours.
LORENZO.   Who comes with her?
MESSENGER. None but a holy hermit[2] and her maid.
I pray you, is my master yet returned?
LORENZO. He is not, nor we have not heard from him.   35
But go we in, I pray thee, Jessica,
And ceremoniously[3] let us prepare
Some welcome for the mistress of the house.

   (*Enter* [*Lancelot the*] *Clown.*)

CLOWN. Sola, sola![4] Wo ha, ho![5] sola, sola!
LORENZO. Who calls?   40
CLOWN. Sola! Did you see Master Lorenzo and Master Lorenzo?[6]
   Sola, sola!
LORENZO. Leave hollowing,° man! Here.   *hollering*
CLOWN. Sola! Where, where?
LORENZO. Here!   45
CLOWN. Tell him there's a post come from my master, with his
   horn[7] full of good news. My master will be here ere morning.

   [*Exit.*]

LORENZO. Sweet soul, let's in, and there expect° their   *await*
   coming.
And yet, no matter. Why should we go in?
My friend Stefano, signify, I pray you,   50

---

1   *holy crosses* Shrines found along the roadside.
2   *holy hermit* Solitary religious devotee, presumably a fabricated detail of Portia's fictional account of her whereabouts while she has been in Venice.
3   *ceremoniously* I.e., for a ceremonious welcome.
4   *Sola, sola* Sounds to mimic a post horn, used to announce a courier.
5   *Wo ha, ho* Call used by a falconer.
6   *Master Lorenzo and Master Lorenzo* The Quarto has an ampersand ("&") here, which may very well have been intended to be a question mark ("?"). This would make this line more sensible. It has also been suggested that the second Lorenzo was intended to be "Mistress Lorenza," but the strength of this conjecture is compromised by the reference to "him" alone in the dialogue that follows.
7   *post* Courier; *horn* Courier's post horn but also a cornucopia, or horn of plenty.

Within the house, your mistress is at hand,
And bring your music° forth into the air.¹   *musicians*

[*Exit Messenger.*]

How sweet the moonlight sleeps upon this bank,
Here will we sit, and let the sounds of music
55   Creep in our ears. Soft stillness and the night
Become° the touches of sweet harmony.²   *Befit*
Sit, Jessica. Look how the floor of heaven³
Is thick inlaid with patens⁴ of bright gold.
There's not the smallest orb which thou behold'st
60   But in his motion like an angel sings,⁵
Still quiring to the young-eyed cherubins.⁶
Such harmony⁷ is in immortal souls,
But, whilst this muddy vesture of decay⁸
Doth grossly⁹ close it in, we cannot hear it.

[*Enter Musicians.*]

65   Come, ho, and wake Diana¹⁰ with a hymn,
With sweetest touches pierce your mistress' ear,
And draw her home with music. ([*The musicians*] *play music.*)
JESSICA. I am never merry° when I hear sweet music.   *lighthearted*

---

1   *into the air*   Outdoors.
2   *touches of sweet harmony*   Strains of musical harmony made by touching an instrument.
3   *floor of heaven*   Sky, as well as the canopy surmounting the Elizabethan stage, which would be decorated to resemble a night sky.
4   *patens*   Delicate circular dishes used to hold the Eucharist. They were frequently made of gold.
5   *There's not ... angel sings*   The planets and stars were thought to occupy fixed positions on a series of "celestial spheres" that surrounded the earth; the movement of these spheres was said to produce a music that living human beings were unable to hear.
6   *quiring*   Singing together as in a choir;   *young-eyed cherubins*   Cherubim were often depicted as young and as having many eyes. Angels were able to hear the music of the celestial spheres.
7   *harmony*   Both serenity and ability to understand musical harmony.
8   *muddy ... decay*   Mortal human vessel.
9   *grossly*   In relation to the physical rather than spiritual.
10   *wake Diana*   Awaken Diana, the moon goddess, suggesting the moon has been obscured by a cloud.

LORENZO. The reason is your spirits are attentive.[1]
  For do but note a wild and wanton herd,   70
  Or race,° of youthful and unhandled colts   *group*
  Fetching mad bounds,[2] bellowing and neighing loud,
  Which is the hot condition of their blood;
  If they but hear, perchance, a trumpet sound,
  Or any air of music touch their ears,   75
  You shall perceive them make a mutual stand,[3]
  Their savage eyes turned to a modest gaze
  By the sweet power of music. Therefore the poet
  Did feign that Orpheus drew trees, stones and floods.[4]
  Since naught so stockish° hard and full of rage   *unfeeling* 80
  But music for the time doth change his nature.
  The man that hath no music in himself,
  Nor is not moved with concord of sweet sounds,
  Is fit for treasons, stratagems and spoils;[5]
  The motions of his spirit are dull as night   85
  And his affections dark as Erebus.[6]
  Let no such man be trusted. Mark the music.

    (*Enter Portia and Nerissa [as themselves].*)

PORTIA. That light we see is burning in my hall.
  How far that little candle throws his beams!
  So shines a good deed in a naughty world.   90
NERISSA. When the moon shone we did not see the candle.
PORTIA. So doth the greater glory dim the less.
  A substitute shines brightly as a king
  Until a king be by, and then his state[7]

---

1 *your ... attentive*   Your mental faculties are concerned with reflection and stillness rather than action.

2 *Fetching mad bounds*   Executing huge jumps.

3 *make a mutual stand*   Stand still all at once.

4 *the poet ... and floods*   Orpheus, a famed musician in ancient Greek legend, was able to enchant non-human entities with his music;   *the poet*   Likely Ovid, who depicted Orpheus's story in *Metamorphoses*;   *feign*   Describe through narrative.

5 *stratagems*   Plots or deceptions conceived in order to take ground from an opponent;   *spoils*   Loot gained from raiding an enemy.

6 *Erebus*   Area of darkness found between Hades and Earth.

7 *state*   Regal bearing, as well as the actual chair of state.

95　　Empties itself, as doth an inland brook
　　　Into the main of waters.[1] Music, hark!
NERISSA.　It is your music, madam, of the house.
PORTIA.　Nothing is good, I see, without respect.[2]
　　　Methinks it sounds much sweeter than by day.
100　NERISSA.　Silence bestows that virtue° on it, madam.　　　*ability*
PORTIA.　The crow doth sing as sweetly as the lark
　　　When neither is attended; and, I think,
　　　The nightingale,[3] if she should sing by day
　　　When every goose is cackling, would be thought
105　　No better a musician than the wren.[4]
　　　How many things by season seasoned[5] are
　　　To their right praise and true perfection.
　　　Peace! How the moon sleeps with Endymion[6]
　　　And would not be awaked.

　　　　　[*Music ceases.*]

LORENZO.　　　　　　　　　That is the voice,
110　Or I am much deceived, of Portia.
PORTIA.　He knows me as the blind man knows the cuckoo:
　　　By the bad voice.
LORENZO.　　　　　　Dear lady, welcome home.
PORTIA.　We have been praying for our husbands' welfare,
　　　Which speed,° we hope, the better for our words.　　　*progress*
115　Are they returned?
LORENZO.　　　　　　Madam, they are not yet,
　　　But there is come a messenger before
　　　To signify their coming.
PORTIA.　　　　　　　Go in, Nerissa.

1　*main of waters*　Ocean.
2　*Nothing is ... respect*　Nothing can be appreciated without a context in which it can be compared.
3　*attended*　Observed or awaited; *nightingale*　Night-time singer, as opposed to the lark, whose song was thought to announce the dawn.
4　*wren*　Very small bird whose voice was considered hollow.
5　*by season seasoned*　Made what they are by their context.
6　*Peace!*　Direction to musicians to stop; *moon sleeps ... Endymion*　Diana's beloved, the shepherd Endymion, was enchanted by the goddess into an eternal sleep on Mount Latmos.

Give order to my servants, that they take
No note at all of our being absent hence,
Nor you, Lorenzo; Jessica, nor you.   120

   [*A tucket*[1] *sounds.*]

LORENZO. Your husband is at hand, I hear his trumpet.[2]
We are no tell-tales, madam, fear you not.
PORTIA. This night, methinks, is but the daylight sick;
It looks a little paler. 'Tis a day
Such as the day is when the sun is hid.   125

   (*Enter Bassanio, Antonio, Graziano and their Followers.*)

BASSANIO. We should hold day with the Antipodes,
If you would walk in absence of the sun.[3]
PORTIA. Let me give light, but let me not be light;°   *licentious*
For a light wife doth make a heavy° husband,   *unhappy*
And never be Bassanio so for me.   130
But God sort all.[4] You are welcome home, my lord.
BASSANIO. I thank you, madam. Give welcome to my friend.
This is the man, this is Antonio,
To whom I am so infinitely bound.
PORTIA. You should in all sense be much bound to him,   135
For, as I hear, he was much bound for you.[5]
ANTONIO. No more than I am well acquitted° of.   *absolved*
PORTIA. Sir, you are very welcome to our house.
It must appear in other ways than words:
Therefore I scant this breathing courtesy.[6]   140
GRAZIANO. [*To Nerissa.*] By yonder moon, I swear you do me
      wrong!
In faith, I gave it to the judge's clerk.

---

1   *tucket*   Trumpet flourish, derived from Italian. *toccato*.
2   *his trumpet*   His own personal flourish, announcing the presence of the lord of the
    estate.
3   *We should ... the sun*   Your presence could light up the night and give us a second day at
    the same time as the day on the other side of the world (the Antipodes).
4   *God sort all*   Let God settle all things.
5   *bound to ... for you*   A play on multiple meanings of "bound": "connected through
    friendship" but also "indebted" or "incarcerated."
6   *scant this ... courtesy*   Will abbreviate this merely verbal show of appreciation.

Would he were gelt° that had it, for my part,   *gelded*
Since you do take it, love, so much at heart.
145 PORTIA. A quarrel ho! Already! What's the matter?
GRAZIANO. About a hoop of gold, a paltry ring
That she did give to me, whose posy[1] was
For all the world like cutler's poetry[2]
Upon a knife: *Love me and leave me not.*
150 NERISSA. What talk you of the posy or the value?
You swore to me when I did give it you
That you would wear it till your hour of death,
And that it should lie with you in your grave.
Though not for me, yet, for your vehement oaths,
155 You should have been respective and have kept it.
Gave it a judge's clerk! No, God's my judge,
The clerk will ne'er wear hair on's face that had it.
GRAZIANO. He will, and if he live to be a man.
NERISSA. Ay, if a woman live to be a man.
160 GRAZIANO. Now, by this hand, I gave it to a youth,
A kind of boy, a little scrubbed° boy,   *stunted*
No higher than thyself, the judge's clerk,
A prating° boy that begged it as a fee;   *prattling*
I could not, for my heart, deny it him.
165 PORTIA. You were to blame, I must be plain with you,
To part so slightly with your wife's first gift,
A thing stuck on with oaths upon your finger
And so riveted with faith unto your flesh.
I gave my love a ring and made him swear
170 Never to part with it, and here he stands.
I dare be sworn for him he would not leave it,
Nor pluck it from his finger, for the wealth
That the world masters.[3] Now, in faith, Graziano,
You give your wife too unkind a cause of grief.
175 And 'twere to me, I should be mad[4] at it.

---

1 *posy* Short phrase, often a verse, inscribed on a ring or other metal accessory.
2 *cutler's poetry* Unsophisticated words that a knife maker might inscribe on a knife.
3 *the wealth ... masters* All the riches the whole world possesses.
4 *mad* Out of my mind with anger.

BASSANIO. [*Aside.*] Why, I were best to cut my left hand off
  And swear I lost the ring defending it.
GRAZIANO. My lord Bassanio gave his ring[1] away
  Unto the judge that begged it, and, indeed,
  Deserved it too, and then the boy, his clerk,   180
  That took some pains in writing, he begged mine,
  And neither man nor master would take aught
  But the two rings.
PORTIA.   What ring gave you, my lord?
  Not that, I hope, which you received of me.
BASSANIO. If I could add a lie unto a fault,   185
  I would deny it: but you see my finger
  Hath not the ring upon it: it is gone.
PORTIA. Even so void is your false heart of truth.
  By heaven, I will ne'er come[2] in your bed
  Until I see the ring.   190
NERISSA. [*To Graziano.*] Nor I in yours
  Till I again see mine.
BASSANIO.   Sweet Portia,
  If you did know to whom I gave the ring,
  If you did know for whom I gave the ring,
  And would conceive for what I gave the ring,   195
  And how unwillingly I left the ring,
  When naught would be accepted but the ring,
  You would abate° the strength of your displeasure.   *lessen*
PORTIA. If you had known the virtue° of the ring,   *power*
  Or half her worthiness that gave the ring,   200
  Or your own honour to contain° the ring,   *retain*
  You would not then have parted with the ring.
  What man is there so much unreasonable,
  If you had pleased to have defended it
  With any terms of zeal, wanted the modesty[3]   205
  To urge the thing held as a ceremony?[4]

---

1 *ring* The word "ring" takes on two meanings throughout this scene, referencing the exchanged jewelry but also carrying a sexual implication wherein the ring represents a vagina.
2 *come* Another word with both a literal and possibly sexual meaning.
3 *wanted the modesty* Was so devoid of courtesy.
4 *urge the ... a ceremony* Demand something considered so sacred.

Nerissa teaches me what to believe.
I'll die for't, but some woman had the ring.

BASSANIO. No, by my honour, madam, by my soul,
210 No woman had it, but a civil doctor,[1]
Which did refuse three thousand ducats of me
And begged the ring, the which I did deny him
And suffered him to go displeased away:
Even he that had held up[2] the very life
215 Of my dear friend. What should I say, sweet lady?
I was enforced to send it after him,
I was beset with shame and courtesy,
My honour would not let ingratitude
So much besmear it. Pardon me, good lady,
220 For, by these blessed candles of the night,[3]
Had you been there, I think you would have begged
The ring of me to give the worthy doctor.

PORTIA. Let not that doctor e'er come near my house.
Since he hath got the jewel that I loved
225 And that which you did swear to keep for me,
I will become as liberal[4] as you;
I'll not deny him anything I have,
No, not my body, nor my husband's bed.
Know[5] him I shall, I am well sure of it.
230 Lie not a night from home; watch me like Argus.[6]
If you do not, if I be left alone,
Now, by mine honour, which is yet mine own,[7]
I'll have that doctor for mine bedfellow.

NERISSA. And I his clerk. Therefore be well advised
235 How you do leave me to mine own protection.

GRAZIANO. Well, do you so; let not me take° him then,   *apprehend*
For if I do I'll mar the young clerk's pen.[8]

---

1   *civil doctor* Doctor of civil law.
2   *held up* Preserved.
3   *candles of the night* Stars.
4   *liberal* Benevolent but also unrestrained sexually.
5   *Know* Recognize, and also know in a sexual way.
6   *Argus* Monster who watched over the nymph Io with a hundred eyes.
7   *is yet mine own* Remains unchanged.
8   *mar the ... clerk's pen* Destroy the clerk's quill, but also his penis.

ANTONIO. I am th'unhappy subject of these quarrels.

PORTIA. Sir, grieve not you. You are welcome notwithstanding.

BASSANIO. Portia, forgive me this enforced wrong,[1]　　　　240
　　And in the hearing of these many friends
　　I swear to thee, even by thine own fair eyes
　　Wherein I see myself.

PORTIA.　　　　　　　Mark you but that.
　　In both my eyes he doubly sees himself,
　　In each eye one. Swear by your double° self,　　　　*duplicitous* 245
　　And there's an oath of credit![2]

BASSANIO.　　　　　　　Nay, but hear me.
　　Pardon this fault, and, by my soul, I swear
　　I never more will break an oath with thee.

ANTONIO. I once did lend my body for his wealth,°　　　*well-being*
　　Which, but for him that had your husband's ring,　　　　250
　　Had quite miscarried.° I dare be bound again:　　　*gone wrong*
　　My soul upon the forfeit, that your lord
　　Will never more break faith advisedly.°　　　*purposefully*

PORTIA. Then you shall be his surety.[3] Give him this,
　　[*Giving Antonio the ring.*]
　　And bid him keep it better than the other.　　　　255

ANTONIO. Here, Lord Bassanio, swear to keep this ring.
　　[*Giving Bassanio the ring.*]

BASSANIO. By heaven, it is the same I gave the doctor!

PORTIA. I had it of him. Pardon me, Bassanio,
　　For by this ring the doctor lay with me.

NERISSA. And pardon me, my gentle Graziano,　　　　260
　　For that same scrubbed boy, the doctor's clerk,
　　In lieu of[4] this, [*Displaying her own ring.*] last night did lie with
　　me.

GRAZIANO. Why, this is like the mending of highways
　　In summer where the ways are fair enough.[5]
　　What, are we cuckolds ere we have deserved it?　　　　265

1　*enforced wrong*　Fault that I have been forced into committing.
2　*oath of credit*　Convincing oath.
3　*surety*　Guarantor.
4　*In lieu of*　In return for.
5　*like the ... enough*　An entirely needless lesson to teach us at this early point in marriage,
　　like repairing roads in a season in which damage has not yet occurred.

PORTIA. Speak not so grossly.¹ You are all amazed.°   *astonished*
 Here is a letter, read it at your leisure;
 It comes from Padua, from Bellario.
 There you shall find that Portia was the doctor,
270 Nerissa there, her clerk. Lorenzo here
 Shall witness I set forth as soon as you
 And even but now returned; I have not yet
 Entered my house. Antonio, you are welcome,
 And I have better news in store for you
275 Than you expect. Unseal this letter soon;
 There you shall find three of your argosies
 Are richly come to harbour suddenly.
 You shall not know by what strange accident
 I chanced on this letter.
ANTONIO.   I am dumb.°   *speechless*
280 BASSANIO. [*To Portia.*] Were you the doctor, and I knew you not?
GRAZIANO. [*To Nerissa.*] Were you the clerk that is to make me
 cuckold?
NERISSA. Ay, but the clerk that never means to do it,
 Unless he live until he be a man.
BASSANIO. [*To Portia.*] Sweet doctor, you shall be my bedfellow.
285 When I am absent, then lie with my wife!
ANTONIO. Sweet lady, you have given me life and living,
 For here I read for certain that my ships
 Are safely come to road.°   *mooring*
PORTIA.   How now, Lorenzo?
 My clerk hath some good comforts too for you.
290 NERISSA. Ay, and I'll give them him without a fee.
 There do I give to you Jessica
 From the rich Jew, a special deed of gift,
 After his death, of all he dies possessed of.
LORENZO. Fair ladies, you drop manna² in the way
295 Of starved people.
PORTIA.   It is almost morning;
 And yet I am sure you are not satisfied

---

1 *grossly* Stupidly or crudely.
2 *manna* Heaven-sent bread that sustained the Israelites in the desert after their flight
 from Egypt in Exodus 16.

Of these events at full.[1] Let us go in,
And charge us there upon inter'gatories,[2]
And we will answer all things faithfully.
GRAZIANO. Let it be so. The first inter'gatory   300
That my Nerissa shall be sworn on is:
Whether till the next night she had rather stay,[3]
Or go to bed now, being two hours to day:
But, were the day come, I should wish it dark
Till I were couching with the doctor's clerk!   305
Well, while I live, I'll fear no other thing
So sore as keeping safe Nerissa's ring.

   (*Exeunt.*)

---

1   *satisfied ... at full*   Completely satisfied with our explanation of how these things have
    come to pass.
2   *charge us ... inter'gatories*   Testify under oath as we would if we were witnesses in a legal
    proceeding;   *inter'gatories*   Interrogatories, questions posed to witnesses in court.
3   *Whether till ... stay*   Whether she would prefer to wait until night falls tomorrow.

In Context

A. The Shakespearean Theater

1. The Swan Theatre

The illustration on the next page, a "Sketch of The Swan Theatre" by Johannes De Witt, is the best visual guide we have of the physical arrangement of the interior of London's four playhouses of the late sixteenth century. The sketch, by a Dutch visitor, is accompanied by the following note (translated here from the Latin):

There are four amphitheatres in London of notable beauty, which from their diverse signs bear diverse names. In each of them a different play is daily exhibited to the populace. The two more magnificent of these are situated to the southward beyond the Thames, and from the signs suspended before them are called The Rose and The Swan. The two others are outside the city towards the north on the highway which issues through the Episcopal Gate, called in the vernacular Bishopsgate. There is also a fifth, but of dissimilar structure, devoted to the baiting of beasts, where are maintained in separate cages and enclosures many bears and dogs of stupendous size, which are kept for fighting, furnishing thereby a most delightful spectacle to men. Of all the theatres, however, the largest and the most magnificent is that one of which the sign is a swan, called in the vernacular The Swan Theatre; for it accommodates in its seats three thousand persons, and is built of a mass of flint stones (of which there is a prodigious supply in Britain), and supported by wooden columns painted in such excellent imitation of marble that it is able to deceive even the most cunning. Since its form resembles that of a Roman work, I have made a sketch of it above.

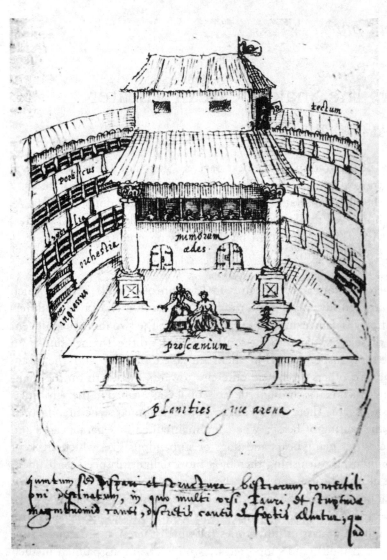

"Sketch of The Swan Theatre" by Johannes De Witt.

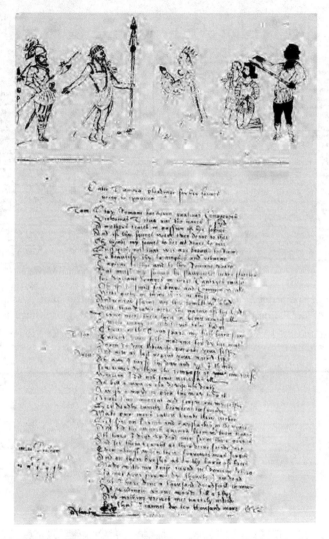

Henry Peacham, from a manuscript in the library of the Marquess of Bath at Longleat (c. 1595). This illustration (known as "the Longleat drawing") is the only surviving image of a play of Shakespeare's in performance during his lifetime. The drawing is accompanied by forty lines of verse from the play.

The plot of *The Seven Deadly Sins* (c. 1590). Originally the "plot" was a physical object listing the scenes of a play, which was hung backstage as an aid for the actors. In this detail of the plot of *The Seven Deadly Sins, Part Two* the square from which the plot hung during a performance is visible.

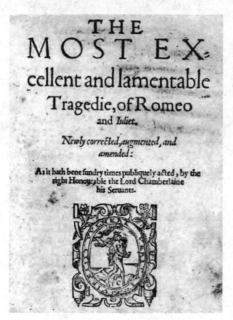

Romeo and Juliet,
Second Quarto
edition (1599).

*A Midsummer Night's
Dream,* First Quarto
edition (1600).

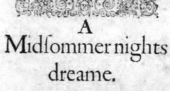

To the Reader.

This Figure, that thou here seeſt put,
  It was for gentle Shakeſpeare cut;
Wherein the Grauer had a ſtrife
  with Nature, to out-doo the life :
O, could he but haue drawne his wit
  As well in braſſe, as he hath hit
Hisface , the Print would then ſurpaſſe
  All, that vvas euer vvrit in braſſe.
But, ſince he cannot, Reader, looke
  Not on his Picture, but his Booke.

                    B. I.

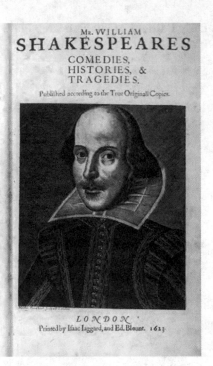

Mʀ. WILLIAM
SHAKESPEARES
COMEDIES,
HISTORIES, &
TRAGEDIES.

Publiſhed according to the True Originall Copies.

LONDON
Printed by Iſaac Iaggard, and Ed. Blount. 1623

The title page of the First Folio (1623), the first collection of Shakespeare's plays, featuring the Droeshout portrait of Shakespeare. The First Folio was assembled by fellow actors John Heminges and Henry Condell after the playwright's death in 1616.

B. Sources and Context

The "pound of flesh," an image that can be traced to antiquity,[1] can be found in England as early as the thirteenth or fourteenth century, in *Cursor Mundi* (*Runner of the World*), a popular medieval poem consisting of 24,000 lines. As the anonymous author explains in the prologue, the poem comprises a series of "rimes" and "gestes" in the vernacular of the north country. One of the tales features a Jewish moneylender who claims a pound of a borrower's flesh. The poem demonstrates other anti-Jewish sentiments typical of medieval England; for example, in a portion of the poem not reprinted here, Jews, having crucified Jesus, take his body to prevent his followers from burying him (lines 16,913–20).

Shakespeare's more direct source for *The Merchant of Venice* was Giovanni Fiorentino's *Il Pecorone* (*The Simpleton*). This fourteenth-century Italian work was not published in English in Shakespeare's lifetime, and yet it clearly influenced Shakespeare's play. This indicates one of several things: *Il Pecorone* may have been circulating in English in a manuscript form that is now lost; it may have been passed to Shakespeare orally; or it may be that Shakespeare knew enough Italian to read the story in its original language.

The Merchant of Venice uses the word "Jew" or "Hebrew" approximately 60 times, and it is often paired with derogatory modifiers such as "villain" or "dog." This tally excludes the many other pronominal references to Jews, including "our sacred nation," "our nation," "tribe," and "infidel," as well as the references to the Torah (also familiar to Christians as the first five books of the Bible). This preoccupation with the supposed evils of Jewry is a common feature of the literature of the time. In Christopher Marlowe's[2] *The Jew of Malta* (c. 1590), for example, the villainy of the title character, the Jewish merchant Barabas, gives full expression to contemporary stereotypes of Jews. The success of this earlier play may have fueled Shakespeare's own enthusiasm for the subject. In *The Jew of Malta*, Barabas, like Shylock, is not simply malevolent—he is also articulate and even, arguably, sympathetic. Marlowe's play also highlights the ruthlessness of some

---

1 See the introduction to this volume for a more complete history.
2 See *Edward II* (F.2) for a brief biography.

Christians and, like *The Merchant of Venice*, takes as its background the expanding commercial world in which England was beginning to play a dominant part.

1. from *Runner of the World*[1] (late 13th or early 14th century)

A cristen man was gode goldsmith
Quatkin thing als scho wald muth
Make till hir ful wele he cutht
Bot pouer he was, and hard in dett
Till a iuu, and terme had sett
A sume of mone for to amunt
þat askid him ful hard acunt
It was wele sene þat hit was hard
For he him asked wid sli forward
If he his mone moght noght gete
þat he suld ȝeild him for his dett
þat ilke weght þat þar war less
He suld ȝeild of his aun fless.

[A Christian man was a good goldsmith,
What[ever] kind of thing she would speak of
He knew how to make to her full satisfaction
But poor he was, and firmly in debt
To a Jew; a fixed time had been set
For him to pay the full amount
To [the Jew], who pressed him hard for it.
It was well seen that it was hard,
For he asked him with such covenant[2]
If he his money might not get,
That he should yield him for his debt
That same weight that there was less,
He should yield of his own flesh.]

---

1   *Runner of the World* Translation by Julie Sutherland, 2013; *late 13th ... 14th century* The date of this poem is unknown. The Oxford University Text Archives designates it a fourteenth-century poem; however, it has also been suggested that the poem was written closer to the end of the thirteenth century, around the time of the expulsion of the Jews. For example, see Murray in *Dialect of the Southern Counties of Scotland*, who determines it was written near Durham (England) in the last quarter of the thirteenth century (30).
2   *covenant* Official agreement.

2. from Giovanni Fiorentino, *The Simpleton*[1] (1378)

… Giannetto[2] told [Ansaldo],[3] he had made a firm resolution, to do all in his power to go again;[4] that he could not bear the shame of living in the manner he must do. When Ansaldo found him resolved, he began to sell every thing he had, and equip another ship; and so he did, and disposed of all he was worth, and left himself destitute, to furnish this other fine ship with merchandise: but, as he wanted still ten thousand ducats, he applied himself to a Jew at Mestre,[5] and borrowed them on condition, that if they were not paid on the feast of St. John in the next month of June, that the Jew might take a pound of flesh from any part of his body he pleased. Ansaldo agreed, and the Jew had an obligation drawn, and witnessed, with all the form and ceremony necessary: and then counted him the ten thousand ducats of gold; with which Ansaldo bought what was still wanting for the vessel. This last ship was finer and better freighted than the other two, and his companions made ready for the voyage, with a design that whatever they gained should be for their friend. When it was time to depart, Ansaldo told Giannetto, that since he well knew of the obligation to the Jew, he entreated him in case any misfortune happened, that he would return to Venice, that he might see him before he died; and then he could leave the world with satisfaction: Giannetto promised to do every thing that he conceived might give him pleasure. Ansaldo gave him his blessing, they take their leave, and the ships set out.…[6]

He continued some time in this happy state, and never had entertained a thought of poor Ansaldo, who had given his bond to the Jew for ten thousand ducats. But one day, as he stood at the window of the palace with his bride, he saw a number of people pass along the

---

1   *The Simpleton* Translation 1755.

2   *Giannetto* A young man who is in love with a woman from Belmont.

3   *Ansaldo* Giannetto's godfather.

4   *to go again* To return to Belmont. He has been there previously and failed to win the lady's love game. The woman from Belmont requires that whoever arrives in her port must go to bed with her; if he pleases her sexually, he must then marry her and become lord of the land.

5   *Mestre* Town connected to Venice by a channel after it was seized from Verona in 1337.

6   *out.…* In the omitted pages, Giannetto succeeds in winning the lady's game, marries her, and becomes lord of the land.

piazza, with lighted torches in their hands, who were going to make their offerings. What is the meaning of this? says he.

The lady answered, they are a company of artificers,[1] who are going to make their offerings at the church of St. John, this day is his festival. Giannetto instantly recollected Ansaldo, and leaving the window, he gave a great sigh, and turned pale; running about the room in great distraction. His lady inquired the cause of his sudden change. He said, he felt nothing. She continued to press with great earnestness, till he was obliged to confess the cause of his uneasiness, that Ansaldo was engaged for the money, and that the term was expired; and the grief he was in, lest his father should lose his life for him: that if the ten thousand ducats were not paid that day, he must lose a pound of his flesh. The lady told him to mount on horseback, and go by land the nearest way, which was better than to go by sea; to take some attendants, and a hundred thousand ducats; and not to stop, till he arrived at Venice: and if he was not dead, to endeavour to bring Ansaldo to her. Giannetto takes horse with twenty attendants, and makes the best of his way to Venice.

The time being expired, the Jew had seized Ansaldo, and insisted on having a pound of flesh. He entreated him only to wait some days, that if his dear Giannetto arrived, he might have the pleasure of embracing him before his death: the Jew replied he was willing to wait, but, says he, if he comes a hundred times over, I will cut off the pound of flesh, according to the words of the obligation: Ansaldo answered, that he was content.

Every one at Venice who had heard of this affair was much concerned: several merchants would have jointly paid the money; the Jew would not hearken to the proposal, but insisted that he might commit this homicide, to have the satisfaction of saying, that he had put to death the greatest of the Christian merchants. Giannetto making all possible haste to Venice, his lady soon followed him in a lawyer's habit, with two servants following her. Giannetto when he came to Venice, goes to the Jew, and (after embracing Ansaldo) tells him, he is ready to pay the money, and as much more as he should demand. The Jew said, he would take no money, since it was not paid at the time due; but that he would have the pound of flesh. And now this

---

1   *artificers* Skilled workers or artisans.

was much talked of, and every one blamed the Jew: but as Venice was a place where justice was strictly administered, and the Jew had his pretensions[1] grounded on public and received forms, nobody dared to oppose him, and their only resource was entreaty; and when the merchants of Venice applied to him, he was inflexible. Giannetto offered him twenty thousand which he refused; then thirty thousand, afterwards forty, fifty, and at last a hundred thousand ducats. The Jew told him, if he would give him as much gold as the city of Venice was worth, he would not accept it; and says he, you know little of me, if you think I will desist from my demand.

The lady now arrives at Venice, in her lawyer's dress; and alighting at an inn, the landlord asks of one of the servants who his master was? The servant having learned his lesson, answered, that he was a young lawyer who had finished his studies at Bologna,[2] and was returning to his own country. The landlord upon this shows his guest great civility: and when he attended at dinner, the lawyer inquiring how justice was administered in that city; he answered, justice in this place is too severe. How comes that? says the lawyer. I will tell how, says the landlord: you must know, that some years ago there came here a young man from Florence, whose name was Giannetto, he was recommended to the care of a relation who is called Ansaldo; he behaved here so well as to possess the esteem and affections of every living creature, and never was a youth so well beloved. Now this Ansaldo sent him out three times, each time with a ship of great value; he, every time, was unfortunate: and to furnish the last, Ansaldo was forced to borrow ten thousand ducats of a Jew, on condition, that if he did not repay them in June, at the feast of St. John, the Jew might take a pound of his flesh. This excellent young man is now returned, and offers to pay a hundred thousand ducats: the wicked Jew won't take them, although the best merchants in the city have applied to him, but to no purpose. Says the lawyer, this question may be easily answered. If you can answer it, says the landlord, and will take the trouble to do it, and save this worthy man from death, you will get the love and esteem of a most deserving young man, and of all the best men of this city. The lawyer caused a proclamation to be made, that whoever had any law matters to determine, they should have recourse

---

1   *pretensions* Legal claims.
2   *Bologna* Site of a celebrated university founded in the eleventh century.

to him: so it was told to Giannetto, that a famous lawyer was come from Bologna, who could decide all cases in law. Giannetto proposed to the Jew to apply to this lawyer. With all my heart, says the Jew; but let who will come, I will stick to my bond. When they came to this judge, and had saluted him, he immediately knew Giannetto; but he did not remember him: for he had disguised his face with the juice of certain herbs. Giannetto, and the Jew, each told the merits of the cause to the judge; who, when he had taken the bond and read it, said to the Jew, I must have you take the hundred thousand ducats, and release this honest man, who will always have a grateful sense of the favour done to him. The Jew replied, I will do no such thing. The judge answered, it will be better for you. The Jew was positive to yield nothing. Upon this they go to the tribunal appointed for such judgments: and our judge speaks in favour of Ansaldo; and desiring that the Jew may stand forth, Now, says he, do you (to the Jew) cut a pound of this man's flesh where you choose. The Jew ordered him to be stripped naked; and takes in his hand a razor, which had been made on purpose. Giannetto seeing this, turning to the judge, this, says he, is not the favour I asked of you.

Be quiet, says he, the pound of flesh is not yet cut off. As soon as the Jew was going to begin, take care what you do, says the judge, if you take more or less than a pound, I will order your head to be struck off: and I tell you beside, that if you shed one drop of blood you shall be put to death. Your paper makes no mention of the shedding of blood; but says expressly, that you may take a pound of flesh, neither more nor less; and if you are wise, you will take great care what you do. He immediately sent for the executioner to bring the block and axe; and now, says he, if I see one drop of blood, off goes your head. The Jew began to be in great fear, and Giannetto in as great joy. At length the Jew, after much wrangling, told him, you are more cunning than I can pretend to be; however, give me the hundred thousand ducats, and I am content. No, says the judge, cut off your pound of flesh according to your bond; I will not give you a farthing: why did not you take the money when it was offered? The Jew came down to ninety, and then to eighty thousand; but the judge was still resolute. Giannetto told the judge to give what he required, that Ansaldo might have his liberty: but he replied, let me manage him. Then the Jew would have taken fifty thousand: he said, I will not give you a penny. Give me at least, says the Jew, my own ten thousand ducats, and a curse confound you all. The judge replies, I will give you nothing: if you will have the pound of flesh, take it; if not, I will order your bond to be protested and annulled. Every one present was greatly pleased; and deriding the Jew, said, he who laid traps for others, is caught himself. The Jew seeing he could gain nothing, tore in pieces the bond in a great rage. Ansaldo was released, and conducted home with great joy by Giannetto. The hundred thousand ducats he carried to the inn to the lawyer, whom he found making ready to depart. You have done me, says he, a most important service, and I entreat you to accept of this money to carry home, for I am sure you have earned it. I thank you, replied the lawyer, I do not want money; keep and carry it back to your lady, that she may not have occasion to say, that you have squandered it away idly. Says Giannetto, my lady is so good and kind, that I might venture to spend four times as much, without incurring her displeasure; and she ordered me, when I came away, to bring with me a larger sum. How are you pleased with the lady? says the lawyer. I love her better than any earthly thing, answers Giannetto: Nature never produced any woman so beautiful, discreet, and sensible, and seems to have done her utmost in forming her. If you will do me the favour to come and see her, you will be surprised at the honours she will show you; and you will be able to judge whether I speak truth or not. I cannot go with you, says the lawyer, I have other engagements; but since you speak so much good of her, I must desire you to present my respects to her. I will not fail, Giannetto answered; and now, let me entreat you to accept of some of the money. While he was speaking, the lawyer observed a ring on his finger, and said, if you will give me this ring, I shall seek no other reward. Willingly, says Giannetto; but as it is a ring given me by my lady, to wear for her sake, I have some reluctance to part with it, and she may think, not seeing it on my finger, and will believe, that I have given it to a woman that I love, and quarrel with me, though I protest I love her much better than I love myself. Certainly, says the lawyer, she esteems you sufficiently to credit what you tell her, and you may say you made a present of it to me; but I rather think you want to give it to some former mistress here in Venice. So great, says Giannetto, is the love and reverence I bear to her, that I would not change her for any woman in the world, she is so accomplished in every article. After this he takes the ring from his finger, and presents it to him; and embracing each the other, I have still a favour to ask, says the lawyer. It shall be granted, says Giannetto. It is, replied he, that you do not stay any time here, but go as soon as possible to your lady. It appears to me a thousand years till I see her, Giannetto answered: and immediately they take leave of each other. The lawyer embarked, and left Venice. Giannetto made entertainments, and presents of horses and money to his former companions; and having made a great expense for several days, he took leave of his Venetian friends, and carried Ansaldo with him, and some of his old acquaintance accompanied them. Everybody shed tears at his departure, both men and women; his amiable deportment had so gained the good-will of all. In this manner he left Venice, and returned to Belmont....

3. from Christopher Marlowe, *The Jew of Malta* (c. 1590)

from ACT 2, Scene 3

BARABAS. As for myself, I walk abroad o' nights,
  And kill sick people groaning under walls.
  Sometimes I go about and poison wells,[1]
  And now and then, to cherish Christian thieves,
  I am content to lose some of my crowns,
  That I may, walking in my gallery,
  See 'em go pinioned° along by my door.   *tied up*
  Being young, I studied physic,° and began   *medicine*
  To practice first upon the Italian;
  There I enriched the priests with burials
  And always kept the sexton's[2] arms in ure°   *use*
  With digging graves and ringing dead men's knells.
  And after that was I an engineer,
  And in the wars 'twixt France and Germany,[3]
  Under pretense of helping Charles the Fifth,

---

1   *poison wells* Reference to a stereotypical misconception about Jewish people commonly held during and after the Middle Ages.
2   *sexton* Church administrator responsible for the burial of the dead.
3   *wars ... Germany* Holy Roman Emperor Charles V (r. 1519–58) struggled for domination of Italy in several wars with Francis I of France (r. 1515–47). The wars continued with their respective successors, Ferdinand I (r. 1558–1564) and Henry II (r. 1547–59).

Slew friend and enemy with my stratagems.
Then after that was I an usurer,
And with extorting, cozening,° forfeiting,[1]   *deceiving*
And tricks belonging unto brokery,
I filled the jails with bankrupts in a year,
And with young orphans planted hospitals,
And every moon made some or other mad,
And now and then one hang himself for grief,
Pinning upon his breast a long great scroll
How I with interest tormented him.
But mark how I am blest for plaguing them:
I have as much coin as will buy the town.

---

1   *forfeiting* Failing to pay bonds.

C. Jews and Christians

1. from the Geneva Bible, John 8.42–49 (1560)

The Geneva Bible was first published in 1560 by a group of English Protestant refugees who had come to Switzerland, fleeing the persecution of Henry VIII's Catholic daughter, Queen Mary—known to history as "Bloody Mary." They smuggled their translation back into England, where it remained an illicit document until Mary's half-sister, Elizabeth I, ascended to the throne and endorsed it. Although Shakespeare had knowledge of other Bible translations, the Geneva Bible is the one he draws on most frequently.

Certain passages in the New Testament (the Book of John in particular) were for centuries used to justify anti-Semitic sentiment. The passage below was understood to show that Jews are the spawn of the devil, do not belong to God, and refuse to honor God.

[42] Therefore Jesus said unto them,[1] If God were your Father, then would ye love me: for I proceeded forth, and came from God, neither came I of myself, but he sent me.

[43] Why do ye not understand my talk? Because ye cannot hear my word.

[44] Ye are of your father the devil, and the lusts of your father ye will do: he hath been a murderer from the beginning, and abode not in the truth, because there is no truth in him. When he speaketh a lie, then speaketh he of his own: for he is a liar, and the father thereof.

[45] And because I tell you the truth, ye believe me not.

[46] Which of you can rebuke me of sin? And if I say the truth, why do ye not believe me?

[47] He that is of God heareth God's words: ye therefore hear them not, because ye are not of God.

[48] Then answered the Jews, and said unto him, Say we not well that thou art a Samaritan,[2] and hast a devil?

[49] Jesus answered, I have not a devil, but I honour my Father, and ye have dishonoured me.

---

1   *them*   Here, Jesus is speaking to a group of Pharisees, a Jewish brotherhood of pious, often well-educated laypeople; they are attempting to have Jesus arrested.

2   *Samaritan*   Member of a Jewish group who remained in ancient Samaria during the Assyrians' invasion of Israel. The Samaritans were later looked upon unfavorably by the other Jewish peoples returning from exile.

2. from *The South English Legendary*: Miracles of the Virgin[1] (c. 1280)

Miracles of the Virgin are short narrative accounts of the miraculous intercessory powers of the Virgin Mary. They were extraordinarily widely circulated from the twelfth century through to the early sixteenth century, and often exist in numerous versions. With the Protestant Reformation this genre of tales involving intercessions in human affairs by the Virgin Mary all but disappears, but the same sorts of anti-Jewish feeling—and many of the same narrative motifs—persist in other literary and cultural forms through the sixteenth century and well into the seventeenth. Many of the tales involve Christians and Jews; they give a powerful sense of the ways in which anti-Semitism was spread through popular narrative in English culture. They also in some cases connect quite directly with the threads of story that are to be found in *The Merchant of Venice*. A number of these accounts involve written contracts between Christians and Jews (or, as in the "St. Theophilus" story below, a contract drawn up with the assistance of a Jew). All are resolved by the intervention of the pure and virtuous Mary; in some stories Mary's intervention involves disguising herself.

The South English Legendary is an anonymous Middle English collection of versified saints' lives and homilies for Christian holidays. It survives in more than 50 manuscripts from the late thirteenth through the fifteenth centuries, and the number and arrangement of items vary considerably between each. In the majority of surviving copies, a series of six Miracles of the Virgin is appended to a life of "St. Theophilus," a pseudo-historical precursor of Faust. St. Theophilus was well known throughout the Middle Ages for contracting his soul to the Devil and obtaining pardon through the Virgin Mary.

St. Theophilus was a great man, and a great clerk[2] also.
He held the position of highest authority under the bishop.
When this high bishop died, Theophilus was elected

---

1 *Miracles of the Virgin* Translated into Modern English and annotated for the *Broadview Anthology of British Literature* by Adrienne Williams Boyarin. The translation is based on the Middle English text in the edition of Charlotte D'Evelyn and Anna J. Mill, *The South English Legendary*, vol. 1, Early English Text Society O.S. 235 (London: Oxford University Press, 1956) 221–38. This material is reproduced here with the permission of Adrienne Williams Boyarin.

2 *clerk* Denotes multiple professions and credentials in Middle English. It can mean cleric or clergyman, scholar or writer, keeper of documents or accounts, or student (especially a university student). The clerical and administerial connotations are likely intended here.

To succeed him as bishop—and, nevertheless, he would not.
Instead, he said that he was not worthy and that he knew too little.
With great magnificence and display, the people readily chose another.
Once the bishop was in power, he cast his anger on Theophilus,
Because he was elected bishop first and was close to the previous
  bishop.
He expelled him from his office and seized his goods[1] for himself,
So that Theophilus quickly came into great poverty.
As wealthy a man as he was before, he was then as much a pauper,
So that he did not know how to survive such woe.
When he was driven into misery, it shamed him very deeply.
Men that honored him before would not do so anymore.
Every man spoke ill of him—and men will do so concerning the poor.
He could not go out among men for shame; he did not know what
  best to do.
Death was the thing he most desired, such that he imagined
That anyone willing to serve the Devil might receive great wealth
  from him.
That night, he went to a Jew who lived nearby.
He begged him for help with what had happened
And begged him to serve the Devil, freely, for wealth's sake.
"It shall be well," said the Jew, "but you must yet wait.
Come another night at this time, here to me in this place,
And I shall give you the finest counsel, which will please you well."
Theophilus did not forget this. He went to the Jew,
To the same place the next night, the better to relieve his need.
"Come along with me," said this Jew, "as I shall guide you,
But no matter what you see or hear, do not be afraid,
Nor make the sign of the cross,[2] nor even think about it.[3]
You never had such wealth as shall be brought upon you."
Theophilus went along with him and did as he told him.
At that point the Jew guided him into a secret place:
He met the high Devil there then, master of all evil,
And all his servants around him ready to record wickedness.
"What is this one," said the evildoer, "that you bring with you there?"

---

1 *goods* Material possessions, property.
2 *Nor make ... of the cross* I.e., Do not cross yourself.
3 *it* The cross.

"He wants to be one of yours," said the Jew, "and he comes to you of
    necessity.
He has been a man of great power, which is now taken from him,
And he wants to become your man in order to restore himself."
"Welcome, *beau frère*,"[1] said the Devil. "Now you do well indeed.
Had you done so earlier you would have been a rich man long before
    this.
But I will help no man unless the debt is guaranteed with a vow.
Become my man and do me homage,[2] and you will be rich enough."
"I become your man," said this other, "as faithfully as anyone can."
"Yet you must do more," said the Devil, "and forsake your law,
Your Christianity that you embrace, which the priest gave to you,
For you cannot have dealings with me any other way."
"And I forsake it," said this other, "and accept you entirely."
"Certainly, *beau frère*," said the Devil, "yet you must forsake more.
You must forsake God who created you, and all saints as well."
"And I forsake them," said Theophilus, "in order to do your will."
"*Sans faille*,[3] *beau frère*," said the Devil. "You can say no better.
You will be a rich man soon enough, but you must give up one thing yet.
Unless you do it, all that we have done is for naught:
You must forsake, along with God, his mother Mary also,
For I am not securely bound to you unless you do this,
For she has taken from me many who were with me."
"And I forsake her," said Theophilus, "her and her son too,
And I commend life and soul to you, to do all your will."
"Oh, *beau frère*," said the Devil, "still I am afraid,
Because Mary has so often led my men away from me.
Words are nothing but wind against her, for though a man forsake her,
She will accept him if he wishes to return his heart joyfully.
Therefore, I want to have a secure agreement before I associate with you:
You will make me a valid charter of this covenant,
Written with your own hand, and indeed sealed also.
When you have done all this, I will do your will."
Theophilus granted all this. He wrote the charter quickly
And indeed sealed it with his ring, as was proper to do.

---

1   *beau frère* French: handsome fellow, literally "fair brother."
2   *Become my man ... homage* The Devil makes a specific request here: that Theophilus
    perform the ceremonial actions associated with feudal pledges of loyalty to a lord.
3   *Sans faille* French: without doubt, assuredly.

He knelt and grasped[1] his master, and kissed his feet also.
"Now, Theophilus," said this evildoer, "you have done everything.
When I get home, I shall lock this charter so securely in hell
That I will not be anxious about Mary taking it away.
So go home and be steadfast, as I shall be to you in return.
You were never so rich a man as you will soon become through me."
The Devil went home to hell, and Theophilus headed home too,
And he enthusiastically thanked the Jew who had done this for him.
The bishop sent for Theophilus immediately the next morning,
So that he went to him in haste, made his way confidently.
He cried out for mercy sorrowfully when he approached him,
And he gave him back all his power, which he had taken from him
    before.
Theophilus quickly became so rich that he had never been richer.
He was esteemed a lord and a knight, so great was his power.
Glad was the man who could please him. Men marveled at the situation,
And said furthermore it was not of this world, *si haut si bas*.[2]
He had sufficient worldly wealth, and worldly joy too—
Alas that any Christian man should also come to that in such a way!
It happened afterwards there, a little while later,
That the Jewish counselor was found to be treasonous.
He was seized and brought to justice, and was put to a horrible death:
He was burned, according to judgment—and too late was he so.[3]
Then Theophilus understood, and he considered in his heart,
That it was the Devil whom he was with that had brought him to
    such death.
He thought, "Am I not with him?" And: "Even if I am wealthy for a
    while,
I will never know in advance the time when he might bring me low.
Then I would be utterly damned—and I am bound to him
So securely that I cannot withdraw! Alas, that moment!
Alas, why did I not choose death instead of that deed?
Have I not forsaken them, each one, who might help and counsel me?
How can I hope for their grace when I have forsaken them?
I am a sinful wretch, alas! My like has never been seen!

---

1   *He knelt and grasped*   I.e., Theophilus is down on one knee and holding the hand of his
    lord, a ceremonial performance of fealty, typical of medieval rites of vassalage.
2   *si haut si bas*   French: whether high (i.e., heavenly) or low.
3   *too late was he so*   I.e., he should have been put to death earlier.

God is so fair-minded that, for that reason, I have no hope with him.
Unless I have Our Lady's[1] grace, I am certainly damned,
For she was always merciful and, even though I have forsaken her,
No matter how I accomplish it, I will cling to her grace."
He went to Our Lady's altar[2] and cried for mercy and grace from her.
He pounded his knees against the ground, weeping in grief.
He cried to her and wept mournfully both night and day.
He would not come out of the chapel, but always lay within it:
Forty days and forty nights he cried to her continually,
To her who was always so good. She appeared to him at last.
For since he cried to her so earnestly, that sweet maiden so mild
Showed her strength and came down from heaven, going to him at once.
"How can I," she said, "find any grace for you, wretched man?
How can I pray to my son for you, when you have forsaken him?"
"Ah, Lady, Lady," said Theophilus. "Lady, now, your pardon—
I have sinned worse than any man, which pains me very sorely.
Have mercy on me, a sinful wretch. I will sin no more.
And if you will grant me your grace, I will do all your teaching."
"You sinful man," Our Lady said, "as much as is permitted me,
I will be very kind to you, and indeed to all Christian men.
For I love Christian men, and I nourish[3] them too,
And I am ever compelled to descend to them and do their bidding:
So much I endure so often to restrain my son,
So that he does not take vengeance as often was he would like—
But confess your sins to him, and that[4] he was born of me,
And that he suffered death for sinful men, and I will pray for you."
"Ah Lady, mercy," said Theophilus, "I am unworthy of it,
To make such a confession to him, with the mouth by which I
    forsook him!"
"Yes, assuredly," said Our Lady, "for he is kind and gentle.[5]
You know that well that he often shows great love to sinful men,

---

1   *Our Lady*   The Virgin Mary.
2   *Our Lady's altar*   An altar dedicated to the Virgin Mary, not the main altar in the church.
3   *nourish*   Feed or comfort spiritually, though the allusion to Mary's maternity is intentional.
    The Middle English verb "norishen" also means "nurse" or "suckle."
4   *and that*   And confess your belief that.
5   *assuredly … kind and gentle*   The Middle English pointedly emphasizes the contrast
    between the truth of Theophilus' statement and Jesus' character, though the opposition
    is somewhat lost in translation: the word "hardliche" is translated here as "assuredly," and
    "softe" is rendered "gentle."

For he was born of sinful men,[1] and put to death for them.
It is necessary that he be kind to them, for birthright dictates it be so."
Then Theophilus began to weep and cry out: "Lord, mercy!" he said.
"I confess my wicked deed to you with a sorrowful heart.
Have mercy on me, as certainly as you were born for us
And endured death for us so that we would not be damned.
Consider my wretchedness, Lord. Sweet Jesus, your pardon!
Give me your mercy, I pray to you, Lord. I will sin no more."
"Theophilus, Theophilus," said Our Lady. "Because of your Christianity,
And because I have loved Christian men ever since my son took flesh,
I will pray to my son on my bare knees for you very soon.
Be steadfast, as you have begun to be, and he will hear your prayer."
At these words, Theophilus did not know where Our Lady went.
He wept and cried out continually, and held on tight to her grace.
He waited there three days without food and drink.
With weeping and suffering and sorrow enough, he cried to Our Lord.
Then Our Lady approached, behind him, and with joyful countenance
　　too:
"Theophilus," she said, "you have done enough penance now.
Be joyful, for I have prayed for my son's kindness and pardon,
Such that he has forgiven you your sin. Sin no more."
"May you be praised, Lady!" said Theophilus. "Praised be your grace!
Praised be the moment that I cried out to you in this place!
Lady, I am always afraid. I am not secure
Until the charter that I made is brought to me.
Lady, you are full of mercy, which you have shown in this place.
Since your mercy is so great, therefore give me your grace."
"Right away now, Theophilus," said Our Lady, "I will yet be kind to you."
At these words, she left again, so that he could not see her.
She revealed her mercy, for she returned to him on the third day
And brought the charter, and went to him as he lay sleeping,
And left again silently. And then Theophilus awoke
And held the charter in his hand, as Our Lady had delivered it to him.
He thanked Our Lady and her grace, as indeed it seems to me he
　　should—
More than he did the wicked Jew who took him to the Devil.

1　*men*　Humankind, though the idea of a birthing from men is perhaps purposefully in
　tension with Mary's miraculous birthing of Jesus.

...

In days long past, in Bourges, a Jew's child   *Miraculum*[1]
Often played, as children happily like to do, with Christian children.
It happened one Easter day that the children began to walk
To church, as children will do when the day requires it.
The Jew's child went with them, and when he entered the church
He paid close attention to everything he saw there.
When his friends kneeled down and cried out to the image on high,[2]
He kneeled down also, and he did everything that he saw the others do.
He felt fitting wonder at the cross he gazed upon intently.
It seemed to him that his heart was most drawn to an image of Our
    Lady.
He devoted himself to that very image, that he might love it above all:
After that first look, she never left his mind.
When the people went forward to take communion, God's flesh and
    blood,
That child went up with them and also did the good deed.
There, with his companions, he accepted God's flesh and blood,
And afterwards he made his way home. While they[3] headed home,
His father and his mother were searching everywhere for him.
They were happy when he arrived at home, because they had been
    worried.
The father asked him where he had been, and he immediately told him
What he had done at church and how it was that he had ended up
    there.
The father was nearly insane with anger. Right away he began to stoke
    his oven.
When the fire was burning hot, he threw that child into the middle
    of it
And shut the mouth of the oven. The mother acted as if she had gone
    insane.
When she saw her child burned, she let out a sorrowful wail.

---

1   *Miraculum*   Latin: miracle. Some *South English Legendary* manuscripts include Latin
    notations like this one in the margins, sometimes to show where a new text or portion of
    text begins, though little else guides readers through divisions within an individual saint's
    life. The story that begins here is a version of one of the oldest and most common Marian
    miracles, usually called by editors "The Jewish Boy" or "The Jewish Boy of Bourges."
2   *image on high*   A crucifix or other image of Jesus.
3   *they*   People who were in the church.

She ran frantically through the streets and cried out miserably.
She told the people how it was, and about all that had happened to her.
The people came immediately to the oven, surrounding it on all sides.
They found that child sitting in the middle of it—and playing with
    the fire!
They asked him if he knew why the fire had not come near him.
"Indeed," he said, "The beautiful woman that I saw at the church,
    Who stood on high, up near the cross, and who, it seemed to me,
Also stood by the altar and beckoned me towards it when I took
    communion—
She afterwards came to me here, and she took her head covering
And embraced me with it so that no fire or heat came near me.
I have never been so happy anywhere as I was there.
I believe in her son, whom the Jews hung on the tree."[1]
The people seized the child's father and stoked the oven until it was hot,
And they threw the lout right into the middle of it and burned him
    to ashes.
The child and his mother, and many others, immediately accepted
    Christianity
And believed in God and his mother and became good people.
Otherwise, except for the miracle of that child, they would have
    been evildoers.
One can yet tell more miracles concerning Our Lady sweet and kind!

...

Jews hate Our Lady intensely, and her sweet son too.   *Miraculum*[2]
That is observable in many of the deeds the evildoers have done.
Once at harvest time, on Our Lady's Day,[3] which is so holy and sweet,
A certain archbishop was singing his Mass in the city of Toledo.[4]
During the Mass, just at the point of the consecration,[5] at the
    moment of that holy deed,

---

1   *tree*   Cross.
2   *Miraculum*   The story that begins here is a version of a Marian miracle commonly called
    by editors "Toledo" or "Jews of Toledo."
3   *at harvest ... Lady's Day*   The feast of the Nativity of the Virgin Mary, 8 September.
4   *Toledo*   In central Spain.
5   *consecration*   I.e., of the bread and wine of communion.

He heard a voice from heaven that said these words:[1]
"The evildoers will put him on the cross once again,
So viciously, and so shamefully hatefully, with such wicked intentions!"
When the archbishop had brought the Mass to an end,
He gathered a very large group of people. He went to the Jewry,[2]
And he had them search everywhere. Finally they found
The likeness of Our Lord on a cross, beaten and bound,
Nailed through the feet and hands, as Our Lord with his five
   wounds.[3]
The Jews had done that. May God grant suffering to them
And to all who show love for them, for many are the vile
And shameful acts that they often do to Our Lord in secret....

3. from Edward I's Edict of Expulsion (1290)

The first substantial Jewish communities to immigrate to England did
so in the eleventh century. Jewish people were also spread throughout
Europe, where their choice of career was often limited by law or custom. Jews were of course not subject to laws and regulations made by
the Church regarding the behavior of Christians—including Pope Alexander III's excommunication of usurers (1179). Christian rulers and
venturesome merchants thus turned to Jews to boost nascent capitalist
economies. Despite their commercial contributions to Christendom,
Jews were largely despised in England and around Europe. In England,
rumors spread about the Jews' rituals. Such rumors included "blood li-
bels"—accusations that Jews murdered Christian children—and outrage at the Jews' alleged sacrilege escalated. An infamous incident in
1190, in which Jews were massacred in York, led many Jews to flee the
country. King Henry III (r. 1216–72) ensured that the remaining Jews
were marked by a distinctive badge; Edward I (r. 1272–1307) then
decreed, in his *Statutum de Judeismo* of 1275, that the badges should
be a conspicuous yellow. He also levied a special tax against the Jewish

---

1   *these words*   At this point, one of the most complete early manuscripts of *The South English
    Legendary* inserts two additional lines: "Allas the Gywes tricherie, allas the lithere fode / That
    among mi sones children, that he boughte mid his blode" (Alas the treachery of the Jews!
    Alas the wicked race / That, along with my son's children, he bought with his blood!).
2   *Jewry*   Area of town where Jews live.
3   *five wounds*   The four wounds caused by nails through both hands and both feet of Jesus,
    plus the wound caused by the spear that stabbed him in the side (cf. John 19.33–35).

people and ordered them not to lend money. (This inevitably drove moneylending underground.) Finally, in 1290, Edward I expelled the Jews from England *en masse*; it was not until 1656 that they began returning to England in large numbers. Although England's Lord Protector, Oliver Cromwell (ruled 1653–58), is frequently remembered for atrocious violence (for instance, against Irish Catholics), it was under his rule that Jews were allowed to return to England's shores and openly practice their faith.

Harsh as England's treatment of its Jewish population was, it was not in any way exceptional in medieval Europe; Jews were expelled several times from France for extended periods, including from the late fourteenth century until the seventeenth; were expelled from Spain in 1492; and were expelled from Portugal in 1496.

Edward ... to the treasurer and barons of the exchequer,[1] greeting. Whereas formerly in our Parliament at Westminster on the quinzaine of St. Michael[2] in the third year of our reign, to the honour of God and the profit of the people of our realm, we ordained and decreed that no Jew thenceforth should lend anything at usury to any Christian on lands, rents or other things, but that they should live by their commerce and labour; and the same Jews, afterwards maliciously deliberating among themselves, contriving a worse sort of usury which they called courtesy, have depressed our people aforesaid on all sides under colour thereof, the last offence doubling the first; whereby, for their crimes and to the honour of the Crucified, we have caused those Jews to go forth from our realm as traitors: we, wishing to swerve not from our former choice, but rather to follow it, do make totally null and void all manner of penalties and usuries and every sort thereof, which could be demanded by actions by reason of the Jewry from any Christians of our realm for any times whatsoever; wishing that nothing be in any wise demanded from the Christians aforesaid by reason of the debts aforesaid, save only the principal sums which they received from the Jews aforesaid; the amount of which debts we will that the Christians aforesaid verify before you by the oath of three good and lawful men by whom the truth of the matter may the better be known, and thereafter pay the same to us at terms convenient to

---

1 *exchequer* Treasury of the state, responsible for all matters related to revenue.
2 *quinzaine of St. Michael* 13 October, the fifteenth day after the feast of St. Michael.

Anonymous, *Desecration of the Host*, from *Rappresentazione d'un Miracolo del Corpo di Cristo* (*Representation of a Miracle of the Body of Christ*), c. 1500. "Desecration of the host" refers to the profane destruction of the sacred bread that Christians consume in memory of Christ's crucifixion. Some Christians believe that when they consume the bread and wine during Holy Communion, it "transubstantiates"—it miraculously changes into the actual body and blood of Jesus. This belief was widespread in medieval Europe, and Jews were frequently arrested and tried for allegedly stealing the "host"—the consecrated bread—and stabbing it to see if it bled. As tales surrounding these circumstances proliferated, they became a kind of conversion narrative in which Jews, astonished when the host did in fact bleed, became Christians. (In versions where they did not become Christians, they were put to death.)

Images of these legends began circulating more widely with the emergence of the printing press. The woodcut was a popular form of book illustration. On the left side of the woodcut above, Jews steal the host. On the right side, they not only stab it, but they also cook it.

them to be fixed by you. And therefore we command you that you cause our said grace so piously granted to be read in the aforesaid exchequer, and to be enrolled on the rolls of the same exchequer, and to be straitly[1] kept, according to the form above noted....

4. from Richard Morison, *A Remedy for Sedition* (1536)

Richard Morison (c. 1510–56) was an English humanist and diplomat. Morison was a protégé first of the powerful Cardinal Wolsey and later of Thomas Cromwell. While serving for Cromwell, Morison wrote, among other things, two anonymous tracts in which he addressed the issue of English rebellion and governmental authority. One of these tracts was *A Remedy for Sedition*.

Morison's attitude in the following passage of *A Remedy for Sedition*—including his acclamation of the way the Jews raise their children to be good scholars and practitioners of their faith, and his description of Jews as a civilized group—stands out amongst the wide variety of anti-Semitic publications that predominated in England at the time.[2] *A Remedy for Sedition* was written following a 1536 rebellion ("sedition") in northern England, and the text in general extols civil obedience to the authority of the king.

… I have oft marvelled, to see the diligence, that the Jews use in bringing up their youth, and been much ashamed to see how negligent Christian men are in so godly a thing. There is neither man, woman, nor child of any lawful age, but he for the most part knoweth the Laws of Moses:[3] and with us he is almost a good curate, that knoweth vi. or vii. of the x. Commandments: amongst the Jews, there is not one, but he can by some honest occupation, get his living. There be few idle, none at all, but such as be rich enough, and may live without labour. There is not one beggar amongst them. All the cities of Italy, many places in Cecilia, many burgs[4] in Germany, have a great number of Jews in them. I have been among them, that are in

---

1   *straitly* Precisely.
2   Of course, even anti-Semitic works might praise Jews for certain attributes within a wider context of condemnation. Thanks to Dr. Julia Garrett for highlighting this.
3   *Laws of Moses* Set of laws believed to have been passed from God to Moses. These are given in the first five books of the Hebrew Bible (called the Old Testament in Christian scripture).
4   *Cecilia* I.e., Sicily; *burgs* I.e., cities.

Italy, I never heard of a Jew, that was a thief, never that was a murderer. No I never heard of a fray between them. I am ashamed to say as I needs must say, they may well think their religion better than ours, if religion be tried by men's lives. Now if Moses' law learned in youth, and but carnally understand,[1] can so stay them, that few or none fall into other vice, than usury, which although they do think permitted by Moses' law, so they use it not one Jew to another, as indeed they do not, but a Jew to a stranger. Might not we learn so much of Christ's law, as were able to keep us from rebellion? ... It is, it is undoubted, one sort of religion, though also it be not right, that keepeth men in concord and unity. Turks go not against Turks, nor Jews against Jews, because they both agree in their faith....

5. from Samuel Usque, *Consolation for the Tribulations of Israel* (1553)

For obvious reasons, there are relatively few texts available by sixteenth-century Jewish writers that are relevant to discussions of Jews and Christians in England during this period. Samuel Usque's *Consolation* is one of the exceptions. Usque's family had been among those forced to leave Spain when that country expelled all Jews in 1492. They moved to Portugal and again came under threat; the Portuguese began forced conversions of Jews and, somewhat later, instituted the Inquisition to root out those suspected of insincerity in the practice of Catholicism. Usque left Portugal, eventually settling in Italy. Like Holinshed below (and, indeed, most chroniclers of "history" at the time), Usque freely mingles legend with fact—recounting, for example, how after the Jews had been expelled from England by one king, another invited them back in order to try to force them to convert to Christianity. The Chronicle is written in the first person, as if from the perspective of a Jew who has personally experienced persecution in all lands and all eras.

In the same country I witnessed another fierce and terrible calamity. After that king[2] had left this life he was succeeded by another, who disregarded the past expulsion and recalled all the Jews who had left the kingdom, offering to take them back and let them live in peace.

---

1 *carnally understand* I.e., understood only superficially, without spiritual depth.
2 *that king* Edward I, who expelled all Jews from England in 1290.

The Jews took counsel among themselves in France, Flanders, Spain, and other lands where they had dispersed. They decided that for no reason, including ease or material gain, would they re-enter a place where they had suffered so great a calamity—except to see the children they had left behind, to talk with them and convince them to return to the faith of their fathers....

O cruel Englishmen, ... so quick to hurt me and so blind to the reason for which you harmed me! How is it that you have not become inured to crime from of old? Are not the ways of your princesses adulterous? Is not the garb of your masses woven of robberies, hatreds, and killing? I do not need to cite ancient histories to tell this, for modern records proclaim it. Consider in the years that King Henry reigned, how many acts of adultery were committed by his own queens; how many treacheries were attempted by the king's noblest and closest associates; how many heads were placed on London Bridge because of these and other ghastly crimes; and how many queens were killed by the sword, and deprived of dominion? The churches where you prayed were demolished by your own hands or converted to stables. Your priests were shamefully expelled.[1]...

According to your religion, all these acts, singly and collectively, are regarded as sins. They manifest extreme wickedness, and you deserved punishment for them. Misfortunes did not come to your land because of the Jews' sins alone, as you say.

6. from Raphael Holinshed, *Chronicles of England, Scotland, and Ireland* (1587 edition)

The first edition of Holinshed's multi-volume work appeared in 1577. Holinshed died in 1580; the second edition was in part written by others. Extremely popular, it is a vital reference point in any exploration of the ways in which late-sixteenth-century educated English minds perceived the history of Christians and Jews. The *Chronicles* readily accept as fact even the most extreme anti-Jewish legends (we may see here the connection between "history" and the sorts of tales presented above). In the context of his time, however, Holinshed was no extremist; on several occasions he expresses strong disapproval of the wholesale murder of Jews by Christians.

---

1   *churches ... expelled*   Usque is referring to the upheavals in the wake of Henry VIII's break with Rome.

... This year was an heinous act committed by the Jews at Norwich, where they put a child to death, in crucifying him upon a cross to the reproach of Christian religion.

1189

... Upon this day of King Richard's coronation, the Jews that dwelt in London and in other parts of the realm, being there assembled, had but sorry hap.... [M]eaning to honour the same coronation with their presence, and to present to the king some honorable gift, the Jews meant to present him with a rich gift whereby they might declare themselves glad for his advancement, and procure his friendship towards them, for confirming of their privileges and liberties, according to the grants and charters made to them by the former kings. [King Richard, being] of a zealous mind to Christ's religion, abhorring [the Jewish] nation (and doubting[1] some sorcery by them to be practiced), commanded that they should not come within the church when he should receive the crown. But at dinner time, among others that pressed in at the palace gate, diverse of the Jews were about to thrust in, till one of them was struck by a Christian, who alleging the king's commandment, kept them back from coming within the palace. Which, some of the unruly people perceiving, and supposing it had been done by the king's commandment, took lightly occasion thereof, and falling upon the Jews with staves, bats and stones, beat them and chased them home to their houses and lodgings. Herewith rose a rumour through the city, that the king had commanded the Jews to be destroyed, and thereupon came running together, to assault them in their houses, which when they could not easily break up nor enter, by reason the same were strongly builded, they set fire on them, so that diverse houses were consumed, not only of the Jews, but also of their neighbours, so hideous was the rage of the fire.... The king being advised of this riotous attempt of the outrageous people, sent some of his councillors ... to appease the tumult: but their authority was nothing regarded, nor their persuasions any whit reverenced, but their threatenings

---

1 *doubting* Suspecting.

rather brought themselves in danger of life among the rude sort of those that were about to spoil, rob, and sack the houses and shops of the Jews: to the better accomplishment of which their unlawful act, the light that the fire of those houses which burned, gave after it was once night, did minister no small help and occasion of furtherance. The Jews that were in those houses which were set on fire were either smouldered and burned to death within, or else at their coming forth most cruelly received upon the points of spears ... of their adversaries....

1209

... Furthermore, about the same time the king taxed the Jews, and grievously tormented and imprisoned them, because diverse of them would not willingly pay the sums that they were taxed at. Amongst other, there was one of them at Bristow, which would not consent to give any fine..., wherefore by the kings commandment he was put unto this penance, that every day, till he would agree to give to the king those ten thousand marks that he was seized at, he should have one of his teeth plucked out of his head. By the space of seven days together he stood steadfast, losing every of those days a tooth, but on the eight day ... he paid the money to save that one [tooth, he] who with more wisdom and less pain might have done so before, and have saved his seven teeth, which he lost with such torments....

1219

... These things being thus brought to pass, and all troubles quieted, the king, as then being at London, there was brought before him by one Polydor Fabian a complaint against the Jews of Norwich, which had stolen a young child, being not past a twelve months old, and secretly kept him an whole year together, to the end that he might (when Easter came) crucify him in despite of our savior Jesus Christ, and the Christian religion.

1253

... Also, upon the two and twentieth of November, were brought into Westminster a hundred and two Jews from Lincoln that were accused for the crucifying of a child in the last summer, in despite of

Christ's religion. They were upon their examination sent to the tower.[1] The child which they had so crucified was named Hugh, about an eight years of age. They kept him ten days after they got him into their hands, sending in the meantime unto diverse other places of the realm, for other of their nation to be present at the crucifying of him. The murder came out, by the diligent search made by the mother of the child, who found his body in a well, on the back side of the Jew's house, where he was crucified: for she had learned that her son was lastly seen playing with certain Jews' children of like age to him, before the door of the same Jew. The Jew that was owner of the house, was apprehended, and being brought before Sir John de Lerinton, upon promise of pardon, confessed the whole matter. For they used yearly (if they could come by their prey) to crucify one Christian child or other. The king, upon knowledge had hereof, would not pardon this Jew that had so confessed the matter, but caused him to be executed at Lincoln, who coming to the place where he should die, opened more matter concerning such as were of counsel and present at the crucifying of the poor innocent. Whereupon at length also eighteen of them that were so brought to London, were convicted, adjudged, and hanged, the other remained long in prison.

1264

... In the Passion week the Jews that inhabited in London being detected of treason, which they had devised against the barons and citizens, were slain almost all the whole number of them, and great riches found in their houses, which were taken and carried away by those that ransacked the same houses.

1290

... The king ordained, that all the wool, which should be sold unto strangers, should be brought unto Sandwich, where the staple thereof was kept long time after. In the same year was a parliament holden at Westminster, wherein the statutes of Westminster the third were ordained. It was also decreed, that all the Jews should avoid out of the land, in consideration whereof, a fifteenth was granted to the king, and so hereupon were the Jews banished out of all the king's domin-

---

1   *to the tower*   I.e., to prison in the Tower of London.

ions, and never since could they obtain any privilege to return hither again. All their goods not moveable were confiscated, with their tallies and obligations; but all other their goods that were moveable, together with their coin of gold and silver, the king licenced them to have and convey with them. A sort of the richest of them, being shipped with their treasure in a mighty tall ship which they had hired, when the same was under sail, and got down the Thames towards the mouth of the river ..., the master mariner bethought him of a wile,[1] and caused his men to cast anchor, and so rode at the same, till the ship by ebbing of the stream remained on the dry sands. The master herewith enticed the Jews to walk out with him on land for recreation. And at length, when he understood the tide to be coming in, he got him back to the ship, whither he was drawn up by a cord. The Jews made not so much haste as he did, because they were not aware of the danger. But when they perceived how the matter stood, they cried to him for help: howbeit he told them, that they ought to cry rather unto Moses, by whose conduct their fathers passed through the Red Sea and if they would call to him for help, he was able enough to help them out of those raging floods, which now came in upon them: they cried indeed, but no succour appeared. Jews drowned, and so they were swallowed up in water. The master returned with the ship, and told the king how he had used the matter, and had both thanks and reward, as some have written. But others affirm (and more truly, as should seem) that diverse of those mariners, which dealt so wickedly against the Jews, were hanged for their wicked practice, and so received a just reward of their fraudulent and mischievous dealing. But now to the purpose.

In the foresaid parliament, the king demanded an aid of money of the spiritualty, for that (as he pretended) he meant to make a journey into the holy land, to succour the Christians there, whereupon they granted to him the eleventh part of all their movables. He received the money aforehand, but [taken up with] other business at home, he went not forth upon that journey.

---

1   *wile*   Clever trick.

Title page, *Coryat's Crudities*, 1611. (Detail.) This image of Coryate being chased by a Jew with a knife is one of several illustrations included on the title page of the first edition of *Coryat's Crudities* (see also below). No such incident is mentioned in Coryate's text, but a poem of commendation included in the volume includes this advice: "fly from the Jews, lest they circumcise thee." Coryate writes briefly in the passage provided below of the practise of circumcision, and notes that he "had not the opportunity to see it" in Venice. He does include elsewhere in the volume a fairly detailed account of witnessing the circumcision of a Jewish baby in Constantinople; as James Shapiro has pointed out, a fascination with (and anxiety over) the Jewish practice of circumcision is a recurrent theme in English writing of the early modern period.

7. from Thomas Coryate, *Coryat's Crudities* (1611)

The son of a rector, Thomas Coryate (or Coryat) (1577?–1617) studied at Oxford but never completed his degree. After a five-month journey around Europe—predominantly on foot—Coryate wrote *Coryat's
Crudities* in 1608. (The work itself was published in 1611.) An ardent
traveler, Coryate also journeyed through countries farther afield, including Turkey, Persia, and Egypt. He died in India in 1617.

Coryat's Crudities is exceptionally long—nearly 800 pages—and
provides its readers with detailed accounts of foreign lands and unique
articulations of the habits and customs of those abroad. Written by an
Englishman who visited Venice, the publication is of particular interest to readers of *The Merchant of Venice*; Coryate's account is the most
extensive description by an Englishman we have of Jewish practices in
Venice during this period.

Coryate presumably left his home country armed with stereotypical English perceptions of Jewish people—including stereotypical associations between Jews and certain physical characteristics regarded
as highly unpleasant. Barabas, for example, in *The Jew of Malta*, is a
"bottle-nosed knave" (3.3.10). In a cookbook entitled *Dyets Dry Dinner*, Henry Buttes claimed in 1599 that "Jews are great goose-eaters;
therefore their complexion is passing melancholious, their colour
swart, and their diseases very perilous." George Sandys noted that he
saw Jewish women in Turkey who were "generally fat, and ranke of the
savors which attend upon sluttish corpulency"—one of many remarks
made by various English writers regarding Jews' supposed stench (or
foetor judaicus). By observing the dissimilarity of Venetian Jewish individuals to English stereotypes, Coryate was quickly disarmed of the
common caricatures as to appearance.

In other respects, however, his prejudice against Jews and against
Judaism has clearly remained undisturbed. Indeed, his presumption
in attempting to persuade a Rabbi to see the error of his ways and
convert to Christianity (accompanied by increasingly venomous commentary about Jews) is a quite extraordinary case study in the psychology of prejudice—all the more striking, perhaps, for Coryate's initial
tone of disinterested curiosity.

I was at a place where the whole fraternity of the Jews dwelleth together, which is called the Ghetto, being an island, for it is enclosed round about with water. It is thought there are of them in all betwixt five and six thousand. They are distinguished and discerned from the Christians by their habits on their heads; for some of them do wear hats and those red, only those Jews that are born in the Western parts of the world, as in Italy, &c. but the eastern Jews (being otherwise called the Levantine Jews), which are born in Jerusalem, Constantinople, and Alexandria, etc., wear turbans upon their heads as the Turks do. But the difference is this: the Turks wear white, the Jews yellow. By that word turban I understand a roll of fine linen wrapped together upon their heads, which serveth them instead of hats, whereof many have been often worn by the Turks in London. They have divers Synagogues Divine in their Ghetto, at the least seven, where all of them, both men, women, and children, do meet together upon their Sabbath, which is Saturday, to the end to do their devotion, and serve God in their kind, each company having a several Synagogue. In the midst of the Synagogue they have a round seat made of wainscot, having eight open spaces therein, at two whereof which are at the sides, they enter into the seat as by doors. The Levite that readeth the law to them, hath before him at the time of divine service an exceeding long piece of parchment, rolled up upon two wooden handles: in which is written the whole sum and contents of Moses' law in Hebrew: that doth he (being discerned from the lay people only by wearing of a red cap, whereas the others do wear red hats) pronounce before the congregation not by a sober, distinct, and orderly reading, but by an exceeding loud yelling, indecent roaring, and as it were a beastly bellowing of it forth.... I think the hearers can very hardly understand him: sometimes he cries out alone, and sometimes again some others serving as it were his clerks ... do roar with him, but so that his voice (which he straineth so high as if he sung for a wager) drowneth all the rest. Amongst others that are within the room with him, one is he that cometh purposely thither from his seat, [in order] to read the law, and pronounce some part of it with him, who when he is gone, another riseth from his seat, and cometh thither to supply his room. This order they keep from the beginning of service to the end. One custom I observed amongst them very irreverent and profane, that none of them, either when they enter the Synagogue, or when they sit down in their places, or when they go forth again, do any reverence or obeisance, answerable to such a place of the worship of God, either by uncovering their heads, kneeling, or any other external gesture, but boldly dash into the room with their Hebrew books in their hands, and presently sit in their places, without any more ado; every one of them whatsoever he be, man or childe, weareth a kind of light yellowish veil ... over his shoulders, something worse than our courser Holland [wool], which reacheth a little beneath the middle of their backs. They have a great company of candlesticks in each Synagogue made partly of glass, and partly of brass and pewter, which hang square about their Synagogue....

I observed some few of those Jews especially some of the Levantines to be such goodly and proper men, that then I said to myself our English proverb: To look like a Jew (whereby is meant sometimes a weather beaten warp-faced fellow, sometimes a frenetic and lunatic person, sometimes one discontented) is not true. For indeed I noted some of them to be most elegant and sweet featured persons, which gave me occasion the more to lament their religion. For if they were Christians, then could I better apply unto them that excellent verse of the Poet, than I can now: *Gratior est pulchro veniens e corpore virtus.*[1]

In the room wherein they celebrate their divine service, no women sit, but have a loft or gallery proper to themselves only, where I saw many Jewish women, whereof some were as beautiful as ever I saw, and so gorgeous in their apparel, jewels, chains of gold, and rings adorned with precious stones, that some of our English Countesses do scarce exceed them, having marvellous long trains like princesses that are borne up by waiting women serving for the same purpose. One thing they observe in their service which is utterly condemned by our Saviour Christ, that is a very tedious babbling, and an often repetition of one thing.... Their service is almost three hours long. They are very religious in two things only, and no more, in that they worship no images, and that they keep their sabbath so strictly, that upon that day they will neither buy nor sell, nor do any secular, profane, or irreligious exercise (I would to God our Christians would imitate the Jews herein), no not so much as dress their victuals, which is always done the day before, but dedicate and consecrate themselves

---

1   *Gratior ... virtus*   Latin: Virtue becomes even more pleasing when it appears in a pleasing form.

wholly to the strict worship of God. Their circumcision they observe as duly as they did any time betwixt Abraham (in whose time it was first instituted) and the incarnation of Christ. For they use to circumcise every male child when he is eight days old, with a stony knife. But I had not the opportunity to see it. Likewise they keep many of those ancient feasts that were instituted by Moses.... Truly it is a most lamentable case for a Christian to consider the damnable estate of these miserable Jews, in that they reject the true Messiah and Saviour of their souls, hoping to be saved rather by the observation of those Mosaical ceremonies, whereof was fully expired at Christ's incarnation, than by the merits of the Saviour of the world, without whom all mankind shall perish. And as pitiful it is to see that few of them living in Italy are converted to the Christian religion. For this I understand is the main impediment to their conversion: All their goods are confiscated as soon as they embrace Christianity: and this I heard is the reason, because whereas many of them do raise their fortunes by usury, in so much that they do not only shear, but also fleece many a poor Christian's estate by their griping extortion; it is therefore decreed by the Pope, and other free Princes in whose territories they live, that they shall make a restitution of all their ill gotten goods, and so dis-clog their souls and consciences, when they are admitted by holy baptism into the bosom of Christ's Church. Seeing then when their goods are taken from them at their conversion, they are left even naked, and destitute of their means of maintenance, there are fewer Jews converted to Christianity in Italy, than in any country of Christendom. Whereas in Germany, Poland, and other places the Jews that are converted (which doth often happen, as Emanuel Tremellius was converted in Germany) do enjoy their estates as they did before.

But now I will make relation of that which I promised in my treatise of Padua, I mean my discourse with the Jews about their religion. For when I was walking in the Jewish court of the Ghetto, I casually met with a certain learned Jewish Rabbi that spake good Latin. I insinuated myself after some few terms of complement into conference with him, and asked him his opinion of Christ, and why he did not receive him for his Messiah; he made me the same answer that the Turk did at Lyons, of whom I have before spoken, that Christ forsooth was a great Prophet, and in that respect as highly to be esteemed as any Prophet amongst the Jews that ever lived before him; but derogated altogether from his divinity, and would not acknowledge him for the Messiah and Saviour of the world, because he came so contemptibly, and not with that pomp and majesty that beseemed the redeemer of mankind. I replied that we Christians do, and will, even to the effusion of our vital blood, confess him to be the true and only Messiah of the world, seeing he confirmed his Doctrine while he was here on earth, with such an innumerable multitude of divine miracles, which did most infallibly testify his divinity; and that they themselves, who are Christ's irreconcilable enemies, could not produce any authority either out of Moses, the Prophets, or any other authentic author to strengthen their opinion ... concerning the temporal kingdom of the Messiah, seeing it was foretold to be spiritual: and I told him that Christ did as a spiritual King reign over his subjects in conquering their spiritual enemies the flesh, the world, and the devil.... and at last [I came] to the persuasion of him to abandon and renounce his Jewish religion and to undertake the Christian faith, without the which he should be eternally damned. He again replied that we Christians do misinterpret the Christian Prophets, and very perversely wrest them to our own sense, and for his own part he had confidently resolved to live and die in his Jewish faith, hoping to be saved by the observations of Moses' Law.

In the end he seemed to be somewhat exasperated against me, because I [had] sharply taxed their superstitious ceremonies. For many of them are such refractory people that they cannot endure to hear any reconciliation to the Church of Christ, in regard they esteem him but for a carpenter's son, and a silly poor wretch that once rode upon an ass, and most unworthy to be the Messiah, whom they expect to come with most pompous magnificence and imperial royalty ... and make the King of Guiana, and all other Princes whatsoever dwelling in the remotest parts of the habitable world his tributary vassals. Thus hath God justly infatuated their understandings, and given them the spirit of slumber (as Saint Paul speaketh out of the Prophet Esau)— eyes that they should not see, and ears that they should not hear unto this day.[1] But to shut up this narration of my conflict with the Jewish Rabbi, after there had passed many vehement speeches to and fro betwixt us, it happened that some forty or fifty Jews more flocked about me, and some of them began very insolently to swagger with

---

1   *spirit of ... this day*   Cf. Romans 11.8.

me, because I durst reprehend their religion: Whereupon, fearing lest they would have offered me some violence, I withdrew myself by little and little towards the bridge at the entrance into the Ghetto, with an intent to fly from them, but by good fortune our noble Ambassador Sir Henry Wotton passing under the bridge in his Gondola at that very time, espied me somewhat earnestly bickering with them, and so incontinently[1] sent unto me out of his boat one of his principal gentlemen, Master Belford his secretary, who conveyed me safely from these unchristian miscreants, which perhaps would have given me just occasion to forswear any more coming to the Ghetto.

Thus much for the Jewish Ghetto, their service, and my discourse with one of their Rabbis.

8. from Leon of Modena, *History of the Present Jews throughout the World* (c. 1616)

A distinguished rabbi with an addiction to gambling, a musician, a failed alchemist, and the author of many books, Leon of Modena (1571–1648) is one of the most interesting figures of the late Renaissance. Sometime around 1616 (according to Leon's autobiography), he was asked by Sir Henry Wotton (then the English ambassador to Venice) to write a description of Jewish religious practices that Wotton could present to King James. The resulting book, *Historia de' Riti Hebraici*, was circulated widely in manuscript in its original Italian, and was translated into a variety of languages (including an English translation by Edmund Chilmead in 1650 under the title *The History of the Rites, Customs, and Manner of Life, of the Present Jews, throughout the World*). The book continued to be widely read and influential in the eighteenth century, having been newly translated by Simon Ockley in 1707. (It is Ockley's translation that appears here.) In its tone as well as its content, Leon's account of Jewish rites and practices makes an instructive point of comparison with, for example, that of Thomas Coryate (see C.7 above). Interestingly, Leon uses the third person throughout—consistently referring to the Jews as "they" rather than as "we." (See appendices E.10 and E.11 for additional excerpts from Leon's work.)

---

1   *incontinently*   Quickly, expeditiously.

from the Introduction

Many Christians, of great piety and learning, have desired to have a faithful and complete account of the rites and customs of the present Jews; the foundation of whose religion, I humbly hope none will deny, ... did originally spring from the fountain of infinite wisdom....

In the management of the whole, I have kept myself strictly to truth, considering myself as a Jew; and therefore ought to be a plain and impartial relator, only I must ingenuously confess that I have endeavored to avoid giving the reader any just occasion to despise the Jews for their multiplicity of ceremonies; but have not in the least taken upon me to apologise for or defend them; my whole design being only to give a just and faithful narration of them, and not to gain proselytes to them.

from Part 1
from Chapter 2: Of Their Houses

They admit of no figure, image or statue in their houses, much less in their synagogues and sacred places, because it is said in Exodus, Chapter 20, Thou shalt not make to thy self any graven image, nor the likeness, etc., and in several other places. However in Italy a great many take the liberty to keep [drawings] and pictures in their houses, especially if they are not in *relievo*,[1] nor a whole body, but only the face.

from Chapter 10: Of Their Synagogues or Schools

They build their synagogues (which they call schools) either little or great.... [Upon the walls] there are written some verses, to put them in mind of being attentive in prayer. Round about there are benches to sit on, [and] above there are a great many lamps and candles ... to enlighten the room. At the doors they have little boxes or chests, where everyone that pleases puts in money, which is afterwards given to the poor....

---

1   *relievo*   Relief sculpture (i.e., sculpture in which certain features are raised off the surface to suggest depth and perspective).

In the midst, or else at the upper end of the synagogue, there is a sort of a desk or little altar, made of wood, raised somewhat high, upon which they rest [the book of laws], and which they lean upon when they preach, and upon other occasions.

They have a place by itself, either above or on the one side, enclosed with wooden lattices, where the women stand to say their prayers, and see everything that is done, but cannot be seen by the men, nor do they mix at all with them: which is done for fear their[1] minds should be diverted from their prayers by any evil thoughts.

Nevertheless, the situation and the particular management of all these things vary according to the different customs of the countries and places where they are.

from CHAPTER 11: OF THEIR PRAYERS

They go to prayers in these synagogues three times a day.... There is one that sings the prayers a good deal louder than the rest [the Chanter, who] goes to the little altar, or stands before the Ark or chest, and begins the prayers in a loud voice, and the rest follow him in a softer tone.... The Italians use a plainer tone [than the German, Levantine, Turkish, or Spanish Jews], and not so loud. These prayers contain more words or fewer, according as the days are common or festival, but in these days also they differ among themselves.

9. from Edward Coke, *The Institutes of the Laws of England*, Part 2 (1642)

Sir Edward Coke (pronounced "Cook," 1552–1634) was Attorney General and later Chief Justice of the King's Bench (a senior court of common law). Politically outspoken, Coke argued against the king's prerogative to override common law, and for a variety of actions— including an attempt to impeach Francis Bacon, one of his successors as Attorney General—was sent to the Tower of London in 1622. Coke was eventually released and continued his maverick existence in Parliament.

Coke's *Institutes of the Laws of England* is a four-volume series (1628–44) in which Sir Edward writes about various statutes of Parlia-

---

1   *their*   I.e., the men's.

ment and provides a history of different English courts. In the second volume, Coke writes venomously about Jewish people's practice of usury and promotes the image of Jews as malicious and greedy. At the same time, he recognizes the benefits of usury to rulers who had the right to seize profits from Jewish financiers.

... [T]wo great mischiefs did follow before the making of this statute upon Jewish usury;[1] now the difficulty was how the same should be remedied. The mischiefs were these:

1. The evils and dishersions[2] of the good men of the land.
2. That many of the sins or offences of the realm had risen and been committed by reason thereof, to the great dishonour of Almighty God.

The difficulty how to apply a remedy was, considering what great yearly revenue the King had by the usury of the Jews and how necessary it was that the King should be supplied with treasure. What benefit the Crown had before the making of this act appeareth by former records, as take one for many: from the 17th of December in the 50 year of King Henry III until the Tuesday in Shrovetide the second year of King Edward I, which was about seven years, the Crown had four hundred and twenty thousand pounds fifteen shillings and four pence ... at what time the ounce of silver was but 20 shillings and now it is more than treble so much....

Many prohibitions were made both by this King and others, some time they [the Jews] were banished, but their cruel usury continued, and soon after they returned. And for respect of lucre and gain, King John in the second year of his reign granted unto them large liberties and privileges, whereby the mischiefs rehearsed in this act without measure multiplied.

Our noble King Edward I and his father King Henry III before him, fought by diverse acts and ordinances to use some mean and moderation herein, but in the end it was found that there was no mean in mischief.... And therefore King Edward I as this act said, in the honour of God, and for the common profit of his people, without all respect (in the respect of these) of the filling of his own coffers,

---

1   *this statute ... usury*   Coke is referring to Edward I's *Statutum de Judaismo* (1275), in which the king of England forbade Jews to lend with interest.
2   *dishersions*   Disinheritances.

did ordain, that no Jew from thenceforth would make any bargain, or contract for usury, nor upon any former contract should take any usury; ... so in effect all Jewish usury was forbidden....

This law struck at the root of this pestilent weed, for hereby usury itself was forbidden; and thereupon the cruel Jews thirsting after wicked gain, to the number of 15,060, departed out of this realm into foreign parts, where they might use their Jewish trade of usury, and from that time that nation never returned again into this realm.

Some are of opinion (and so it is said in some of our histories) that it was decreed by the authority of Parliament that the usurious Jews should be banished out of the realm; but the truth is that their usury was banished by this act of Parliament, and that was the cause that they banished themselves into foreign countries, where they might live by their usury.[1] And for that they were odious both to God and man, that they might pass out of the realm in safety, they made petition to the King, that a certain day might be preferred to them to depart the realm, to the end that they might have the King's writ[2] to his sheriffs for their safe conduct, and that no injury, molestation, damage, or grievance be offered to them in the meantime....

And thus this noble King by this means banished forever these infidel usurious Jews; the number of which Jews thus banished was fifteen thousand and threescore.[3] ...

---

1 *Some are ... their usury* Edward I's 1290 edict (see C.3) did in fact banish Jews from the country. Coke may be deliberately distorting the facts, or he may be mistaken; generally speaking, historians of this period did not know a great deal about the expulsion.

2 *writ* Official document.

3 *threescore* Sixty.

D. Revenge

1. from the Geneva Bible,[1] Exodus 21.12–25 (1560)

Lex talionis literally means "the law of retaliation" but is equivalent to the much-used phrase "an eye for an eye." A code of justice that endorses striking back against an aggressor, it is found in the biblical book of Exodus, where it serves as part of the laws of the nation of Israel. As a principle of punishment, it has often been wrongly used to justify unharnessed aggression against an aggressor. In its original context, however, the law is a call for moderation; rather than taking a whole body for an eye, the law suggests the retaliator take only his or her "due." This is in stark contrast to many revengers on the late sixteenth- and early seventeenth-century stage, who leave a bloodbath in their wake, wreaking complete and utter havoc against those who have wronged them.[2]

12 He that smiteth[3] a man, and he die, shall die the death.

13 And if a man hath not laid wait, but God hath offered him into his hand, then I will appoint thee a place whither he shall flee.

14 But if a man come presumptuously upon his neighbour to slay him with guile,[4] thou shalt take him from mine altar, that he may die.

15 Also he that smiteth his father or his mother, shall die the death.

16 And he that stealeth a man, and selleth him, if it be found with him, shall die the death.

17 And he that curseth his father or his mother, shall die the death.

18 When men also strive together, and one smite another with a stone, or with the fist, and he die not but lieth in bed.

19 If he rise again and walk without upon his staff, then shall he that smote him go quit, save only he shall bear his charges for his resting, and shall pay for his healing.

20 And if a man smite his servant, or his maid with a rod, and he die under his hand, he shall be surely punished.

---

1   *Geneva Bible*   For a brief history of the Geneva Bible, please see the introduction to John 8.42–49 (C.1 above).

2   For a discussion of Shylock as a revenger, see the introduction to this volume.

3   *smiteth*   Assaults with a sharp blow.

4   *guile*   Deceit or treachery.

²¹ But if he continue a day or two days, he shall not be punished: for he is his money.[1]

²² Also if men strive and hurt a woman with child, so that her child depart from her and death follow not, he shall be surely punished, according as the woman's husband shall appoint him, or he shall pay as the Judges determine.

²³ But if death follow, then thou shalt pay life for life.

²⁴ Eye for eye, tooth for tooth, hand for hand, foot for foot,

²⁵ Burning for burning, wound for wound, stripe for stripe.

2. Francis Bacon, "Of Revenge" (1625)

In the dedication of his *Essays*, Francis Bacon (1561–1626) predicted that his works would "last as long as books last." Now considered one of the most important writers of the English Renaissance, Bacon is remembered for his philosophical writings, his contributions to the development of the scientific method, and his *Essays*—the first work in English to be published using that term—a collection of brief, incisive pieces on a wide variety of moral, political, religious, and other subjects. Bacon also achieved greatness as a lawyer and statesman, serving as Attorney General and later as Lord Chancellor, official head of the Court of Chancery.

The following piece was first published in the third edition of Bacon's *Essays*. "Of Revenge" is not so much a polemic against retributive justice as it is a reminder to leave justice in the hands of the authorities. Legal justice, Bacon argues, is distinct from private revenge—a kind of retaliation that he contends has no place in a civil society. Rather than addressing those biblical passages condoning an eye for an eye, such as we see in the verses from Exodus (above),[2] Bacon draws on other Old Testament material to argue for forgiveness and patience.

Revenge is a kind of wild justice; which the more man's nature runs to, the more ought law to weed it out. For as for the first wrong, it doth but offend the law; but the revenge of that wrong, putteth the law out of office. Certainly, in taking revenge, a man is but even with

---

1   *for he … his money*   I.e., the slave belongs to the master.
2   For a more detailed explanation of the "eye for an eye" form of justice, see the introduction to Exodus 21.12–25 (D.1 above).

his enemy; but in passing it over, he is superior: for it is a prince's part to pardon. And Solomon,[1] I am sure, saith, It is the glory of a man to pass by an offence. That which is past, is gone, and irrevocable; and wise men have enough to do, with things present, and to come: therefore, they do but trifle with themselves, that labour in past matters. There is no man doth a wrong, for the wrong's sake; but thereby to purchase himself profit, or pleasure, or honour, or the like. Therefore why should I be angry with a man, for loving himself better than me? And if any man should do wrong, merely out of ill nature, why, yet it is but like the thorn, or briar, which prick, and scratch, because they can do no other. The most tolerable sort of revenge, is for those wrongs which there is no law to remedy: but then, let a man take heed the revenge be such as there is no law to punish: else, a man's enemy is still before hand, and it is two for one. Some, when they take revenge, are desirous the party should know whence it cometh: this is the more generous. For the delight seemeth to be, not so much in doing the hurt, as in making the party repent: but base and crafty cowards are like the arrow that flieth in the dark. Cosmus, duke of Florence,[2] had a desperate saying, against perfidious or neglecting friends, as if those wrongs were unpardonable: You shall read (saith he) that we are commanded to forgive our enemies; but you never read, that we are commanded to forgive our friends. But yet the spirit of Job,[3] was in a better tune; Shall we (saith he) take good at God's hands, and not be content to take evil also? And so of friends in a proportion. This is certain; that a man that studieth revenge, keeps his own wounds green, which otherwise would heal, and do well. Public revenges, are, for the most part, fortunate; as that for the death of Caesar; for the death of Pertinax; for the death of Henry the Third of France;[4] and many more. But in private revenges it is not so. Nay rather, vindictive persons live the life of witches; who as they are mischievous, so end they unfortunate.

---

1   *Solomon*   King of Israel (c. tenth century BCE) associated with wisdom.

2   *Cosmus, duke of Florence*   Cosimo "The Great" Gherardini, 1st Duke of Florence (c. 870–950).

3   *Job*   Subject of the Old Testament book of the same name. He endured many trials and misfortunes without wavering in his faith.

4   *Caesar ... of France*   Julius Caesar (r. 49–44 BCE), Roman Emperor Publius Helvius Pertinax (r. 193 CE), and Henry III (r. 1574–89), were all assassinated during times of instability in the states over which they ruled.

E. Commercial Life: Of Venice, Merchants, Usurers, and Debtors

1. The Geneva Bible (1560) on Usury and Generosity

The biblical verses below all deal in one way or another with lending, borrowing, and usury. The passage from Deuteronomy contains the most contentious set of verses; the interpretation of the Hebrew word "ger" (commonly translated as "stranger" or "foreigner") led to a great divide over issues relating to the practice of moneylending. Whereas most Christians interpreted it to mean that usury was a sin, most Jews interpreted it to mean lending "upon usury" to fellow Jews was a sin, but not to non-Jews. There was further disagreement as to what constituted usury; did the charging of interest constitute usury? Did the charging of a fee constitute usury? Did the charging of a substantial penalty for non-payment of a bond constitute usury? On all these questions opinions differed—and also changed over time. According to the most widespread Jewish interpretation of the text, lending at interest by Jews to non-Jews was not exploitative, since there was potential mutual advantage in the transaction. When, in 1571, England legalized lending money at interest, one of the justifications used was a similar concept of mutually beneficial exchange: it formed a relationship between those in need of money and those who had it. Shylock references this principle in 1.3 when he determines that he can borrow some of the three thousand ducats Bassanio requires from his fellow "wealthy Hebrew," Tubal.

a. Exodus 22.22–27

²² Ye shall not trouble any widow, nor fatherless child.
²³ If thou vex or trouble such, and so he call and cry unto me, I will surely hear his cry.
²⁴ Then shall my wrath be kindled, and I will kill you with the sword, and your wives shall be widows, and your children fatherless.
²⁵ If thou lend money to my people, that is, to the poor with thee, thou shalt not be as a usurer unto him: ye shall not oppress him with usury.

^{26} If thou take thy neighbour's raiment[1] to pledge, thou shalt restore it unto him before the sun go down.

^{27} For that is his covering only, and this is his garment for his skin: wherein shall he sleep? Therefore when he crieth unto me, I will hear him: for I am merciful.

b. Leviticus 25.35–37

^{35} Moreover, if thy brother be impoverished, and fallen in decay with thee, thou shalt relieve him, and as a stranger and sojourner, so shall he live with thee.

^{36} Thou shalt take no usury of him, nor vantage, but thou shalt fear thy God, that thy brother may live with thee.

^{37} Thou shalt not give him thy money to usury, nor lend him thy vittles[2] for increase.

c. Deuteronomy 23.19–20

^{19} Thou shalt not give to usury to thy brother: as usury of money, usury of meat, usury of anything that is put to usury.

^{20} Unto a stranger thou mayest lend upon usury, but thou shalt not lend upon usury unto thy brother, that the Lord thy God may bless thee in all that thou settest thine hand to, in the land whither thou goest to possess it.

d. Psalms 15.1–5

15 Lord, who shall dwell in thy Tabernacle?[3] who shall rest in thine holy Mountain?

^{2} He that walketh uprightly and worketh righteousness, and speaketh the truth in his heart.

^{3} He that slandereth not with his tongue, nor doeth evil to his neighbour, nor receiveth a false report against his neighbour.

^{4} In whose eyes a vile person is contemned, but he honoureth them that fear the Lord: he that sweareth to his own hindrance and changeth not.

---

1   *raiment*   Clothing.
2   *vittles*   Stores of food and other supplies.
3   *Tabernacle*   Temporary haven, or community worship house.

⁵ He that giveth not his money unto usury, nor taketh reward against the innocent: he that doeth these things, shall never be moved.

e. Ezekiel 18.7–13

⁷ Neither hath oppressed any, but hath restored the pledge to his debtor: he that hath spoiled none by violence, but hath given his bread to the hungry, and hath covered the naked with a garment,

⁸ And hath not given forth upon usury, neither hath taken any increase, but hath withdrawn his hand from iniquity, and hath executed true judgment between man and man,

⁹ And hath walked in my statutes, and hath kept my judgments to deal truly, he is just, he shall surely live, saith the Lord God.

¹⁰ If he beget a son, that is a thief, or a shedder of blood, if he do any one of these things,

¹¹ Though he do not all these things, but either hath eaten upon the mountains,[1] or defiled his neighbour's wife,

¹² Or hath oppressed the poor and needy, or hath spoiled by violence, or hath not restored the pledge, or hath lifted up his eyes unto the idols, or hath committed abomination,

¹³ Or hath given forth upon usury, or hath taken increase, shall he live? He shall not live: seeing he hath done all these abominations, he shall die the death, and his blood shall be upon him.

2. from Thomas Wilson, *A Discourse upon Usury* (1572)

Thomas Wilson (1523/24–81) was a Protestant humanist who served as a successful diplomat and later as a Privy Councillor and as Secretary of State for Elizabeth I. Of the six books he wrote, Wilson's most enduring composition is *The Art of Rhetoric* (1554).

Wilson's diplomatic missions exposed him to a wide variety of foreign commercial practices; he drew on this knowledge to write *A Discourse upon Usury* (1572), in which he denounced the act of moneylending for interest. While he presents arguments in the form of orations delivered by a lawyer and a merchant on one side and a preacher on the other, the victory of the preacher makes Wilson's message clear; his extended commentary on biblical injunctions against

---

1 *eaten ... mountains* I.e., made sacrifices to false idols (and eaten the sacrificed food). Such rituals often took place in mountain settings.

usury[1] aligns him with other conservatives. Though the lending of money at interest had been legalized in England the year before *A Discourse upon Usury* was published (Wilson, as an MP for London in 1571, had been closely involved in the debates over the bill), the controversy over these issues continued, and it remained illegal to charge *excessive* rates of interest. (Interestingly, Shakespeare's own father would be accused twice under this law.)

A COMMUNICATION OR SPEECH BETWEEN THE RICH WORLDLY MERCHANT, THE GODLY AND ZEALOUS PREACHER, THE TEMPORAL AND CIVIL LAWYERS, TOUCHING USURY, OR THE LOAN OF MONEY FOR GAIN.

About two years past (as I remember) a jolly merchant of London, after he had heard a most earnest sermon against usury in his parish church, did invite the preacher to dinner, having purposed before to have certain of his friends and acquaintances the same day at dinner also with him....

PREACHER. ... [T]ouching lending of money, I think men rather seek their own gain, than anything the benefit of their Christian neighbour.

LAWYER. Nay, both, and who I pray you would lend but to have some benefit of his money? And is that any harm when both do gain?

MERCHANT. God's blessing of your heart for so saying, for I did never lend money in my life but for gain, and whether my neighbour gained, or no....

PREACHER. Herein you wanted charity, and showed yourself not to be a perfect Christian.

LAWYER. I cannot tell what you call a Christian. They that will live in this world must do so....

PREACHER. Theft is counted so horrible amongst some nations, that men commonly will rather starve then steal, and here in England he that can rob a man by the highway is called a tall fellow.[2] Again, they do less oppress their neighbours elsewhere, they are more temperate in their speech, and more spare of diet than we

---

1   See E.1 above for more on usury in the Bible.
2   *tall fellow*   Brave man.

commonly are, and that which grieveth me most [is that there are fewer] extortioners, and fewer usurers elsewhere than are here in England.

LAWYER. All countries have their faults, and I cannot excuse England, but yet I will not so accuse my country that I will make it altogether worse than others…. And as every one of these countries hath his especial faults, so have they their proper virtues and several qualities, more excellent than any other nation.

PREACHER. My desire is that England might be most perfect and without any fault, if it were possible, and would Christ there were none other fault in England than gluttony in the most, theft in many mean[1] men, and treason in some great folk. But I say there wanteth charity, without which there cannot be perfection in any man…. You go about, sir, to persuade the rich man that his treasure is his chief assurance and best friend, whereas he ought to lay up his treasure where neither moths nor rust should corrupt and consume it, and so he should have the reward at God's hand. Therefore I say still, charitable dealing is the most assured and best wealth that a man can purchase upon earth, for where all other worldly substance faileth and consumeth away, this continueth for ever, and is a token of perfect Christianity, when men show their faith and belief by their good living and well doing.

MERCHANT. When I am dead, I may perhaps do good; but so long as I live, I will save one, and be sure not to want. Lay it up in heaven quoth he? A merry jest indeed! So long as I live, I will keep it in a chest, and have the key about me.

LAWYER. Indeed I must needs say that willful poverty is the greatest folly in the world, and for a man to want himself,[2] by giving to others, is the eighth deadly sin, the which I call extreme folly or madness.

PREACHER. If you will not, when you have it in your own possession, bestow it upon others for Christ's sake, because you fear to want, then be you assured, if you give your goods after your decease when they can do you no good at all, because then you are not, as being dead and without sense, God will little esteem such….

---

1   *mean* Lowly, poor.
2   *want himself* Put himself in a position of poverty.

Therefore I say still, use charity while you may, and help the needy and poor, and not only lend friendly, but also give freely to your power.

LAWYER. ... This is a hard thunderbolt, and such a one as, I think, all men are afraid of, for very few follow that lesson, say you what you will. But I see you are much grieved with usury, amongst all other sins, and in all your sermons and preachings you rattle so greatly against this offence, that you shake the blood of some, till they blush as red as their cloaks....

PREACHER. The Saint Augustine and all the doctors are so much against usury, that they will not have any good deed done, nor alms bestowed, nor orphans aided, nor widows relieved, nor captors redeemed, by way of usury, but wholly and utterly forbid it as a most wicked and detestable sin, according to the saying of St. Paul: man must not do any evil, that good may come thereof.[1] And whereof cometh this foul usury? For sooth of covetousness, which, as St. Paul saith, is the root of all mischief.[2] ... [W]hat can be worse than the usurer, who is without all love and charity, and hath no pity of his neighbour, in what misery or want so ever he be? The poor may starve, and die in the streets, for any mercy or charity that they will show, whereas, if they were of God, they should remember the poor and needy, and not only to lend freely but also give alms frankly.... And in the law of Moses God saith: when one of thy brethren among you is waxen poor in any of the cities within thy land which the lord thy God giveth thee, see thou harden not thine heart, nor shut thy hand from thy poor brother, but open thy hand unto him, and lend him sufficient for his need which he hath, and let it not grieve thine heart to give, because that for that thing the lord thy God shall bless thee in all thy works, and in all that thou puttest thy hand to, for the land shall never be without poor, wherefore I command thee saying: open thine hand unto thy brother that is needy and poor in thy land.[3] Yet, all this notwithstanding, the usurer is as deaf as a door nail, as blind as a

---

1   *Saint Augustine*   Theologian (354–430) and bishop of Hippo whose teachings strongly influenced medieval and later Catholic philosophy;   *doctors*   I.e., Doctors of the Church, people who have been officially recognized by the Catholic Church for their work in theology;   *saying of ... come thereof*   See Romans 3.7–8.

2   *covetousness ... mischief*   See 1 Timothy 6.10.

3   *when one of ... land*   See Deuteronomy 15.7–11.

beetle, and as hard hearted as a flint stone, whose mind God for his great mercy soften....

What is the matter that Jews are so universally hated wheresoever they come? Forsooth, usury is one of the chief causes, for they rob all men that deal with them, and undo them in the end. And for this cause they were hated in England, and so banished worthily, with whom I would wish all these Englishmen were sent that lend their money or their goods whatsoever for gain, for I take them to be no better than Jews. Nay, shall I say: they are worse than Jews. For go whither you will throughout Christendom, and deal with them,[1] and you shall have under ten in the hundredth,[2] yea sometimes for six at their hands, whereas English usurers exceed all God's mercy, and will take they care not how much....

THE MERCHANT OR GROMWELL GAINER.[3]   I have heard you say, master Preacher, and I have heard it also of others, that God in the scriptures affirmeth it to be an easier matter for a camel to go through the eye of a needle, than for a rich man to enter into the kingdom of heaven.[4] Surely I believe it to be true, except God's goodness be the greater, for we merchants are marvellously given to get goods without conscience....   And this world is a great temptation for man to advance his welfare, and hardly can one avoid the sweet enticements thereof. For what is he nowadays that is of any estimation, if he want[5] wealth? Who maketh any account of him, be he never so learned, never so virtuous, or never so worthy, that hath not the goods of this world?

... But fie of this world, in respect of the world to come! And I thank you master Preacher, for such your heavenly doctrine. For I promise you I am now become through the same (as I trust) a new man, praised be God and you therefore. And now I do as much abhor to lend money for gain hereafter, as I do abhor to steal by the highway, or to murder any man violently for his goods, which God forbid that ever I should think or mind to do....

---

1   *them*   I.e., Jews.
2   *in the hundredth*   Per cent.
3   *Gromwell Gainer*   I.e., penny-pincher, hoarder.
4   *easier ... heaven*   See Matthew 19.24.
5   *want*   I.e., lacks.

3. from Zuane di Andrea Zane and Brothers, Petition to the Senate[1] (31 July 1550)

The tale of misfortune told by these brothers provides some sense of the perils that maritime merchants could be exposed to. It is of course possible that the family may have painted their misfortunes in the most disastrous light to assist their appeal for aid, but even if some allowance is made for that possibility, the account remains an extraordinary record of suffering.

We will not count among our losses the damage inflicted by the Rialto fire,[2] nor what the sea took from us at that time, nor yet the large sums borne away by debtors, nor yet the marriage portions of our three sisters ...—although these things amount to a great deal of money. We will speak only of the disasters which have overtaken us since the year 1524. In April of that year we sent a ship of 1,300 butts to England, and our brother Beneto was aboard it, armed with the most ample safe-conduct from the Most Christian King.[3] On its return voyage from England in May this ship was attacked off Cádiz[4] ... and captured after a lengthy fight. In defending himself our brother received seventeen wounds, and, being so dreadfully torn and mutilated, he was taken prisoner. It was not God's will that he should die then, but ill fortune kept a far worse fate in store for him. Upon that ship were our wools, kerseys, cloths and tin, and a large sum in cash to buy salt at Ibiza[5] if other business should be lacking—so that, taking account of the ship itself, equipped as it was with guns and with everything else necessary to sailing such seas and encountering so many different peoples, and taking account too of our own merchandise and money, the loss amounted to over 22,000 ducats. We say nothing of the cargo of sugar we were due to take on in Cádiz and the profit expected from the merchandise and from various freight charges of more than 8,000 ducats, and there was a clear

---

1 *Petition to the Senate* Translated by Brian Pullan, from David Chambers and Brian Pullan, eds., *Venice: A Documentary History, 1450–1630*. Reprinted with permission.

2 *Rialto fire* Major city fire in 1514.

3 *butts* Barrels; *safe-conduct* Official document ensuring protection on a journey through a particular area; *Most Christian King* I.e., the king of France.

4 *Cádiz* Port and popular trade destination in southwestern Spain.

5 *kerseys* Rough wool fabrics; *Ibiza* Western Mediterranean port.

Pieter Bruegel the Elder, *The Storm at Sea*, 1568. *The Storm at Sea* aptly captures the perils of marine travel in the second half of the sixteenth century. The artist, Pieter Bruegel the Elder (c. 1525–69), came from a long line of artists; he continues to be remembered as one of the finest Flemish painters. His work ranged widely, from landscapes to religious scenes; *The Storm at Sea* is one of many drawings and paintings in which Bruegel took the sea as his subject. An unfinished oil on panel, it is probably his last painting.

loss of another 11,000 ducats and more—a thing one shudders even to hear about, let alone suffer oneself, and all the worse because at that time we were debtors on Rialto for more than 7,000 ducats.

A year later, our brother Beneto escaped from the captain's clutches. He then went to the Most Christian King to recover what he could and he engaged in prolonged dispute with the captain and his men for eight months and more at a stretch. At last his case was brought before His Royal Majesty ... [and the king] promised him a prompt and fair judgement. After this was known, when our brother, accompanied by the secretary Don Hieronimo da Canal, was returning from a visit to the Grand Chancellor's secretary concerning the lawsuit, at about the first hour of the night, he found armed men waiting for him at the Venetian ambassador's door, and was wounded many times and killed. So we lost our beloved brother and everything with him, and all the disasters overtook us, so that we suffered inestimable losses, were impoverished at the instance of our creditors, and were deprived of all hope. But, since we deserve justice, because we suffered such terrible violence despite that very full safe-conduct which we had and still have from that Most Christian King, ... we hope that through your boundless goodness and mercy this just reprisal[1] may be converted into some other form of redress and that this may be offered to us.[2]

4. from William Thomas, *The History of Italy* (1549)

Thomas was an Englishman who lived mostly in Italy from 1544 to 1549. In addition to his *History of Italy* he was the author of a work defending Henry VIII and of an Italian-English dictionary. On his return to England he served as an advisor to Edward VI; a Protestant, he fell out of favor under Queen Mary and was executed in 1554. Thomas's account of life in Venice in the late 1540s is in several respects in marked contrast to that provided in 1612 by Dudley Carleton (see the Introduction to this volume), as well as to that depicted in

---

1   *reprisal* Payment made in compensation for a loss.
2   *some other ... to us* The Zane brothers were each granted a monthly pension of ten ducats, to last for the rest of their lives. If any of them died within the first six years of the commencement of this pension, that pension was to be shared among the others for the rest of the six years.

The Merchant of Venice. Though impressions are of course subjective, it is reasonable to think that much of the difference may be attributed simply to societal change—that, for example, the typical Venice merchant of 1612 had acquired a substantially more profligate character than his predecessor of three generations earlier.

The principal merchants [in Italy as a whole] are for the most part gentlemen. For when there be of one house three or four brethren, [often] two or three of them dispose themselves to merchandise.... They carry neither weapon nor armour but do what they can to live in peace, not only searching the trades of all countries with their merchandise but also occupying at home the most substantial farms, and possessions by their factors [i.e., agents] as hereafter more plainly it followeth.... There be such numbers of wealthy men in that country as the like is not to be found any otherwhere. For in diverse cities in Italy it is no marvel to see twenty persons in a city with 100,000 crowns apiece, and upwards.[1]...

... He that beholdeth the place where Venice standeth ... should say it were the rudest, unmeetest, and unwholesomest place to build upon or to inhabit that were again to be found throughout an whole world. It standeth upon the main sea, four miles from the nearest mainland, in such a march as every low water leaveth the muddy ground uncovered....

It is almost incredible what gain the Venetians receive by the usury of the Jews, both privately and in common. For in every city the Jews keep open shops of usury, taking gages of ordinary for fifteen in the hundred by the year, and if at the year's end the gage be not redeemed it is forefeet, or at the least done away to a great disadvantage, by reason whereof the Jews are out of measure wealthy in those parts....

... The statutes and customs of the city ... are so many that in manner they suffice of themselves. But he that substantially considereth the manner of their proceedings shall plainly see that all matters are determined by the judges' consciences and not by the ... laws....

To speak of the greater number [of Venetians], strangers use to report that the gentleman Venetian is proud, disdainful, covetous, a great niggard, ... spare of living, tyrant to his tenant, finally never

---

1 *in diverse cities ... upwards* Historian George B. Parks estimates in commenting on this passage that the equivalent amount in English currency would have been £25,000.

satisfied with hoarding up of money. For though ... he hath eight, nine, ten thousand ducats of yearly revenue, yet he will keep no more persons in his house but his wife and children, with two or three women servants and one man, or two at the most, to row his gondola. He will go to the market himself and spend so miserably that many a mean[1] man shall fare better than he.... Besides all this, he hath two or three Jews that chop and change with him daily, by whose usury he gaineth out of measure. And yet he would rather see a poor man starve than relieve him with a penny.... Finally, his greatest triumph is when [the Venetian government] hath need, to be able to disburse an huge sum of money in loan, to receive yearly till he be repaid ten, twelve, or fifteen of the hundred. This kind of [financial transaction] the Signoria useth to take (borrowing of all them that are able to lend) when they happen to have wars. And they that may, do the more willingly lend because they are not only well paid again with the usury but also the more honoured and favoured....

... Further, he that dwelleth in Venice may reckon himself exempt from subjection. For no man there marketh another's doings, or that meddleth with another man's living. If thou be a papist, thou shalt want no kind of superstition to feed upon. If thou be a gospeler,[2] no man shall ask why thou comest not to church. If thou be a Jew, a Turk, or believest in the devil (so [long as] thou spread not thine opinions abroad) thou art free from all controlment. To live married or unmarried, no man shall ask thee why.... And generally, of all other things, so [long as] thou offend no man privately, no man shall offend thee, which undoubtedly is one principal cause that draweth so many strangers thither....

5. from Yehiel Nissim Da Pisa, *The Eternal Life* (1559)

Da Pisa (1507–c. 1573) was trained in Pisa in northern Italy both as a banker and as a religious scholar. His treatise *The Eternal Life*, which appears to have circulated only in manuscript form in the sixteenth century, is focused on the various issues regarding the charging of interest.

---

1   *mean*   Less well-off.
2   *gospeler*   Evangelist, Protestant. As in the rest of Italy, churches in Venice were with few exceptions Catholic.

from Chapter 1

... [W]e shall, by way of introduction, offer two introductory statements that will serve as the fundamentals and bases on which our treatise will be built.... The first principle is that whosoever goes by the name of an Israelite and enters the religion of Moses, of blessed memory, is consequently obliged to observe the ... commandments of the Torah....

The second principle is that the matter of lending on interest between Jew and Jew is prohibited from the Torah....

from Chapter 10

Interest which is proscribed by the Torah is that which is lent from one Jew to another, as it is written, "Thou shalt not lend on interest to thy brother." This means that anyone who enters into the realm of the Torah of Moses and takes upon himself God's commandments, even if he be originally a gentile ... is in the category of "thy brother," and one may not lend to him upon interest. However, one may lend on interest to a gentile, for the Torah has specifically permitted such a practice by stating "Unto a foreigner thou may lend upon interest." Though we say that one may not defraud a gentile, one may lend to him on interest since he has voluntarily and of his own accord chosen to pay the sum. The codifiers are divided on this point [as to whether one is merely permitted to charge interest to gentiles, or positively required to do so;] Maimonides[1] counted this among the positive commandments.... Rabbi Moses of Coucy[2] and others did not count this among the positive precepts, but have declared it to be merely a permissive act—that is, when one lends to a gentile, one may receive interest from him.... My opinion is that this is merely a permissive act.... In our times, it is the practice to permit lending on interest to gentiles for more than a mere living. In all the nations of Christendom, the practice of lending money is as widespread as other business enterprises.

---

1   *Maimonides*   Prominent Sephardic Jewish philosopher (1138–1204).
2   *Rabbi Moses of Coucy*   Moses ben Jacob of Coucy, thirteenth-century scholar of Jewish law.

6. from Thomas Lupton, *The Second Part and Knitting Up of the Book Entitled Too Good to Be True* (1581)

Thomas Lupton (fl. 1572–84), who wrote in multiple genres, was the author of several works focused on money, including a dialogue on greed titled "A Dreame of the Devil and Dives" and a morality play, *All for Money*, which suggests that money leads to the ruin of society, religion, and law.

The first part of *Siuqila Too Good to Be True* appeared in 1580; a second part Dedicated to William Cecil, Lord Burghley, the chief advisor to Elizabeth I, was issued a year later. The work is a satire calling for changes to England's laws and customs. In its utopian dialogue structure, it is reminiscent of Thomas More's much more famous *Utopia* (1516). *Too Good to Be True* features a citizen of Lupton's fictional commonwealth, Mauqsun—a play on *nusquam* (Latin: nowhere). The resident's name is Omen—a play on *nemo* (Latin: nobody)—and he discusses the utopia's foundations with an English traveler named Siuqila, whose name is a play on *aliquis* (Latin: someone). The utopia, which is presented as a preferable alternative to England, is distinguished by its devoutness, which is ensured by a vigilant government that fiercely punishes nonconformists. One object of Lupton's satire was the then-new practice of punishing defaulting debtors with imprisonment. The excerpt below recounts an absurd episode in which two charitable men vie for the privilege of paying a £20 debt owed by a prisoner (and thereby securing his release from prison).

OMEN. And on a certain day, it was two men's chances to meet at one time at one prison, to visit what prisoners were there: and the keeper answered them, that then there was but only one in prison, which when they heard, they earnestly desired the keeper, that they might speak with him. You shall with a good will, said he. And so they both went unto the prisoner, whom they asked, how long he had been there: the prisoner said, I have been here yet scant[1] a whole day: wherefore do you lie here, said the one of them: Forsooth, said he, for debt, and that is twenty pounds, which I am not able to pay, yet I was once within this twelve

---

1   *scant*   Hardly.

month, worth a hundred pounds, and all my debts paid: but through God's good prudence, not by mine own negligence, I am now not worth a groat:[1] wherefore I thank him as much, as though I were as rich as I was before. What is he, (said one of the charitable men) that keepeth you in prison? a very honest man, said he, who, through necessity is urged to do it, in hope, thereby to get some of my friends to pay him, thereby to release me. Have you any friends or kinsfolks that dwell nigh here, said one of them, or that knoweth of this your imprisonment? No truly, said the prisoner, but within a hundred miles I have such friends, I hope, that would quickly release me, if they knew of it. Well, said the one of them, if your friends were here, they should not need to trouble themselves about the delivering of you, for I will pay your debt, and release you out of prison: therefore tell me his name, said he, and where he dwelleth, to whom you owe the money, for I will not dine before I have paid him thy debt, that he may release thee. No, said the other, you shall not pay his debt, for I will pay it for him: you shall not, said the other, for I was within the prison door before you. And thus they were at contention one with another, which of them should release the poor man out of prison.... Yea, said the other, I will have a remedy for that, & he seeing an officer there at the prison door, said, I pray thee arrest this man at my suit for such matter as I have against him: and that he may appear this day in the afternoon before the judge. And when he had given him his fee, he departed thence, and then the officer arrested him by and by, and told him it was at the suit of such a one. Well, said he that was arrested, I will put in sureties[2] for my appearance: and so he did.

SIUQILA. I think few sergeants with us can say, that ever they arrested any in such a case: But did he appear before the judge at afternoon?

OMEN. Yea I warrant you. At which time the plaintiff ... met him, who said then unto the judge: my Lord, it was my chance this day to go to a prison, where I found but only one prisoner, who layeth there for twenty pounds debt, which prisoner I would have released, and paid his said debt to his creditor, but this man

---

1   *groat*   English coin with a value equal to four pennies.
2   *sureties*   Money pledged as an assurance that an agreement will be carried out.

whom I have caused to appear before you, would not suffer me, for when I was going unto him that imprisoned the poor man, he said he would go to him, and discharge the prisoner, wherein me thought he offered me great wrong, to take that charitable work out of my hand that I was determined to do.

SIUQILA. But saving your tale: me think, that he had no lawful cause to arrest him in this case.

OMEN. You think so: but it is as lawful with us to sue a man for preventing him of a charitable deed, as it is lawful for a man to arrest one with you for preventing him of any worldly commodity.... Then the judge ... examined them privately, ... [and] then said the judge, you are both charitable & godly men, you strive to do well, where as many strive to do evil. But for as much as you are both willing, to show a great deed of charity of the poor prisoner, and that one of you will needs pay his said debt of twenty pound: my judgement is, that you that are the plaintiff, partly for that you were first within the prison door, but chiefly for that you were first determined to visit the prison, to do such a charitable work, that you shall pay the said twenty pounds to his creditor, thereby to release him out of prison. And further, because you that are defendant, were so desirous to pay the same for him, and to release him: therefore I decree that you shall give the said poor man, when he is released out of prison, twenty pounds also, to help to maintain & succour him withal, for that I understand he hath nothing to live on: for it is as charitable a deed, to relieve poor men (that can not tell how to live) when they be out of prison, as to help to release them out of prison....

7. from Anthony Copley, *Wits Fits and Fancies* (1595)

The English poet Anthony Copley (1567–c. 1609) has the dubious distinction of having been called "the most desperate youth that liveth" by Elizabeth I's notorious interrogator Richard Topcliffe in a 1592 report to the queen. Despite his hot-headed temperament, Copley, a layperson of the Catholic gentry, called on other Catholics to remain loyal to their Protestant monarch.

Wits Fits and Fancies was printed in 1595 and again in 1614. It comprises a series of jokes, stories, and proverbs, many of which were translated from a Spanish book, *La floretta spagnola*. The excerpts below take a low view of both merchants and misers, often deeming them one and the same.

OF MERCHANTS AND MISERS

... Hernando de Pulgar[1] used to say, that who so desires to be soon rich, must have two Muches, and two Littles: Much Avarice, and Much Diligence: Little Shame, and Little Conscience....

A merchant had agreed with a wood-monger for all his faggots[2] at pence a piece one with another: The wood-monger after having thus bargained, told him, that unless he would give him somewhat over & above, he would not unload them. Go too then (said the merchant) I am content thou shalt &c. With that the wood-monger unloaded, and when he had done, did also help to carry them down into the cellar, in hope of &c. Then the merchant paid him for his faggots: and he demanding his &c. the merchant answered: My meaning was that thou shouldst help to carry the faggots down into the cellar over and above thy bargain: So art thou paid thy &c....

A merchant that ought[3] much, and was not able to correspond, fled the country, and for haste left much of his goods undisposed of: Which his creditors seizing upon, and selling at the street door to the most givers: one came & bought a featherbed, and said: It is good sleeping in his bed, that ought so much money....

A miserly merchant asking one whom he greatly disdained, how he came by so rich a widow, he answered: Even as a man may come by yours after you are dead.

A miser said unto his man: Sirrah, you had best be gone lest I give you that you would not willingly have. The serving man answered: Sir, I believe you not, for you never give.

---

1 *Hernando de Pulgar* Spanish writer (c. 1436–c. 1492) and secretary to Queen Isabella I.
2 *faggots* Bundles of kindling.
3 *ought* Owed.

A rich churl[1] was so miserly minded, that he thought all mischiefs that befell any of his neighbours, was in respect that they wished him ill, or went about to do him some despite. It chanced that his man riding in an evening to water his horse, both he and the horse drowned: Whereupon the miser said: See, see, out of doubt the varlet[2] hath done this to spite me....

One asked a rich usurer how many sons he had, who answered eighteen: Eighteen (replied the other). Believe me, had you as many more, the country hath curses enough for ye all....

8. from Thomas Lodge, *Wit's Misery, and the World's Madness* (1596)

Thomas Lodge (1558–1625), who as a poet and dramatist exerted a notable influence on Shakespeare, was the son of Sir Thomas Lodge, Lord Mayor of London. Despite the notability of his family, young Lodge knew all too well the sting of financial strain: when he was five, his father went bankrupt. Lodge, who did not inherit any money or land from either of his parents, seems to have been tormented by unpaid dues for much of his life. He grew to despise moneylenders as unprincipled men, and attacks them both in *An Alarum against Usurers* (1584) and in *Wit's Misery* (1596). The following passage of physical description from his 1596 publication supplies a vivid example of the way in which the appearance and bearing of the usurer were often described.

This Usury is jump of the complexion of the baboon his father; he is haired like a great ape, and swart like a tawny Indian, his horns are sometimes hidden in a button cap (as Th. Nashe[3] described him), but now he is fallen to his flat cap, because he is chief warden of his company: he is narrow-browed, and squirrel-eyed, and the chiefest ornament of his face is, that his nose sticks in the midst like an embossment in terrace work, here and there embellished and decked

---

1   *churl* Miser.

2   *varlet* Scoundrel.

3   *jump* Precisely; *Th. Nashe* Thomas Nashe, British satirist, pamphleteer, and playwright. In his pamphlet *Pierce Penniless* (1592), the unfortunate protagonist encounters a hideous Jewish usurer who wears "a sage button-cap, of the form of a cow-shard [a cow-turd] overspread very orderly."

with *verrucae* for want of purging with agaric; some authors have compared it to a rutter's cod-piece,[1] but I like not the allusion so well, by reason the tyings have no correspondence. His mouth is always mumbling, as if he were at his matins:[2] and his beard is bristled here and there like a sow that had the lousy.[3] Double-chinned he is, and over his throat hangs a bunch of skin like a money-bag. Band wears he none, but a welt of coarse holland,[4] and if you see it stitched with blue thread, it is no workaday wearing. His truss[5] is the piece of an old packcloth, the mark washed out; and if you spy a pair of Bridges' satin[6] sleeves to it, you may be assured it is a holiday. His points are the edging of some cast packsaddle, cut out sparingly (I warrant you) to serve him and his household for trussing[7] leather. His jacket forsooth is faced with moth-eaten budge, and it is no less than Lisle grogram[8] of the worst. It is bound to his body with a cordelier's girdle,[9] dyed black for comeliness' sake: and in his bosom he bears his handkerchief made of the reversion of his old tablecloth. His spectacles hang beating over his codpiece like the flag in the top of a maypole. His breeches and stockings are of one piece I warrant you, which, having served him in pure kersey for the tester[10] of a bed some twenty years, is by the frugality of a dyer and the courtesy of a tailor for this present made a sconce for his buttocks. His shoes of the old cut, broad at the toes and cross-buckled with brass, and have loopholes like a sconce for his toes to shoot out at. His gown is suitable, and as seemly as the rest, full of threads I warrant you, wheresoever the wool is employed, welted on the back with the clipping of a bare

---

1 *verrucae* Warts; *agaric* Treatment made from dried fungus; *rutter* Mounted soldier; *codpiece* Fabric flap tied over the opening of a pair of hose or breeches; also a colloquial term for "penis."
2 *matins* Morning prayer.
3 *had the lousy* I.e., was infected by lice.
4 *Band* Belt; *welt* Ornamental band; *holland* Roughly woven linen often used for household furnishing.
5 *truss* Waistcoat.
6 *Bridges' satin* Fabric made of a combination of linen and silk. It was used as a budget alternative to silk satin.
7 *points* Laces or cords used to attach clothing; *trussing* Bundling.
8 *budge* Lambskin made into a cheap fur trim; *Lisle grogram* Twisted thread made of rough-hewn silk.
9 *cordelier's girdle* Belt made of knotted cord.
10 *kersey* Rough wool; *tester* Canopy.

cast velvet hood, and faced with foins[1] that had kept a widow's tail warm twenty winters before his time.

Thus attired, he walks Paul's,[2] coughing at every step as if he were broken-winded, grunting sometime for the pain of the stone and strangury:[3] and continually thus old, and seeming ready to die, he notwithstanding lives to confound many families.

9. from Giovanni Botero, *Relations, of the Most Famous Kingdoms and Commonweals through the World*[4] (1595)

The Italian Giovanni Botero (1544–1617) was trained as a Jesuit but never took his final vows. From 1580, he was a political secretary and diplomat, and a prolific and influential writer. Ben Jonson, for example, quotes Botero directly in *Cynthia's Revels* (1601) and *Volpone* (1606).

The excerpt below is from Botero's *Relazioni Universali*, printed in Italian in 1595. The first English edition was printed in England in 1601. Commonly known as *The Traveller's Breviat*, it has also been printed as *Relations, of the Most Famous Kingdoms and Common-weales through the World*. The following excerpt conveys a sense of Venice's wealth, and also of its commercial vitality. Botero's optimistic account is glaringly different from the harsh reality presented by merchants such as Zuane di Andrea Zane and his brothers (see E.3 above).

… The city, amongst many other channels which do encircle it, is divided by one main channel (for his largeness, called the Grand Canal) into two parts, whereof the one part looketh south-west, the other north-east. This channel in his winding, maketh the form of the letter S backward: and it is the more famous for the admirable prospect of so many most curious and goodly palaces, as are built all the length of it on either side, to the astonishment of the beholders. On the middle of this channel, standeth the bridge of Rialto, built first of wood, but in our time re-edified[5] and built of stone, and that

---

1   *foins* Fur of a marten, weasel, or similar animal.
2   *walks Paul's* Walks the central aisle of St. Paul's Cathedral, where people frequently went to learn the latest news and to conduct business.
3   *the stone and strangury* Disease causing painful urination released drop by drop.
4   *Relations … the World* Translation 1611.
5   *re-edified* Rebuilt.

with such excellency of workmanship, that it may justly be numbered amongst the best contrived edifices of Europe. This bridge, joineth together the two most and best frequented parts of the city, the Rialto and Saint Mark's.[1] Many less channels fall into this, which are passed over either by bridges, or boats appointed for that purpose. The city hath in circuit seven miles, and yieldeth an inestimable revenue....

Fame reporteth, the Venetians to be exceeding rich: But besides opinion, there is great reason, why they should be so indeed. First, they are lords of a large territory, both by land and sea: but chiefly on land: where they have cities of the best rank of Italy, with large and opulent territories adjoining unto them, and full of people, industrious and thrifty. They have also rich bishoprics, wealthy abbeys, with the fattest and most commodious benefices[2] of Italy: families both for nobility and revenue, worshipful; and buildings, for state and magnificence, singular. Besides which, they have also very wealthy commonalties.[3] Amongst which, to omit many, Brescia[4] alone hath 18 thousand crowns of yearly revenue: and Asola which is but a town, subject to Brescia, ten thousand.

Another reason, is the great advantage which the Venetian hath for traffic, both in drawing unto himself other men's commodities, and in vending his own. [T]he flower of gain, and emolument[5] to the state, is the traffic of the great Sea of Soria[6] and Egypt, which the Venetian had altogether in his hand, especially the ancient traffic for spice, which hath always been, and yet is, of great consequence unto them. In some, all the trade of cloves, nutmegs, ginger, cinnamon, pepper, wax, sugars, tapestries, cloths, silks, and leather, with all the commodities of the east to pass this way, and are uttered from hence into the greater part of Italy, and a good part of Germany. The greatness of this trade, may the better be perceived by the greatness and multitude of private shipping, belonging to citizens and other strangers, merchants of Venice & other haven-towns belonging to the state: as also by the multitude and wealth of the said merchants, and

---

1   *Rialto* Famous exchange market; *Saint Mark's* Busy public square and site of Saint Mark's Basilica.
2   *bishoprics* Areas administered by bishops; *benefices* Positions for Church officials.
3   *commonalties* Lower-class peoples.
4   *Brescia* Northern Italian city located in Lombardy at the base of the Alps.
5   *emolument* Profit.
6   *the great Sea* The Mediterranean Sea; *Soria* Spanish province.

of the great stirring and bartering, that is there every day. In which kind the merchants only of the Dutch nation, in Venice do dispatch as much, as were thought sufficient to furnish a whole world....

10. from Leon of Modena, *History of the Present Jews throughout the World* (c. 1616)

Just as Christians disagreed heatedly as to what constituted usury and what charges (if any) it was legitimate to levy when lending money, so too did Jews. The writings of Leon of Modena on this topic form an interesting counterpoint to those of, for example, Yehiel Nissim Da Pisa (see E.5 above), who was in this matter expressing the majority view. (Modena's *History of the Present Jews* is also discussed above; see C.8.)

from PART 2, CHAPTER 4: OF THEIR TRADING, AND USURY

They are obliged, not only by the laws of Moses, but also by the oral law also, to be exact in their dealings, and not to defraud or cheat any one, let him be who he will, either Jew or Gentile, observing at all times and towards all persons those good rules of dealing which are so frequently commanded in the scripture, especially in Leviticus 19 from verse 11 to the end.[1]

As for that which some have spread abroad, both in discourse and in writing, viz., that the Jews take an oath every day to cheat some Christian, and reckon it a good work: it is a manifest untruth, published to render them more odious than they are. So far is it that many rabbis have written ... that it is a much greater sin to cheat one that is not a Jew, than one that is, both upon the account that the thing is bad in itself, and because the scandal is greater.... Therefore if there are any found among them that cheat or defraud, it ought to be attributed to the ill disposition of that particular person, for no such practice is in any wise allowed, whether by their laws or [by the] rabbis.

'Tis very true, that the narrowness of their circumstances which their long captivity has reduced them to; and their being almost

---

1 *Leviticus 19 ... to the end* Leviticus 19.11 prohibits stealing, lying, and deceit.

everywhere prohibited to purchase lands, or to use several sorts of merchandizes, and other creditable and gainful employments, has debased their spirits, and made them degenerate from the ancient Israelitish sincerity.

For the same reason, they have allowed themselves to take usury, notwithstanding it is said in Deuteronomy 23.20: *Unto a stranger thou mayst lend upon usury, but unto thy brother thou shalt not lend upon usury*. In which place, the Jews cannot understand by the word *stranger* any other besides these seven nations, the Hittites, Amorites, Jebusites etc., which God commanded be destroyed by the sword. But because they are not [allowed] to use the same means of getting a living as others which are brethren by nature, they pretend they may do it[1] lawfully.

11. from Leon of Modena, "Refutation of What Fra Sisto Writes in His Holy Library"[2] (1627)

Fra Sisto was a convert to Christianity who became influential as a Dominican friar—and who adopted extreme views in condemning his former religion, suggesting that the Talmud encourages Jews to deceive Christians, to commit incest, and to engage in various other nefarious practices. Leon was refused permission from the Venetian authorities to publish his twenty-three page pamphlet refuting Sisto's charges. It is an extraordinary document for its time—not least of all for its expression of principles of situational ethics that we tend to associate with a much later era.

[I write] to refute the false and contrived calumnies of a certain Fra Sisto Senese.... When the Talmud discusses whether it is possible to defraud the Gentile, the conclusion in any event is no. Many say

---

1 *do it* I.e., lend upon usury. Leon is suggesting that the prohibitions on Jews taking other forms of employment led them to bend their own laws in the area of providing loans. According to Leon's way of thinking, Christians are to be considered brethren to Jews (despite the long history of Christian ill treatment of Jews); the only "foreigners" or "strangers" being referred to according to this reading are the other groups of Israelites (Hittites, Amorites, etc.) referenced in Deuteronomy 20.17 who were to be destroyed when the Israelites took possession of the land God had set out to be theirs.

2 *Refutation of ... Library* As translated in Riccardo Calimani, *The Ghetto of Venice*, pp. 15–59.

that it is indeed a greater sin to deceive a Gentile than another Jew, because the Jew attributes it to the dishonesty of the particular Jew who cheats him, but the Gentile is scandalized by the entire Hebrew nation and law, which he believes allows it.... It is true that the law is not always observed by this Jew or that, both because in every nation there are many of little conscience, and also because need and poverty, in which the Hebrew nation finds itself in this long captivity, intrinsically give a certain freedom (albeit neither just nor legitimate) to act against conscience for survival's sake....

[Here Leon recalls a relevant incident that occurred in 1605 in Ferrara.]

A Jew was claiming repayment of a large debt from a gentleman of Ferrara; it included hundreds of ducats of interest, and that gentleman alleged it was illegal, even according to the Jew's own law, for the Jew to take interest from a Christian.... The most illustrious Cardinal sent for me and asked me whether or not I thought it was legitimate for a Jew to take interest from a Christian. My answer was both "no, sir" and "yes, sir."

"Explain yourself," said he.

"[Yes, sir,] I believe it is legitimate," said I.... "By *foreigner* [in Deuteronomy 23.19], certainly no other is meant but those seven nations [Hittites, Amorites, etc.] The others are considered brothers.... So the Christian is a brother and cannot be lent to at interest. [But on the other hand] I said 'No, sir.' If the Christian treated us as brothers and let us live as citizens and subjects, and did not forbid us familiarity in all dealings, in the purchase of real estate, in many trades, and—in places such as Venice—even in the mechanical arts, and in infinite other prohibitions, we would be equally obliged to acknowledge him as a brother. But if he treats us like slaves, we, as slaves, may feel it legitimate for the sake of survival to do what should not be done, which is to lend at interest. And therefore I [said both yes and no]."

The most illustrious Cardinal, with a grave laugh, placed a hand on my shoulder and, dismissing me, ruled in favor of the Jew.

12. Francis Bacon, "Of Usury" (1625)

"Of Usury" first appeared in the third edition of Francis Bacon's *Essays*.[1] In the essay, Bacon takes a pragmatic, secular approach to the subject of usury, noting ways in which lending money with interest can benefit the state—an approach that contrasts starkly with religion-fueled arguments such as that put forward by Thomas Wilson (see E.2 above). Bacon had presented an earlier version of this essay to the king's principal secretary in 1623 (and he may have written it as early as 1612).

By Bacon's era, decades after the usury statute of 1571 had legalized lending with interest, the Crown was looking for new means of raising money and stimulating the economy; Bacon made a persuasive case for managing moneylending to the economic benefit of the nation.

Many have made witty invectives against usury. They say, that it is pity, the devil should have God's part, which is the tithe.[2]

That the usurer breaketh the first law that was made for mankind, after the fall; which was, *in sudore vultus tui comedes panem tuum*; not, in *sudore vultus alieni*.[3] That usurers should have orange-tawny bonnets, because they do Judaise.[4] That it is against nature, for money to beget money; and the like. I say this only, that usury is a *concessum propter duritiem cordis*:[5] for since there must be borrowing and lending, and men are so hard of heart as they will not lend freely, usury must be permitted. [F]ew have spoken of usury usefully. It is good to set before us the incommodities, and commodities of usury; that the good may be either weighed out, or culled out....

The discommodities of usury are: first, that it makes fewer merchants. For were it not for this lazy trade of usury, money would not

---

1 For a brief discussion of the *Essays* and of Bacon's life, see the introduction of Bacon's "Of Revenge" (D.2).

2 *tithe* Charitable contribution of a tenth of one's income, especially one made to the Church.

3 *in sudore ... tuum* Latin: by the sweat of your brow you will eat your bread. See Genesis 3.19; *sudore vultus alieni* Latin: by the sweat of strangers.

4 *orange-tawny bonnets* Colored hats that commonly marked their wearers as Jewish. In many jurisdictions Jews were forced to wear yellow or orange hats as an identifying mark. *Judaise* Practice Judaism or Jewish cultural customs.

5 *concessum ... cordis* Latin: allowed because of the hardness of heart. See Matthew 19.8.

lie still, but would, in great part, be employed upon merchandising; which is the *vena porta*[1] of wealth in a state.

On the other side, the commodities of usury are, first, that howsoever usury in some respect hindereth merchandising, yet in some other it advanceth it: for it is certain, that the greatest part of trade is driven by young merchants, upon borrowing at interest: so as if the usurer either call in, or keep back his money, there will ensue presently a great stand of trade. The second is, that were it not for this easy borrowing upon interest, men's necessities would draw upon them a most sudden undoing, in that they would be forced to sell their means (be it lands or goods) far under foot;[2] and so, whereas duty doth but gnaw upon them, bad markets would swallow them quite up.... [Moreover], it is a vanity to conceive that there would be ordinary borrowing without profit; and it is impossible to conceive the number of inconveniencies that will ensue, if borrowing be cramped. Therefore, to speak of the abolishing of usury is idle. All states have ever had it, in one kind or rate, or other. So as that opinion must be sent to Utopia.

To speak now, of the reformation and reglement[3] of usury; how the discommodities of it may be best avoided, and the commodities retained. It appears by the balance of commodities and discommodities of usury, two things are to be reconciled. The one, that the tooth of usury be grinded, that it bite not too much: the other, that there be left open a means to invite moneyed men to lend to the merchants, for the continuing and quickening of trade. This cannot be done, except you introduce two several sorts of usury; a less, and a greater....

To serve both intentions, the way would be briefly thus. That there be two rates of usury, the one free, and general for all; the other under licence only, to certain persons, and in certain places of merchandising. First therefore, let usury, in general, be reduced to five in the hundred; and let that rate be proclaimed to be free and current; and let the state shut itself out, to take any penalty for the same. This will preserve borrowing from any general stop or dryness ... his, by like reason, will encourage and edge industrious and profitable improve-

---

1 *vena porta* Latin: portal vein, a vein that transports blood from several major organs to the liver.
2 *under foot* I.e., under their actual value.
3 *reglement* Regulation.

ments.... Secondly, let there be certain persons licensed to lend, to known merchants, upon usury at a higher rate; and let it be with the cautions following. Let the rate be, even with the merchant himself, somewhat more easy, than that he used formerly to pay: for, by that means, all borrowers shall have some ease by this reformation, be he merchant, or whosoever. Let it be no bank or common stock, but every man be master of his own money: not that I altogether mislike banks, but they will hardly be brooked, in regard of certain suspicions.[1] ... Let these licensed lenders be in number indefinite, but restrained to certain principal cities and towns of merchandising: for then they will be hardly able to colour other men's monies in the country: so as the licence of nine will not suck away the current rate of five: for no man will send his monies far off, nor put them into unknown hands.

If it be objected that this doth, in a sort, authorize usury, which before was, in some places, but permissive: the answer is; that it is better to mitigate usury by declaration, than to suffer it to rage by connivance.[2]

---

1   *bank or common stock* I.e., jointly held stock; *brooked* Accepted; *certain suspicions* Though Bacon does not specify his suspicions here, early bankers were widely mistrusted; common complaints included that they controlled the rate of exchange and that they conspired to move funds outside England.
2   *connivance* Implicit support of a misdeed.

F. Friendship and Love between Men

Repeatedly in *The Merchant of Venice* we hear of Antonio's warmth of feeling for Bassanio. "My purse, my person, my extremest means," he says to the younger man, "Lie all unlocked to your occasions." When Salerio describes how Antonio has wrung Bassanio's hand "with affection wondrous sensible," Solanio gives voice to the thought that "he only loves the world for him." What are we to make of Antonio's feelings? To what degree is it reasonable to read his love for Bassanio as being romantic or sexual in nature? To what extent should same-sex friendship, love, and sexual desire in the Elizabethan era be understood differently from in our own?

Research of the past generation has increased our appreciation of the ways in which same-sex desire is mediated by history and by culture, and our awareness of the complexity of the issues involved. In any historical or cultural context it is important to distinguish between homosexuality (a term that did not exist until the late nineteenth century), and homoeroticism, which takes a wide variety of historically and culturally determined forms that might or might not involve the adoption of a specific sexual identity. In reading back into history it is far from easy for the modern reader always to keep in mind the ways in which same-sex desire differs from era to era in its meaning and modes of expression.

That said, one of the most striking developments of English literature of the early modern period is the widespread appearance of same-sex eroticism. Not surprisingly, given the transgressive nature of such love at the time (homosexual acts were a capital offence—though an offence for which virtually no one seems ever to have been punished according to the letter of the law), such eroticism appears in an often conflicted or ambiguous fashion, frequently adopting as a model the conventions of male-female love. In Shakespeare's twentieth sonnet, for example—one of the sonnets that first indicates his speaker's love of another man as a central theme—the poet exploits some of the tropes of Petrarchan poetry in contrasting this love with that of "false" women. The poem is perhaps the most famous expression of ambiguity in Shakespeare's sonnets, one that both admits and denies simultaneously.

The nature of homoeroticism in literature was not always openly acknowledged by the writers of the time even when it was openly expressed. Of some of his clearly homoerotic sonnets, for example, Richard Barnfield offered utterly implausible denials of the clear sense of his verse, saying that he had merely been trying to write like Virgil. Imitating the classics proved to be useful in giving homoerotic verse a good cover story, so to speak. But the groundbreaking literary expressions are quite real. In this as in so many other respects Shakespeare and Marlowe (in this case along with Barnfield, a much lesser poet) were pioneers; in the 1590s they are the first literary figures we know of to write openly and unequivocally homoerotic literature. Marlowe imagines Neptune making a pass at the naked young Leander as he swims the Hellespont in the poem "Hero and Leander," and in his play *Edward II* depicts the king's alienation from his kingdom and his wife as a direct consequence of being "love sick for this minion," Piers Gaveston. (In the end Edward is reduced to a despairing hope that he may have "some nook or corner left / To frolic with" his "dearest Gaveston.") Barnfield is more explicit, whatever his odd denials in his prefatory material, about the transgressive nature of the desires being expressed: "If it be sin to love a lovely lad / Oh then sin I."

We have only minimal evidence as to whether the homoerotic expressions of feeling by any of these poets extended beyond the literary. In the case of Shakespeare, at least, we know that such expressions did not preclude marriage and children. More generally, we know that "cross-over" activity of several sorts was characteristic of the age. When Marlowe's Gaveston paints an idyllic picture of the world he desires, for example, it is one featuring "men like satyrs grazing on the lawns" but also young men resembling women:

Sometime a lovely boy in Diane's shape,
With hair that guilds the water as it glides,
Crownets of pearl about his naked arms
And in his sportful hands an olive tree,
To hide those parts which men delight to see …

If the male-male erotic landscape had different features in the 1590s than it does today, neither was male-male friendship quite as it is now. Much as Montaigne, for example, rejects any suggestion of male unions being consummated through sexual activity, his language is of a sort that today we would take to be infused with romantic feeling: "In the amity I speak of, [two minds] intermix and confound themselves one in the other, with so universal a commixture that [one cannot find] the seam that hath conjoined them together."

The selections below will not settle any questions regarding the nature of Antonio's feelings for Bassanio or the nature of the relationship between the two. The intent in including them is rather to provide historical context—to give a sense of the range of male-male feeling, and of male-male interactions during the period.

1. from Cicero, *Of Friendship*[1] (44 BCE)

Marcus Tullius Cicero (106–43 BCE) is ancient Rome's most famous orator. His *De Amicitia* (*Of Friendship*) presents a fictional dialogue between the historical Roman statesman Gaius Laelius and his two sons-in-law, Quintus Mucius Scaevola and Gaius Fannius. The occasion for the conversation, set in 129 BCE, is the death of Laelius's good friend, Scipio Minor. Cicero's discussion of friendship between men draws on Greek philosophers, including Plato; it was, in turn, influential in the early modern period, inspiring thinkers such as the English writer Sir Thomas Elyot (c. 1490–1546) and the French essayist Michel de Montaigne (1533–92) to similarly celebrate male-male relationships.

… What sweeter thing can there be than to have one with whom thou darest so boldly talk all matters, as with thine own self? How should the profit of welfare and prosperity be so great if you had not some which should rejoice so much thereat as yourself? But as for evil plight and adversity, it were hard to bear them without such a one as would bear the same more grievously than yourself. To conclude, all other things that are desired, each one to each man serveth the turn, as riches for use, wealth for worship, honour for praise, pleasure for delight, health to want grief and to do the office of the body. Friendship containeth more things in it. Whithersoever you turn, it is at hand. It will be kept out of no place; it is never unreasonable, nor ever troublous.[2] Therefore, neither water, nor fire, nor air, as they say, do we in more places use than this friendship. And now do I not speak of the common or mean sort of friendship, which yet delighteth and

---

1 *Of Friendship* Translation by Sir John Harrington, 1550.
2 *troublous* Characterized by trouble.

profiteth, but of the true and perfect, as theirs was, which being few are soon told. For friendship maketh welfare the goodlier, and evil-fare—by sundering and parting of griefs—the lighter.

And where friendship hath in it many and great commodities, yet this exceedeth all the rest, that she forecomforts us with the good hope that is to come. She suffereth men's hearts neither to faint nor yet to fall, but he that beholdeth his friend doth, as it were, behold a certain pattern of himself. Wherefore in friendship the absent be present, the needy never lack, the sick think themselves whole, and—that which is hardest to be spoken—the dead never die. So great honour, remembrance, and desire breedeth in them toward their friends. By reason whereof their deaths be thought happy, and others' lives be much praised. But if you should take out of the world the knot of friendship, neither can there any house, neither any city be able to continue; no, not the tillage of the land can endure. And if this cannot be understood hereby, yet of strife and debate it may well be perceived, how great the power of concord and friendship is. For what house so steady, or what city stands so fast, but through hatred and strife it may be utterly overthrown? Whereupon, how much goodness resteth in friendship it may be easily judged.

2. from Christopher Marlowe, *Edward II* (1594)

A reputed atheist and spy for Elizabeth I's Secretary of State, Christopher Marlowe (1564–93) led a brief but full and dramatic life. He was part of a group of virtuoso playwrights that included such literary powerhouses as Thomas Kyd, Robert Greene, Ben Jonson, Thomas Middleton, and Shakespeare. Marlowe's plays dazzled the burgeoning commercial stages of London, and his innovative and effective use of blank verse contributed to its establishment as a standard form for playwrights of the period. His career was cut short when he was killed in a tavern, allegedly on account of a dispute over the bill—though conspiracy theories have thrived.

Marlowe was in all probability attracted to men: he is (perhaps falsely) reported to have said, "All they that love not tobacco and boys were fools." The playwright's own sexuality aside, an erotic same-sex relationship appears in his play *Edward II*, between King Edward II (r. 1307–27) and his confidant, Piers Gaveston, Earl of Cornwall (c.

1284–1312). The dynamic between these characters has a historical basis; the king was known to be exceptionally close to Gaveston. In underscoring this relationship (to which Edward II seemed more devoted than he did to his people or his crown), the play raises questions about what we should do when personal desires are pitted against public duty.

from ACT 1, Scene 1

GAVESTON. "My father is deceased; come, Gaveston,
And share the kingdom with thy dearest friend."[1]
Ah, words that make me surfeit with delight!
What greater bliss can hap[2] to Gaveston
Than live and be the favourite of a king?
Sweet prince, I come. These, these thy amorous lines
Might have enforced me to have swum from France
And like Leander[3] gasped upon the sand,
So thou wouldst smile and take me in thy arms.
The sight of London to my exiled eyes
Is as Elysium[4] to a new come soul,
Not that I love the city or the men,
But that it harbours him I hold so dear,
The king, upon whose bosom let me die
And with the world be still at enmity.
What need the arctic people love starlight,
To whom the sun shines both by day and night?
Farewell base stooping to the lordly peers,
My knee shall bow to none but to the king.
As for the multitude, that are but sparks
Raked up in embers of their poverty,
Tanti![5] I'll fan first on the wind
That glanceth at my lips, and flieth away.

---

1   *My father ... friend*   After the death of Edward I, Edward II reversed his father's decision to exile Gaveston to Gascony.
2   *hap*   Happen by chance.
3   *Leander*   Character from Greek mythology who drowns tragically while swimming across a river to reunite with his lover Hero.
4   *Elysium*   Paradise of classical mythology where the blessed reside after death.
5   *Tanti*   Italian utterance of contempt, translating roughly as "So much for that."

3. from Richard Barnfield, *Cynthia, with Certain Sonnets, and the Legend of Cassandra* (1595)

Richard Barnfield (1574–1627) has the distinction of being one of the first writers to name Shakespeare in print. Along with the much more celebrated writer whom he names, Barnfield produced some of the period's most explicitly homoerotic poetry: *Cynthia* (1595), for example, includes 20 sonnets addressed to a boy. Evidence suggests that during his lifetime Barnfield's overt homoeroticism was received with outrage. In the preface to *Cynthia*, he defends an earlier (also homoerotic) poem by claiming it to be merely an imitation of the great Roman poet Virgil, who—like other admired classical writers—was appreciated despite the homoerotic content of his work.

Sonnet 8

Sometimes I wish that I his pillow were,
So might I steal a kiss, and yet not seen,
So might I gaze upon his sleeping eine,°   *eyes*
Although I did it with a panting fear:
But when I well consider how vain my wish is,
Ah foolish bees (think I) that do not suck,
His lips for honey; but poor flowers do pluck,
Which have no sweet in them: when his sole kisses,
Are able to revive a dying soul.
Kiss him, but sting him not, for if you do,
His angry voice your flying will pursue:
But when they hear his tongue, what can control,
Their back-return? For then they plain may see,
How honey-combs from his lips dropping be.

4. from William Shakespeare, *Sonnets* (1609)

The 1609 publication of a volume of 154 sonnets by Shakespeare occasioned little reaction in the seventeenth century, and for centuries they remained relatively neglected among Shakespeare's works. Though some eighteenth-century editions of Shakespeare included the sonnets, others omitted them on clearly homophobic grounds.

George Stevens, for example, the editor of a multi-volume edition of Shakespeare's works published in 1793, declared that it was "impossible to read this fulsome panegyric, addressed to a male object, without an equal measure of disgust and indignation." In the nineteenth century some (such as Robert Browning) regarded Shakespeare as representing a pinnacle in the history of sonnet writing in English, but others were distressed; as late as 1930 published comments continued to allude with discomfort to the poems' sexual content. It is only relatively recently, then, that the homoeroticism of the sonnets has ceased to be regarded as a taint—and that the poems themselves have been accepted unequivocally and universally as central to the Shakespearian canon.

Of the 154, the first 126 are generally accepted as being addressed to a young man (with most of the remainder written to or about a "dark lady"). The three included here are all of interest not only in that they are among the group addressed to the young man, but also for the degree to which they use the language of money and wealth.

20

A woman's face with nature's own hand painted
Hast thou, the master mistress of my passion;
A woman's gentle heart, but not acquainted
With shifting change, as is false women's fashion;
An eye more bright than theirs, less false in rolling,[1]
Gilding the object whereupon it gazeth;
A man in hue,° all hues in his controlling,   *appearance*
Much steals men's eyes and women's souls amazeth;
And for a woman wert thou first created;
Till nature as she wrought thee fell a-doting,
And by addition[2] me of thee defeated,
By adding one thing to my purpose nothing:
     But since she pricked[3] thee out for women's pleasure,
     Mine be thy love, and thy love's use[4] their treasure.

---

1   *rolling*   Glancing at lovers.
2   *by addition*   I.e., of male genitals.
3   *pricked*   Selected; "prick" was also slang for genitals.
4   *love's use*   Sexual pleasure and probably the suggestion of reproduction and increase, with a pun on "usury."

When, in disgrace with fortune and men's eyes,
I all alone beweep my outcast state,
And trouble deaf heav'n with my bootless° cries, *unavailing*
And look upon myself, and curse my fate,
Wishing me like to one more rich in hope,
Featured like him,[1] like him with friends possessed,
Desiring this man's art° and that man's scope, *skill*
With what I most enjoy contented least;
Yet in these thoughts myself almost despising,
Haply° I think on thee, and then my state, *By chance*
Like to the lark at break of day arising,
From sullen° earth sings hymns at heaven's gate; *dark, gloomy*
    For thy sweet love remembered such wealth brings
    That then I scorn to change my state with kings.

87

Farewell—thou art too dear[2] for my possessing,
And like enough thou know'st thy estimate.° *value*
The charter of thy worth gives thee releasing;[3]
My bonds in thee are all determinate.° *expired*
For how do I hold thee but by thy granting,
And for that riches where is my deserving?
The cause of this fair gift in me is wanting,
And so my patent° back again is swerving. *title to property*
Thy self thou gav'st, thy own worth then not knowing,
Or me to whom thou gav'st it else mistaking;
So thy great gift, upon misprision° growing, *error*
Comes home again, on better judgement making.
    Thus have I had thee as a dream doth flatter:
    In sleep a king, but waking no such matter.

---

1 *Featured like him* With physical attractions like his.
2 *too dear* Both "too expensive" and "too much loved."
3 *The charter ... releasing* The document stating your value releases you (from any associated debts).

5. from Michel de Montaigne, "Of Friendship"[1] (1580)

Michel de Montaigne (1533–92), now best known as an essayist, practiced law in Bordeaux and served as a councillor in the Bordeaux parliament before retiring early to his family's estate. Secluded there, he spent years writing, then expanding and revising his *Essais* (1580–95). In the work, he coined a new term—"essays," from the French word meaning "attempts" or "trials"—and applied it to writings in which he held his own beliefs up for scrutiny, assessing himself and the world around him through myriad contemplations. His compositions are conversational, rich in classical quotation, and wide-ranging, addressing subjects from education to drunkenness.

Montaigne's essays were first published in English in 1603, and it is certain that Shakespeare read at least some of them. Echoes of Montaigne are most clearly heard in *The Tempest*, but the French essayist's ideas may also have influenced Shakespeare's thought more generally. Whether or not it directly impacted Shakespeare, Montaigne's essay "On Friendship" is a significant contribution to writing in praise of friendships between men.

… To compare the affection toward women unto it [friendship between men], although it proceed from our own free choice, a man cannot, nor may it be placed in this rank: Her fire, I confess it to be more active, more fervent, and more sharp. But it is a rash and wavering fire, waving and diverse: the fire of an ague[2] subject to fits and stints, and that hath but slender hold-fast of us. In true friendship, it is a general and universal heat, and equally tempered, a constant and settled heat, all pleasure and smoothness, that hath no pricking or stinging in it, which the more it is in lustful love, the more is it but a raging and mad desire in following that which flies us,

> *Come segue la lepre il cacciatore*
> *Al freddo, al caldo, alla montagna, al lito,*
> *Ne piu l'estima poi che presa vede,*
> *E sol dietro a chi fugge affretta il piede.*

---

1   *Of Friendship*   Translation by John Florio, 1603.
2   *ague*   Fever.

Ev'n as the huntsman doth the hare pursue,
In cold, in heat, on mountains, on the shore,
But cares no more, when he her ta'en espies
Speeding his pace only at that which flies.[1]

As soon as it creepeth into the terms of friendship, that is to say, in the agreement of wits, it languisheth and vanisheth away: enjoying doth lose it, as having a corporal[2] end, and subject to satiety. On the other side, friendship is enjoyed according as it is desired, it is neither bred, nor nourished, nor increaseth but in jouissance,[3] as being spiritual, and the mind being refined by use custom. Under this chief amity, these fading affections have sometimes found place in me, lest I should speak of him, who in his verses speaks but too much of it.[4] So are these two passions entered into me in knowledge one of another, but in comparison never: the first flying a high, and keeping a proud pitch, disdainfully beholding the other to pass her points fare under it. Concerning marriage, besides that it is a covenant which hath nothing free but the entrance, the continuance being forced and constrained, depending elsewhere than from our will, and a match ordinarily concluded to other ends: a thousand strange knots are therein commonly to be unknit, able to break the web, and trouble the whole course of a lively affection; whereas in friendship there is no commerce or business depending on the same, but itself. Seeing (to speak truly) that the ordinary sufficiency of women cannot answer this conference and communication, the nurse of this sacred bond: nor seem their minds strong enough to endure the pulling of a knot so hard, so fast, and durable. And truly, if without that, such a genuine and voluntary acquaintance might be contracted, where not only minds had this entire jouissance, but also bodies, a share of the alliance, and where a man might wholly be engaged. It is certain, that friendship would thereby be more complete and full. But this sex could never yet by any example attain unto it, and is by ancient schools rejected thence....

---

1   [Montaigne's note] ARIOST. can. x. st. 7. [Ludovico Ariosto, *Orlando Furioso* (*Mad Orlando*, 1516–32).]

2   *corporal*   Relating to the body or material realm.

3   *jouissance*   Delight.

4   *him, who ... of it*   Étienne de la Boétie (1530–63), Montaigne's close friend. Montaigne is referring to la Boétie's love sonnets.

As for the rest, those we ordinarily call friends and amities, are but acquaintances and familiarities, tied together by some occasion or commodities, by means whereof our minds are entertained. In the amity I speak of, they intermix and confound themselves one in the other, with so universal a commixture, that they wear out and can no more find the seam that hath conjoined them together. If a man urge me to tell wherefore I loved him, I feel it cannot be expressed, but by answering: Because it was he, because it was my self. There is beyond all my discourse, and besides what I can particularly report of it, I know not what inexplicable and fatal power, a mean and Mediatrix[1] of this indissoluble union. We sought one another before we had seen one another, and by the reports we heard one of another; which wrought a greater violence in us, than the reason of reports may well bear; I think by some secret ordinance of the heavens, we embraced one another by our names. And at our first meeting, which was by chance at a great feast, and solemn meeting of a whole township, we found ourselves so surprised, so known, so acquainted, and so combinedly bound together, that from thence forward, nothing was so near unto us as one unto another.

6. from Leon of Modena, *Treatise on Ethics*[2] (1587)

Despite the prevalence of discrimination and mistrust, there was considerably more cultural intermingling and goodwill between Christians and Jews in late sixteenth- and early seventeenth-century Italy than in most other parts of Europe; scholars such as Moses Avigdor Shulvass have termed the period an era of relative "harmony and rapprochement." One interesting reflection of this is Leon of Modena's *Zemah Zaddik* (or *Tzemah Tzaddik*), *Treatise on Ethics*, a work of forty short chapters printed in Venice in 1587, and reissued in 1600. Leon's work was based closely on a Christian Italian treatise, *Dior di Virtu*; he deleted many purely Christian references and added numerous references to rabbinical authorities. The passages below form an interesting point of comparison on the subject of friendship and love.

---

1   *Mediatrix*   Intermediator, personified as female.
2   *Treatise on Ethics*   Translated by Ralph Anzarouth and an anonymous friend.

The third category, which is also called love, fraternity, peace and friendship, involves pleasing each other [and treating each other] with truth and justice. It is pleasant, agreeable and precious for people to establish between themselves this love, based on fraternity and joining together. This love can result from one of three causes: the first is the gain and benefit one hopes to receive from his fellow man and this is what our Sages of blessed memory said (Ethics of the Fathers 5, 16): "Every love which is dependent upon something, when this thing vanishes love is extinguished with it." For this reason, it is an inferior and despicable kind of love. The second is providing mutual benefit in the same way as one hand washes the other; and for this reason it is called a worthy love. The third is when the one who loves seeks to benefit his friend in every way even if he himself will suffer damage or loss as a result. This is the perfect love which cannot be surpassed. The proof of this pure love is when one loves his friend with all his heart and will try to do everything he can think of to please him and refrain himself from doing anything which he deems unworthy or harmful to him. In fact, one acquires and keeps a friend with three things: by respecting him in his presence, by praising him when not in his presence and by rendering him service when needed. In addition, he will not show friendship in good times and turn away and distance himself in times of trouble. Talmud Bavli says (treatise Shabbat 32a): "It is well known that at the thresholds of wealthy shops abound friends and sympathizers; whereas at the thresholds of misery there are no friends or sympathizers." It is further known that the prime example of faithful friends is David and Jonathan, whose wonderful friendship in life and death is related in the Bible.

The wise man said that there are four things which improve with age: wine, fish, oil and above all, friendship. Aristotle said that in the same way as a large tree needs a lot of attention, an important man needs many friends, since man can only be happy in this world in the company of friends and not when he is alone. And [our Sages] said (Talmud Bavli, treatise Taanit 23a): "Either friendship or death." Archita the philosopher said that if man were to ascend to the heavens and see the sun and its course in its extremities, the beauty of the moon and the stars in their positions in firmament and all the rest of the supernal renewals—and then descend [back to Earth] and see the marvels of the universe and all its contents—if he were alone and could not describe them to a company of friends he would have no pleasure and only great pain from them.

Our Sages of blessed memory said (Talmud Bavli, treatise Berachot, 17a): "A pearl of wisdom from Abaye was that man should always be wise in his awe of Hashem, he should give his replies gently, answer with warmth and spread peace among his brothers, his relations and all his fellow men, so that he will be loved in Heaven, desired in this world and accepted among all creatures."

Bear in mind that man changes and transforms himself according to his circle of friends. He should therefore acquire for himself a good friend. Seneca used to say: "Before you choose a friend, test him and try him, and after he passed the test love him with all your heart."

We found in Roman literature a tale concerning a king of Sicily[1] who decreed upon a man called Pythias a sentence of death by beheading. Pythias asked from the king a reprieve of eight days in order to give him time to return to his home and put his affairs in order. The king replied by way of joke that his request would be granted if he could find somebody who would remain in prison in his place and would undertake to be beheaded in his place if he failed to return at the appointed time. Pythias sent for his friend Damon, who shared with him a very close mutual friendship and told him his predicament. Damon immediately went to the king and undertook to be beheaded if Pythias did not return by the end of the eight days. They imprisoned him until [the time fixed for] Pythias's return. As the deadline approached and Pythias had not come, everybody made fun of poor Damon for undertaking what he did. Damon, however, was not at all concerned since he fully trusted his loyal friend. And so it was that when the deadline was reached Pythias returned as he had promised. When the king saw such intense and faithful friendship, he pardoned Pythias since he did not want to separate by death two friends such as these.

---

1 *a king of Sicily* Dionysius I (r. 406–367 BCE), a famously despotic king of Syracuse.

Chapter 5: Natural Love

The fourth category is natural love, which is beyond the power of man's will to control and it is his nature which compels him and inclines him to love what resembles him either in substance, form or deed: [the object of his love] and his conduct will find favor in his eyes, whether they are good or bad. He will continue loving even without receiving any pleasure or benefit. The wonder of this is seen in the animal realm where each species will like its own kind without possessing intelligence or knowledge. And every raven will settle with its own kind without receiving any benefit at all.

Similarly, practitioners of the same craft will befriend each other, in spite of the mutual rivalry and aversion between fellow craftsmen. Since each person places his own interests before those of his fellow man, therefore, due to his jealousy and fear of being damaged by him, he will dislike him.

Plato said: "If you want to recognize somebody who is like you, look for somebody who befriends you without obvious motives." Our Sages of blessed memory said (Talmud Bavli, treatise Bava Kama 92b): "Why does the starling mix with the raven, if not because he is of the same species?"[1]

This sums up the whole matter.

Chapter 6: Love of Women

The fifth category is emotional love which is totally physical and most of it stems from the love of women; for this reason it will be classified as good or bad according to its ultimate goal. Therefore many people have been drawn to talk in excess about women either in disparaging terms or in praise of them. This can be explained by the fact that there are people who love women solely for their own pleasure and this is animal lust, which is shameful and depends totally on the physical senses, in particular on the sense of touch. It is a disgrace for us, because someone who engages in it ignores and disregards whether it will cause harm or benefit, shame or honor, flaw or perfection. In

---

1 [translators' note] This is Rabbi Eliezer's interpretation of Leviticus 11, 15 ["Every raven after his kind"], whereas the Sages disagree and think that the starling belongs to a pure species.

this respect, King Solomon peace be upon him said (Eccl. 7, 26): "I consider the woman more bitter than death, since she tends only to trap and ensnare." Our Sages of blessed memory remind us that the first woman introduced death into the world;[1] however, our Sages despised only evil women.

A philosopher said: "There are three things which cause man to leave his home: smoke, a roofless house and a bad wife." Hippocrates told about a woman who was bearing fire: "Here comes fire carrying fire. And the carrying fire burns more than the fire which is carried." Sorcina said about a woman who was learning to write: "Why add evil upon evil?"

However, one who loves a woman of worth in order to perpetuate mankind is called a holy man, as it is written (Genesis 29, 18): "And Jacob loved Rachel" and other examples. And the principle of this love is intellectual and spiritual. It is well known that Solomon in his wisdom used as his parable in the Song of Songs a beloved and loving woman, so that details of physical love will be used as an example for love of Hashem; in fact, the righteous loves Him with a true love in the same way as when one desires a woman he will not sleep or rest nor will he eat or drink and will suffer the intense heat of the day and the extreme cold of the night out of love for her.

Our Sages of blessed memory said in the Midrash (Bereshit Raba 80): "Rabbi Shimon said etc. that the Holy one blessed be He expressed His affection for the Jewish People with three different terms of endearment: attachment, longing and desire etc." We learn these three expressions from the episode of that evil man:[2]

attachment—[from the verse] "And his soul felt attachment to Dina, the daughter of Jacob";
longing—[from the verse] "The soul of my son Shechem longs for your daughter";
desire—[from the verse] "Since he desired Jacob's daughter."

---

1   [translators' note] Until Adam ate from the forbidden fruit in the Garden of Eden, he was immortal. But by persuading him to eat it, Eve introduced sin into the world. Thus Hashem [God] decided that man should be mortal, so that death will be an atonement for man's sin.
2   [translators' note] Shechem the son of Chamor kidnapped and raped Dina, the daughter of our Patriarch Jacob. The full story and the three quotes are in the Genesis, chapter 41.

Rabbi Abba bar Elisha adds a further two to these, namely love and speech etc.

[King] Solomon said concerning proper love (Proverbs 18, 22): "When one finds a wife, one finds goodness etc." He says further (ibid. 5, 18): "And rejoice in the wife of your youth." It is written in the book of Ben Sira "A good wife is a fine gift." It is further written (Psalms 128, 3): "Your wife is like a fruitful vine within your home etc."

Happy is the one who loves with his head rather than with his heart, since this is what elevates man above beast and regarding this it is said (Song of Songs 8, 6): "Embers [of love] are like burning embers, a divine flame."

G. Women, Family, and Obedience

1. from Baldassare Castiglione, *The Book of the Courtier*[1] (1528)

Courtesy books dictating appearance and behavior for men and women circulated Europe from the Middle Ages into the early modern period. One of the most influential was Baldassare Castiglione's *The Courtier* (published as *Il Cortegiano* in 1528), translated from the Italian into English by Thomas Hoby in 1561. The work delineates the characteristics of an ideal courtier, emphasizing intense classical education, refined tastes, and noble carriage. In the excerpt below, Castiglione underscores the distinct differences he perceives between men and women and outlines how those should be publicly conveyed.

The L. Julian[2] proceeded: ... [W]hereas the L. Gaspar[3] hath said, that the very same rules that are given for the Courtier, serve also for the woman, I am of a contrary opinion. For albeit some qualities are common and necessary as well for the woman as the man, yet are there some other more meeter[4] for the woman than for the man, and some again meet for the man, that she ought in no wise to meddle withal. The very same I say of the exercises of the body. But principally in her fashions, manners, words, gestures and conversation (me think) the woman ought to be much unlike the man. For right as it is seemly for him to show a certain manliness full and steady, so doeth it well in a woman to have a tenderness, soft and mild, with a kind of womanly sweetness in every gesture of hers, that in going, standing and speaking what ever she lusteth, may always make her appear a woman without any likeness of man.

2. Juan Luis Vivès, *The Instruction of a Christen Woman*[5] (1524)

Juan Luis Vivès, a Spanish humanist, addressed the subject of women's roles in *The Instruction of a Christen Woman* (*De Institutione Foeminae*

---

1   *The Book of the Courtier*   Translated by Thomas Hoby, 1561.
2   *L. Julian*   Lord Julian de Medici. *The Book of the Courtier* is structured as a dialogue, and Lord Julian is one of the participants.
3   *L. Gaspar*   Lord Gaspar Pallavicin, another participant in the dialogue.
4   *meeter*   More suitable.
5   *The Instruction of a Christen Woman*   Translated by Richard Hyrde, 1529.

Christianae). Originally published in Latin in 1524, the text was soon translated into English by the humanist scholar Richard Hyrde. In this book, Vivès promotes education for women of all social classes. The publication further serves as a conduct book and advice column for women, from childhood to widowhood. While he may be a champion for women's scholarship, Vivès is still conservative where other aspects of conduct are concerned; in the excerpt below, he unequivocally advocates obedience as a chief attribute of women.

Now then, what woman will be so presumptuous and so haute,[1] to disobey her husband's bidding, if she consider that he is unto her in stead of father and mother and all her kin, and that she oweth unto him, all the love and charity that were due to them all? A ragious[2] and foolish woman doth not consider this, the which is disobedient unto her husband. Except paraventure[3] she would say, she oweth none obedience, neither to father nor to mother, nor to none of her kin. For if she obey them, she must needs obey her husband: in whom by all rights, by all customs, by all statutes and laws, by all precepts and commandments, both natural, worldly, and heavenly, she ought to account all thing to be. The woman is not reckoned the more worshipful[4] among men, that presumeth to have mastery above her husband: but the more foolish, and the more worthy to be mocked: Yea and more over than that cursed and unhappy: the which turneth backward the laws of nature, like as though a soldier would rule his captain, or the moon would stand above the sun, or the arm above the head. For in wedlock the man resembleth the reason, and the woman the body: Now reason ought to rule and the body to obey, if a man will live. Also Saint Paul saith: The head of the woman is the man.[5]

3. from Thomas Becon, *The Catechism* (c. 1550)

Thomas Becon (c. 1512–67), a staunch Protestant with a degree from Cambridge and a burning desire for reform, was a Canon of Canter-

---

1   *haute* High or lofty.
2   *ragious* Enraged.
3   *paraventure* Perhaps.
4   *worshipful* Worthy of respect.
5   *Saint Paul ... man* See 1 Corinthians 11.4.

bury Cathedral as well as a theological writer. Becon articulates his views on duty and obedience in the following chapters of his *Catechism*, a contribution to a popular genre of guidebooks of Christian education. In "Of the Duty of Children toward Their Parents," he teaches sincere filial piety; in "Of the Duty of Maids and Young Unmarried Women," while he maintains that wives are subordinate to their husbands, he also claims that unmarried women should be able to influence their fathers regarding the choice of their husbands.

from OF THE DUTY OF CHILDREN TOWARD THEIR PARENTS

...

SON. The most worthy apostle St. Paul describeth the office and duty of children toward their parents on this manner: "Children, obey your fathers and mothers in the Lord; for that is right. Honour thy father and mother (the same is the first commandment in the promise), that thou mayest prosper, and live long on the earth."[1] Again he saith: "Ye children, obey your fathers and mothers in all things; for that is well-pleasing to the Lord."[2] Here see we, that the office and duty of children toward their parents consisteth in two things.

FATHER. What two things are they?

SON. Honour and obedience. That child, which will do his office truly and faithfully according to the commandment of God, must both honour and obey his father and mother.

FATHER. In what points doth the honour of parents consist?

SON. First of all, in having a reverent opinion of them, of their prudence and wisdom, of their state and vocation, of their regiment and governance; being persuaded that they are our parents, not by fortune and chance, but by the singular providence and good will of God, given unto us of God for our great commodity, profit, and wealth.

Secondly, in loving them, yea, and that not feignedly, but from the very bottom of the heart; and in wishing unto them all good things from God, as unto persons which, next unto God, have and do best deserve of us.

---

1   *Children ... the earth* See Ephesians 6.1–3.
2   *Ye children ... Lord* See Colossians 3.20.

Thirdly, in giving them that reverence and honour outwardly, which by the commandment of God is due from children to their parents; as to bow the knee unto them, to ask them blessing, to put off their cap, to give them place, reverently and meekly to speak unto them, and with all outward gestures to show a reverent honour and honourable reverence toward them, as persons representing the majesty of God.

Fourthly, in labouring to the uttermost of their power to be thankful, and to requite their parents for such and so great benefits as they have received of God by them and their labours. As for an example, if their parents be aged and fallen into poverty, so that they are not able to live of themselves, nor to get their living by their own industry and labour, then ought the children, if they will truly honour their parents, to labour for them, to see unto their necessity, to provide necessaries for them, and by no means, so much as in them is, to suffer them for to lack any good thing; forasmuch as their parents cared and provided for them, when they were not able to care and provide for themselves.

Fifthly and finally, in concealing, hiding, covering, and in interpreting all their parents' faults, vices, and incommodities unto the best, never objecting nor upbraiding them by any thing done amiss; but quietly and patiently to bear all things at their hands, considering that in thus doing they greatly please God, and offer unto him an acceptable sacrifice; and by no means to follow the wicked manners of the most wicked Ham, which, when Noah his father was drunken and lay uncovered in the tent, went and told his two brethren without; but rather to practice the godly behaviour of Shem and Japheth, which, taking a garment, laid it upon their shoulders, and, coming backward, covered the nakedness of their father, namely, their faces being turned away, lest they should see their father's nakedness. By this means were they blessed, and Ham cursed.[1]

It becometh a good and godly child, not to display, but to conceal the faults of his father, even as he wisheth that God should cover his own offences, as the wise man saith: "Rejoice not when

---

1 *Ham cursed* This story, often called "the curse of Ham," concludes with Noah placing a curse on Ham's son Canaan and his descendants, saying that they would be slaves to their brothers' descendants (see Genesis 9.20–25).

thy father is reproved; for it is not honour unto thee, but shame. For the worship of a man's father is his own worship; and where the father is without honour, it is the dishonesty of the son. My son, make much of thy father in his age, and grieve him not as long as he liveth. And if his understanding fail, have patience with him, and despise him not in thy strength. For the good deed that thou showest to thy father shall not be forgotten; and when thou thyself wantest, it shall be rewarded thee,"[1] etc.

FATHER. Wherein consisteth the obedience of a child toward his father?

SON. In two things principally.

First, in showing himself obedient, not feignedly, but from the very heart, to the will and commandment of his father in executing, performing, and accomplishing the same with all diligence, evermore seeking to do that which may please him, and eschewing again at all times whatsoever in any point may displease him.

FATHER. But what if the father command the child to do that thing which is contrary to the word of God?

SON. Here the child oweth unto the father no obedience. For "we must obey God more than men."[2] But of this matter we spake when we talked of the fifth commandment.

Secondly, in attempting no grave or weighty matter without the counsel of his father, but to desire and crave his father's advice and judgement in all things; as not to enterprise marriage without his consent, nor to entangle himself with any weighty cause without the counsel and consent of his father; always preferring his father's judgement before his own, as one of more experience, larger wisdom, and greater knowledge, yea, as one that tendereth his commodity and profit no less than his own.

FATHER. What ought to move children to show this honour and obedience unto their parents?

SON. First, the commandment of God, which saith: "Honour thy father and thy mother."[3] Again: "Ye children, obey your fathers and mothers in the Lord."[4]

---

1 *Rejoice not ... rewarded thee*   See Ecclesiasticus (also called Sirach) 3.1–15.
2 *we must ... men*   See Acts 5.29.
3 *Honour ... mother*   See Exodus 20.12.
4 *Ye children ... the Lord*   See Ephesians 6.1.

Secondly, the promise which is annexed to the commandment; even this, that they which honour and obey their parents shall prosper and live long on the earth.[1]

Thirdly, the commination or threatening of God's anger and vengeance against all disobedient children. "Whoso laugheth his father to scorn, and setteth his mother's commandment at nought," saith the wise man, "the ravens pick out his eyes in the valley, and devoured be he of the young eagles."[2] How miserably perished Absalom[3] for his disobedience against his father! Is not the commandment of God, that such children as are stubborn and disobedient to their parents should be stoned unto death? Fourthly, the great labours and pains which the parents take, and the infinite charges and costs which they also bestow, in bringing up of them....

from OF THE DUTY OF MAIDS AND YOUNG UNMARRIED WOMEN

...

FATHER. Thou holdest then, that parents ought to place their children in marriage, and that children in this behalf also owe obedience unto their parents.

SON. Yea, verily.

FATHER. Ought not the consent of the children also to be considered in this behalf no less than the authority of the parents?

SON. God forbid else! For we read, that when Rebecca was promised that she should go with Abraham's servant to be married unto Issac, they said: "We will call the damsel, and inquire at her mouth. And they called forth Rebecca, and said unto her, Wilt thou go with this man? and she answered, I will go," &c.[4] Here see we, that though the authority of the parents be great over their children, yet in the matter of marriage the consent of the children may not be neglected. For parents must so use their authority that they do not abuse it. They abuse it, when it turneth unto the

---

1 *the promise ... the earth* See Exodus 20.12.

2 *Whoso ... eagles* See Proverbs 30.17.

3 *Absalom* Biblical son of David, king of Israel; Absalom attempted to usurp his father's throne and was eventually executed by his father's followers at the Battle of Ephraim after his head was caught in the branches of an oak tree. See 2 Samuel 18.

4 *We will ... &c.* See Genesis 14.57–58.

hinderance, incommodity, and destruction of their children. The parents therefore must so place their children in marriage, as may profit, and not hinder them, yea, and that with the good-will and consent of the children, to whom the matter chiefly pertain; that the authority of the parents and the consent of the children may go together, and make perfect a holy and blessed marriage.

FATHER. This is commendable. But some parents greatly abuse their authority, while they sell their children to other for to be married for worldly gain and lucre,[1] even as the grazier[2] selleth his oxen to the butcher to be slain, having no respect to the person, whether he be godly or ungodly, honest or unhonest, wise or foolish, &c. If money, if riches, if the muck of the world come, let the child go. The person is godly enough, honest enough, wise enough, &c., though he be never so ungodly, without all honesty, and a very fool.

SON. These be wicked parents, and marriages thus made for the most part have never good success, as experience daily teacheth. It becometh therefore all godly and Christian parents to provide for their children such mates and yoke-fellows as fear God, love his word, and will diligently provide for their family; and, such ones provided, it becometh all faithful children to obey the authority of their parents, and to take such unto them to be their companions in matrimony as their fathers and mothers have appointed, and so to live together in the fear of God, loving one another as Christ loveth the congregation....

4. from Elizabeth Cary, *The Tragedy of Mariam, the Fair Queen of Jewry* (1613)

Elizabeth (Tanfield) Cary (c. 1585–1639) was a playwright, a poet, a historian, and a translator well-versed in several languages. Though published female playwrights were virtually unheard-of at the time, Cary was a popular success until her public conversion to Catholicism left her abandoned both by her husband and by the public. Neglected for several centuries, much of her work has been lost; she is now best known for her first published play, *The Tragedy of Mariam*.

---

1 *lucre* Money or wealth (often with a disreputable connotation).
2 *grazier* Person who grazes livestock to fatten them for sale.

The Tragedy of Mariam is a closet drama based on a story recorded by the first-century historian Flavius Josephus. In a political move to secure his throne, Herod, King of the Jews, has divorced his first wife and married the title character. Then, by duplicitous means, he has secured the deaths of Mariam's relatives who have nearer titles to the throne. Twice, Herod has been called to Rome and faces a potential death sentence; each time, he has arranged that if he dies, Mariam will also be killed to prevent her marriage to anyone else. Both times, Mariam has been informed of the plot—the second time by Herod's councillor Sohemus, who had been charged with the deed. The play begins when Mariam learns of a rumor that Caesar has put Herod to death. In the excerpt here, Sohemus announces—to Mariam's surprise—that the king has returned home, very much alive. When Sohemus encourages her to overlook her husband's behavior and submit to him, she responds with outrage.

ACT 3, SCENE 3

([*Enter*] *Mariam and Sohemus.*)

MARIAM. Sohemus, tell me what the news may be
That makes your eyes so full, your cheeks so blue?
SOHEMUS. I know not how to call them. Ill for me
'Tis sure they are: not so I hope for you.
Herod—
MARIAM. Oh, what of Herod?
SOHEMUS.   Herod lives.
[MARIAM.] How! Lives? What in some cave or forest hid?
SOHEMUS. Nay, back returned with honour. Caesar gives
Him greater grace then ere Antonius[1] did.
MARIAM. Foretell the ruin of my family,
Tell me that I shall see our city burned:
Tell me I shall a death disgraceful die,
But tell me not that Herod is returned.
SOHEMUS. Be not impatient Madam, be but mild,
His love to you again will soon be bred.

---

1   *Caesar ... Antonius*   Both Julius Caesar (c. 100–44 BCE) and Mark Antony (83?–30 BCE) were political allies with Herod and his family, appointing Herod and his father Antipater to positions of power.

MARIAM. I will not to his love be reconciled,
  With solemn vows I have foresworn his bed.
SOHEMUS. But you must break those vows.
MARIAM.   I'll rather break
  The heart of Mariam. Cursed is my fate:
  But speak no more to me, in vain ye speak
  To live with him I so profoundly hate.
SOHEMUS. Great Queen, you must to me your pardon give,
  Sohemus cannot now your will obey:
  If your command should me to silence drive,
  It were not to obey, but to betray.
  Reject, and slight my speeches, mock my faith,
  Scorn my observance, call my counsel nought
  Though you regard not what Sohemus saith,
  Yet will I ever freely speak my thought
  I fear ere long I shall fair Mariam see
  In woeful state, and by her self undone:
  Yet for your issue's° sake more temp'rate be,   *offspring's*
  The heart by affability is won.
MARIAM. And must I to my prison turn again?
  Oh, now I see I was a hypocrite:
  I did this morning for his death complain,
  And yet do mourn, because he lives ere night.
  When I his death believed, compassion wrought,
  And was the stickler° twixt my heart and him: *mediator*
  But now that curtain's drawn from off my thought,
  Hate doth appear again with visage grim:
  And paints the face of Herod in my heart,
  In horrid colours with detested look:
  Then fear would come, but scorn doth play her part,
  And saith that scorn with fear can never brook.°   *abide*
  I know I could enchain him with a smile:
  And lead him captive with a gentle word,
  I scorn my look should ever man beguile,
  Or other speech, then meaning to afford.
  Else Salome in vain might spend her wind,
  In vain might Herod's mother whet her tongue:

In vain had they complotted[1] and combined,
For I could overthrow them all ere long.
Oh what a shelter is mine innocence,
To shield me from the pangs of inward grief:
'Gainst all mishaps it is my fair defence,
And to my sorrows yields a large relief.
To be commandress of the triple earth,[2]
And sit in safety from a fall secure:
To have all nations celebrate my birth,
I would not that my spirit were impure.
Let my distressed state unpitied be,
Mine innocence is hope enough for me.

(*Exit* [*Mariam*].)

SOHEMUS. Poor guiltless Queen. Oh that my wish might place
A little temper now about thy heart:
Unbridled speech is Mariam's worst disgrace,
And will endanger her without desert.
I am in greater hazard. O'er my head,
The fatal axe doth hang unsteadily:
My disobedience once discovered,
Will shake it down: Sohemus so shall die.
For when the King shall find, we thought his death
Had been as certain as we see his life:
And marks withal I slighted so his breath,
As to preserve alive his matchless wife.
Nay more, to give to Alexander's[3] hand
The regal dignity. The sovereign power,
How I had yielded up at her command,
The strength of all the city, David's Tower.[4]
What more than common death may I expect,
Since I too well do know his cruelty:
'Twere death, a word of Herod's to neglect,

---

1 *complotted*   Plotted together.
2 *triple earth*   Probably referring to the lands over which the major military powers often struggled: Rome, Jerusalem, and Egypt.
3 *Alexander*   Son of Mariam.
4 *David's Tower*   Citadel said to have been built during Herod's reign but named for David in the Middle Ages.

What then to do directly contrary?
Yet life I quit thee with a willing spirit,
And think thou could'st not better be employed:
I forfeit thee for her that more doth merit,
Ten such were better dead than she destroyed.
But fare thee well chaste Queen, well may I see
The darkness palpable, and rivers part:
The sun stand still. Nay more retorted be,
But never woman with so pure a heart.
Thine eyes grave majesty keeps all in awe,
And cuts the wings of every loose desire:
Thy brow is table to the modest law,[1]
Yet though we dare not love, we may admire.
And if I die, it shall my soul content,
My breath in Mariam's service shall be spent.

   [*Exit Sohemus.*]

CHORUS. 'Tis not enough for one that is a wife
  To keep her spotless from an act of ill:
  But from suspicion she should free her life,
  And bare her self of power as well as will.
    'Tis not so glorious for her to be free,
    As by her proper self restrained to be.

  When she hath spacious ground to walk upon,
  Why on the ridge should she desire to go?
  It is no glory to forbear alone,
  Those things that may her honour overthrow.
    But 'tis thank-worthy, if she will not take
    All lawful liberties for honour's sake.

  That wife her hand against her fame doth rear,
  That more than to her lord alone will give
  A private word to any second ear,
  And though she may with reputation live.

---

1 *brow ... law* Allusion to the tablets containing the Ten Commandments that God gave to
Moses in Exodus 19–20.

Yet though most chaste, she doth her glory blot,
And wounds her honour, though she kills it not.

When to their husbands they themselves do bind,
Do they not wholly give themselves away?
Or give they but their body not their mind,
Reserving that though best, for others pray?
    No sure, their thoughts no more can be their own,
    And therefore should to none but one be known.

Then she usurps upon another's right,
That seeks to be by public language graced:
And though her thoughts reflect with purest light,
Her mind if not peculiar is not chaste.
    For in a wife it is no worse to find,
    A common body, than a common mind.

And every mind though free from thought of ill,
That out of glory seeks a worth to show:
When any's ears but one therewith they fill,
Doth in a sort her pureness overthrow.
    Now Mariam had (but that to this she bent[1])
    Been free from fear, as well as innocent.

---

1   *but that ... she bent*   I.e., if she had acted according to this advice.

Permissions Acknowledgments

Ralph Anzarouth and an anonymous friend, Translators. Excerpts from *Treatise on Ethics (Tzemach Tzaddik)* by Leon of Modena, 1587. Retrieved from http://www.anzarouth.com/. Reprinted with the permission of Ralph Anzarouth.

David Chambers and Brian Pullan. Excerpt from *Venice: A Documentary History, 1450-1630*. Oxford UK and Cambridge USA: Blackwell Publishers, 1992. Copyright © 1992 by David Chambers and Brian Pullan. All rights reserved. Reprinted with permission.

Rabbi Martin A. Cohen, Translator. Excerpt from Samuel Usque's *Consolation for the Tribulations of Israel*. Jewish Publication Society of America, 1965, 1977.

Gilbert S. Rosenthal, Translator and Editor. Excerpt from "The Eternal Life" (1559) by Yehiel Nissim De Pisa, from *Banking and Finance among Jews in Renaissance Italy*. Bloch Publishing, 1962. Reprinted with the permission of Rabbi Gilbert S. Rosenthal.

Katharine Silverblatt Wolfthal, Translator. Excerpt from *The Ghetto of Venice* by Riccardo Calimani. Mondadori, 1995. M. Evans, 1987.

The publisher has endeavoured to contact rights holders of all copyright material and would appreciate receiving any information as to errors or omissions.

from the publisher

A name never says it all, but the word "broadview" expresses a good deal of the philosophy behind our company. We are open to a broad range of academic approaches and political viewpoints. We pay attention to the broad impact book publishing and book printing has in the wider world; we began using recycled stock more than a decade ago, and for some years now we have used 100% recycled paper for most titles. As a Canadian-based company we naturally publish a number of titles with a Canadian emphasis, but our publishing program overall is internationally oriented and broad-ranging. Our individual titles often appeal to a broad readership too; many are of interest as much to general readers as to academics and students.

Founded in 1985, Broadview remains a fully independent company owned by its shareholders—not an imprint or subsidiary of a larger multinational.

If you would like to find out more about Broadview and about the books we publish, please visit us at **www.broadviewpress.com**. And if you'd like to place an order through the site, we'd like to show our appreciation by extending a special discount to you: by entering the code below you will receive a 20% discount on purchases made through the Broadview website.

Discount code: **broadview20%**

Thank you for choosing Broadview.

Please note: this offer applies only to sales of
bound books within the United States or Canada.

The interior of this book is printed on 30% recycled paper.